D1236773

EX LIBRIS
Pace University
New York · Westchester
PACE UNIVERSITY
OPPORTVNITAS
MCMVI
NEW YORK
NEW YORK & WESTCHESTER
PACE PLAZA
NEW YORK

Prisoners of society: attitudes and after-care

International Library of Social Policy

General Editor Kathleen Jones
Professor of Social Administration
University of York

Arbor Scientiae
Arbor Vitae

A catalogue of the books available in the **International Library of Social Policy** and other series of Social Science books published by Routledge & Kegan Paul will be found at the end of this volume

Prisoners of society

attitudes and after-care

Martin Davies
Department of Social Administration
University of Manchester

Routledge & Kegan Paul
London and Boston

First published in 1974
by Routledge & Kegan Paul Ltd
Broadway House, 68–74 Carter Lane,
London EC4V 5EL and
9 Park Street,
Boston, Mass. 02108, USA
Set in 10-point Times New Roman
and printed in Great Britain by
Unwin Brothers Limited
The Gresham Press
Old Woking, Surrey

ISBN 0 7100 7989 3
Library of Congress Catalog Card No. 74–83377

Contents

Figures and tables

Figures

Tables

Preface

'If you send someone to prison, the prison does what it can and then the man comes out and we start again outside.' This frank statement by the Home Office's Principal Probation Inspector reflects the limitations inherent in the prison after-care process.[1] In 1972, 41,655 men and women were received into the prison system following sentence; about a half of them would have come into contact with an after-care officer following discharge, but for most the relationship would be short-lived. The effectiveness of after-care would be judged by its consumers to the extent that it succeeded in minimizing the damaging impact of their prison experience, rather than as an integral part of the original sentence. Could it provide them with basic material help to enable them to travel, to find lodgings, to get a job? Could it provide a base for rebuilding their shaken self-confidence? Could it provide direction for resettlement out of an alien culture back into the outside world? Could it undo that which prison had done?

After-care in the penal system (and in any system in which an individual is forcibly taken into and then ejected from a total institution) must be seen largely as society's apology for the hurt inflicted; in a culture where we did not feel the need to impose a system of moral apartheid, men and women might be more usefully employed than in building bridges previously broken down by the normal processes of the penal system. But so long as deterrence, retribution and social protection are demanded from the courts in their dealings with offenders, then so also will the social services be expected to 'start again outside' in their task of achieving some degree of integration between the individual and society.

In recent years it has become increasingly apparent that the extent and complexity of relevant research in criminology is such that academic justice can no longer be done to the many parts of the penal system involved with offenders solely through the medium of comprehensive texts. The subject of after-care may appear at first sight to represent only a small, if expanding, area within penology. But the range of work undertaken by the probation service is now extremely wide, and a great deal of officers' time is taken up directly or indirectly with prisons, prisoners or ex-prisoners. This development – which has gathered pace since the publication in 1963 of an advisory report on *The organisation of after-care*[2] – is important, not only because of its impact on the work of the probation service, but because it has brought into the arena of public debate important issues of principle concerning the purpose and function of the penal system. The very juxtaposition of social work and custodial detention that is inherent in the idea of prison welfare and after-care compels us to consider their compatibility. This book examines in detail the implications of the probation service's involvement in after-care, prison welfare and parole.

A major emphasis is on published research evidence. The field of after-care is not short of experiments, good intentions or novel ideas; but few of these have been adequately explored before their introduction, and even fewer are subjected to disciplined monitoring or evaluation afterwards. The probation service itself is now deeply involved in trying out new schemes, both in regard to the provision of residential facilities and in exercising intensive community care, and yet our ignorance in both these areas far outstrips our knowledge. A little has been done in relation to the need for different kinds of accommodation for ex-prisoners, and there is a considerable body of literature in the USA reporting the results of using small or specialized caseloads in the supervision of offenders; but in Britain, there have been as yet no more than a handful of investigations into the use of hostels in the penal system, and virtually nothing which offers convincing evidence about the efficacy of after-care in the community.

The work of Apex in the employment sector is reviewed at some length, mainly because of the first-rate monitoring and evaluation independently carried out within the project by Keith Soothill; but as an innovatory exercise, Apex was exceptional in having a director willing to submit his convictions and his efforts to microscopic investigation in this way. Much other after-care research has been carried out in the Home Office Research Unit, where its Director, T. S. Lodge, and Senior Research Officer, Steven Folkard, proved the possibility of taking an independent research line within a government department; this is something that can never be assumed in central or local government research, but as a result of the Research Unit achieving a position of relative strength and organizational autonomy in the Home Office, some of the most thorough –

and hence most critical – analyses of developments in probation and after-care have been published under the Stationery Office imprint.

There are many areas covered by this volume which are as yet almost totally unexplored in research terms, as a result of which it has been necessary at times to make educated guesses or rely on conventional wisdom; there are also areas where the research surveyed is fairly rudimentary, and where the methodology used leaves serious doubts about reliability and validity. However, it is hoped that this review of the literature – which would have been a futile exercise ten years ago – might encourage workers to recognize those spheres where further research would prove most fruitful, and that future editions might then have a wider range of material on which to draw. With this thought in mind, I would be grateful to any reader willing to draw my attention to relevant studies – especially where these are unpublished, or circulated only within a restricted area.

Of course many of the topics covered in this study are relevant to much that the probation officer does in areas other than after-care and prison welfare, but it has been found possible to make a conceptual distinction between the twin aspects of the work of the probation and after-care service. A companion volume will review the service's original brief of supervising offenders allocated to them by the courts, its work of social enquiry, and the rapidly accruing tasks that officers are now being required to accept in order to provide sentencers with a wider range of alternative forms of penal disposal. In the study that follows, however, the focus is on the relationship between the probation service and offenders who are or have been in custody.

I would like to express my gratitude to the librarians of the Prison Staff Training College, Wakefield, the *Guardian*, the *Reading Evening Post* and John Burrows Newspapers; to Kenneth Norman of the Portia Trust, Freddie Pentney of Apex, Nick Hinton and Cathy Mordue of NACRO; and especially to J. W. Marsh, the Principal Probation Officer of south-east Lancashire, and his colleagues, whose generosity and interest have helped me to overcome one of the major snags facing the university researcher in social work – that of being cut off from the reality of the client and his would-be helpers. In a volume of this kind, considerable reliance must be placed on official government publications, and two reports in particular have been used extensively: *The organisation of after-care*, produced by the Advisory Council on the Treatment of Offenders in 1963; and *Explorations in after-care*, produced by the Home Office Research Unit. Extracts from these and other official documents are included with the permission of the Controller of Her Majesty's Stationery Office.

I would like to express my appreciation to Mr A. S. Greenhorn of the Home Office Statistical Division for his kind assistance in up-dating the statistics contained in the 1969 White Paper, *People in prison*.

Finally, I would say a deep thank you to my wife Judy, whose patience, encouragement and understanding have enabled me to spend many hours at this and other tasks at times when she might justifiably have expected me to provide better companionship.

University of Manchester MARTIN DAVIES

1 The reality of after-care

After-care is not a large-scale activity in society, although it probably has symbolic importance to our contemporary situation out of proportion to its size; in it we see reflected the growing concern that is felt about the way we behave towards disadvantaged or deviant minorities in a civilized community.

Who is concerned in the provision of after-care for ex-prisoners? It is important to begin with the recognition that, as in all sectors of social need, many men and women who have served jail sentences are able to turn to families, friends and other non-professional networks in order to obtain material and moral support; for them, after-care is available in an indigenous form. But for many men on discharge, such resources are either inadequate for their needs, or non-existent, and it is then that the basic element in after-care hinges on the professional relationship between probation officer and client. Whether the offender has served his sentence in a borstal, detention centre or prison, whether he has been released on licence or is looking for help on a voluntary basis, and whatever his feelings about the custodial experience, it is to the probation service that he will turn for help, and in some of the biggest urban centres, he will find a specialist after-care unit provided.

Probation officers are increasingly aware of their service's unique position within the penal system as it steadily extends its range of activities with adult offenders; their traditions and their training, however, are still derived from a social work background, and a primary emphasis on casework with the individual client has always been, and still is, central to the probation officer's approach.

The probation officer is employed by a Probation and After-care Committee; 80 per cent of the service's money comes from the Treasury and 20 per cent from the local authority. Until recently the proportions were fifty-fifty and neither party exercised more than technical control over committee policy, but it seems probable that the influence of central government will now increasingly make itself felt at the local level. The responsible department is contained within the Home Office, and its influence is felt in a number of ways:

for example, in the distribution of Home Office Circulars concerned with such matters as the use of voluntary associates in the provision of after-care, the authorization of increased cash payments to enable ex-prisoners to buy working clothes, secure accommodation, and so on; and in the visits paid by Home Office Inspectors to probation offices, as a result of which local policy concerning such matters as pre-release visits to prospective after-care clients might be encouraged or discouraged. (In this particular example, policy has been rather ambiguous in recent years. On the one hand, the value of pre-release contact is recognized and visits are sanctioned; but on the other there is a recognition that, because of the geographical spread of prisoners, the involvement of officers in full-day trips for an interview lasting perhaps thirty to sixty minutes is costly in both time and money.)

Home Office policy, while it develops a certain momentum of its own (though just how much initiative is exercised either by administrative civil servants or by professional advisers in political development is still one of the most under-explored areas in social administration), is a reflection of the work of politicians in Parliament. The most significant step in the growth of after-care followed the acceptance by Parliament and the Government in 1963 of the report on *The organisation of after-care*[1], as a result of which the task was largely redefined as one requiring a professional social work approach both before and after release.

The politicians themselves represent, and to some extent reflect, conflicting aspects of public opinion, both in their concern for the extension of welfare provisions in the penal system and in their continuing support for a punitive approach to sentencing. The sentencers send offenders to prison, but, through the magistracy, make up the majority membership of probation and after-care committees. Borstals, detention centres and prisons are provided by the Home Office Prison Department, which is ever anxious to emphasize that the institutions contain as much of a positive element as is consistent with a mainly custodial commitment.

On the duly appointed day, at 8.00 a.m., an act occurs which has been represented innumerable times in films and on television screens: the gates open and another batch of ex-prisoners walk out into freedom. A few may have spent ten years inside – perhaps one-third of their whole life – and for them, society will seem like a foreign land; but most will have been away for a year or less. Have they learned their lesson? Are they bitter? Are they determined to 'get' whoever shopped them? Have they a wife and family waiting for them? Will they get a job? Have they been taught anything that will be of any use to them now? And, above all, from the point of view of the probation officer with after-care to offer, do they only want to forget that they have been prisoners, or will they be glad of the proffered helping hand?

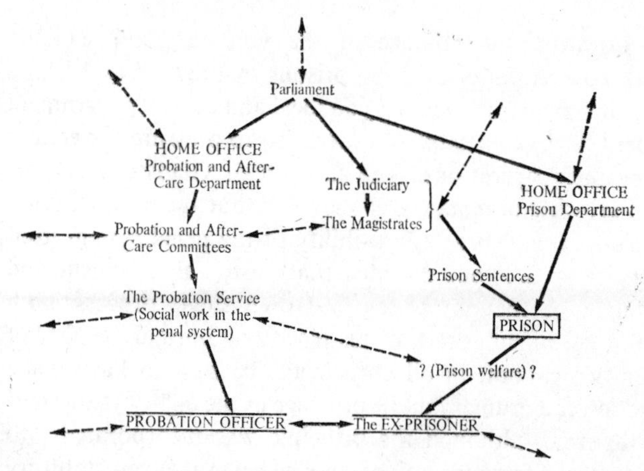

Figure 1 The after-care relationship

The diagram represents the formal structure that lies behind the after-care relationship. The dynamic nature of the links between the constituent parts is, however, crucial and reflects the fact that each of them influences and is influenced by attitudes and pressure-groups in the open society (represented by the space outside the administrative circle). The dotted lines across the circle illustrate two ways in which internal links have been forged between the two sides: magistrates make up the bulk of the membership of probation and after-care committees, and probation officers are employed inside prisons as welfare officers.

The voluntary tradition

The historical separation of the avowedly supportive role of the after-care agent from the destructive process of imprisonment ('destructive' in effect, if not always in intention) was organizationally reflected until the 1960s in the distinct roles fulfilled by voluntary and statutory bodies:[2]

> After-care in this country originated, as did so many other forms of social service, in voluntary work by individuals who were moved by a spirit of charity to relieve distress among their

fellows and to seek their moral reformation. The private philanthropy of the late eighteenth and early nineteenth centuries, often inspired by strong religious convictions, found expression in this field in the formation of Discharged Prisoners' Aid Societies, attached to the local city and county gaols. Without initiation and planning from the centre, these early societies grew up spontaneously and independently.

Inevitably, however, the reliance of the voluntary aid societies (whose work covered almost all the prisons in England and Wales by the end of the nineteenth century) on local and central government to supplement their charitable resources led to pressure for greater control over their operations. The far-sighted Gladstone Report 'encouraged growing acceptance of the view that the rehabilitation of offenders was as much a responsibility of the penal system itself as of society at large',[3] but the idea that custodial treatment and after-care might be thought of 'as part of a single process, both designed to fit the offender to take his place as a normal member of the community'[4] cannot, in all conscience, be said to have made much impact on the ordinary adult prisoner in the eighty years since Gladstone reported, although the principle was incorporated into the borstal system for young offenders when it was given statutory recognition in 1908. The borstal licence, which took effect immediately on his release, was intended primarily to bring about the positive rehabilitation of the offender, and although not all borstal trainees have understood the position, the imposition of a borstal sentence has always carried with it the twin elements of a period in custody and a complementary period of community supervision. During the twentieth century a number of other sentences have worked on a similar basis; penal servitude, preventive detention, corrective training (all of which no longer exist), life sentences, and extended sentences.

During the seventy years following the Gladstone Report, the Discharged Prisoners' Aid Societies continued their voluntary responsibility for the mass of ordinary prisoners. Their employees worked both inside and outside the institutions giving material aid, advice and support to offenders and their families. Inevitably standards varied greatly, and a number of committees reported on the need for increased central control. The pattern of proposal and counter-proposal, attack and defence, with the separate societies determined to retain their independence for as long as possible, is a classic example of charity politics (in which the welfare of the assumed recipient of service seems at times to have been quite unimportant beside the personal and organizational clashes that ensued). In 1937 the societies won their battle for independence, although their interests were to be represented in a reorganized national association (NADPAS). Sixteen years later, however, the problem of money had again become critical, and the publication of the Maxwell Report effectively transferred most of the societies' responsibilities for giving material aid to men on discharge to public agencies, and led to a switch of emphasis away from money and clothing towards constructive after-care and casework. It was but a short step from this to the recommendations of the Advisory Council in 1963 'that after-care whether it is compulsory or voluntary, should be available according to individual need and that one service – the probation and after-care service – should be responsible for the provision of both forms of after-care'.[5] These recommendations, linked to the more ambitious concept of through-care ('a process which starts on the offender's reception into custody, is developed during his sentence, and is available for as long as necessary after his release'[6]) echoing Gladstone but still far from being an accurate image of prison reality in the 1970s, nevertheless identify after-care as having the primary function of *treatment* or *rehabilitation* – although rehabilitation in such a context may still be as much concerned with overcoming the effects of incarceration as with counteracting the factors allegedly associated with criminal behaviour.

In the event, the Government went even further than the Council had recommended, and in the course of the 1960s, the probation service became responsible not only for all after-care, voluntary and compulsory (with the consequent winding-up of most of the voluntary organizations previously concerned with this work), but from 1966 for all prison welfare work, and from 1969 for social worker posts in remand centres, detention centres and borstal allocation centres. The only effective welfare area from which the probation service is now excluded is that in boys' borstals where responsibility for welfare remains part of the function of the assistant governors in charge of houses.

But although the organization of after-care passed into the hands of the probation service during the 1960s, nobody was anxious to destroy the voluntary tradition of work with ex-prisoners, and the voluntary sector has continued to develop on four fronts.

Following recommendations contained in the ACTO Report,[7] the probation service has increasingly involved voluntary associates in a variety of tasks with ex-prisoners; the role is generally that of an *aide* working in support of a professional social worker, and the work can range from providing transport for families to visit a man in prison to developing long-term friendships with ex-prisoners to an extent quite impossible for the probation officer working under normal conditions. A more recent trend has been for the probation service to organize volunteers into 'setting up and running fully-fledged visiting centres adjacent to prisons where wives and relatives can wait in reasonable comfort for visits to begin, obtain refreshments, wash and tidy themselves and their infants and, if they wish, leave children in friendly care while they make their visit'.[8] By the contrast that they provide, such activities serve well to emphasize the still archaic and often inhumane attitudes of the penal system itself, but they are none the less important for that; indeed it is arguable that the most valuable contribution that the voluntary sector can make is to keep at least one step ahead of statutory effort, and to press for its more successful innovations to be taken over by the system and to be made comprehensive.

The potential role of voluntary organizations in providing accommodation for ex-prisoners was emphasized by the Reading Report in 1966. By the end of 1971 over a hundred hostels were receiving special Home Office grants to help with running costs, and they were continuing to open at the rate of about twenty a year. These hostels reflect the same sort of balance between voluntary effort and government money that characterized the Discharged Prisoners' Aid Societies in their later years, and the fact that the Criminal Justice Act 1972 authorizes probation and after-care committees to set up their own hostels, is an indication that voluntary effort alone is felt by the Home Office to be unlikely to meet the growing need for accommodation – especially among homeless single men.

The third front on which voluntary effort is concentrated is in the organizations which exist for purposes other than the provision of accommodation. Some, like the National Association for the Care and Resettlement of Offenders (NACRO), are involved in both, but others are concerned with improving opportunities for employment, providing specialist treatment facilities (in respect, for example, of alcoholism, gambling and drug abuse), and encouraging self-help among ex-prisoners. NACRO in particular has made an impact on the scene since its creation in 1966 out of the ashes of the National Association of Discharged Prisoners' Aid Societies. In addition to its concern with accommodation, NACRO has drawn attention to shortcomings in the provision of training for residential work and has itself tried to fill the gap; in addition, it has taken on a pressure-group role, using its special relationship with the Home Office to express critical opinions about aspects of the penal system.

The fourth front is quite different, and receives little recognition and no approval in official Home Office reports: it represents the growth of self-awareness and the striving for a political voice among prisoners, ex-prisoners and some of their closest sympathizers. Of necessity the pattern is somewhat confused: although there is some membership overlap, Preservation of the Rights of Prisoners (PROP) and Radical Alternatives to Prison (RAP) have both asserted opinions more radical than those of NACRO, and have expressed resentment that middle-class liberal organizations should presume to speak on behalf of underprivileged offenders denied their freedom. Such radical groups are not primarily interested in concepts of after-care, because for them the reality of after-care is only a reflection of the iniquities of imprisonment. Even though it is difficult to see PROP in particular exerting any great influence on its own in the immediate future because of its very weak bargaining position and its inevitably transient support, its arguments and its actions cannot be ignored by those concerned with the task of returning disadvantaged and dehumanized ex-prisoners to society, for compromise, though often politically necessary, is not always morally right.

The natural history of after-care: four faces of reality

To read Home Office reports or descriptions of work undertaken by the probation service or the voluntary organizations can be very deceptive, because the concentration on developments and innovations may give a misleading picture of the reality as it is perceived by the working probation officer or his client. One of the commonest errors in penology is to confuse good intent with actual effect, and in order to illustrate after-care in practice, the experience of four men will now be presented in detail. When one gets down to individuals, there is no such thing as a typical or representative case; but these people are *more* representative of *personal* reality than the administrative emphasis of the foregoing historical description, for they illustrate, not the cool policy-making decisions of the civil servant, the politician, or the committee member, but the direct experience of the ex-prisoner himself.

Case example 1

Offenders who are committed to life imprisonment are eligible for release under supervision on the direction of the Home Secretary.

Sam Bell was sentenced to life imprisonment for murdering a woman who, two years earlier, had left him after they had cohabited for twelve years. They had remained on friendly terms, but on the day of her death they had been arguing all day. He had become jealous because he thought she was associating with another man. He said if he could not have her, no-one would and he knocked her to the floor; he then jumped on top of her and strangled her.

Four years after his sentence, the case was brought to the attention of a probation officer in the West Country, as the Home Office were considering possible release. Sam Bell was handicapped by chronic arthritis, but was able to shuffle along with the aid of walking sticks. During the next three years, before he was eventually freed, the probation officer visited the prison from time to time, liaised with the welfare officer regarding possible accommodation, and tried to get a grant from NACRO or the British Legion to pay for petrol for Sam's invalid carriage, which had been obtained for him while he was in prison. After Sam's release, the probation officer saw him almost weekly; it was an occasion which Sam obviously looked forward to with considerable pleasure. He was a lonely man, in his middle fifties, with few people to talk to: 'Tends to treat appointments (with the probation officer) as "natter" sessions.' Interviews were 'basically about everyday events and occurrences and just the opportunity for him to discuss any topics he wishes'.

It is apparent that the probation officer deliberately adopted a policy of making himself available to provide support as and when it was required. Considerable help was given in the way of accommodation. At first Sam found an uneasy situation as a lodger in a run-down farm; the woman had said she would be glad to have him on his release, but eventually Sam moved because of the hostility of her cohabitee. (The probation officer also noticed that he lay in bed till lunch-time, made no effort to go out, and expected to be waited on hand and foot.) Sam then went to his sister's, until a row with his brother forced him to leave. From there the probation officer helped him move in with an elderly lady 'who wished to help offenders by offering accommodation'. Finally he progressed, through a long spell in a block of drab, depressing and cheerless twilight dwellings, to a perfectly respectable and pleasant flat with a television set 'provided by a friend of the probation service'. Financially he seemed to manage quite well, but there was clearly no prospect of employment: 'There is really very little for him to do apart from potter around.'

Every so often, Sam would want to talk about the offence for which he had been sentenced – 'whether he was testing me out or not, I don't know' – or about his experiences in prison. In general, the probation officer did not find the need for a great deal of environmental intervention in this case; in many ways, it represents the rare example of a situation in which the simple availability of a probation officer – time-consuming though this might be – was sufficient to enable the ex-prisoner to find the initiative and staying power to survive.

Case example 2

Damien Vernon is now forty-seven. He lived with his parents until he was thirty, and gradually accumulated a number of minor offences which appeared to reflect a degree of inadequacy in coping with the adult world. He had done mainly unskilled work and experienced spells of unemployment. Damien was sent to prison two years ago for stealing money from his mother with whom he had been living; he had committed similar offences previously.

He is the kind of man who seems to set up a negative reaction in those who deal with him, despite a superficial pleasantness. On reception in prison, he was described as not very bright, and living off Social Security, 'a bone idle type who takes it for granted that he will return to an open prison'; it was recommended that he should be left in the local prison to show that this was not a holiday camp. The welfare officer found him affable but effeminate, and the probation service described him as 'a quiet unassertive, almost servile man who has little self-confidence'. It was noted at the time of sentence that Damien did not get on with his two sisters, and that, as his mother had now gone to live with one of them, he might have to go it alone on discharge.

He was released in September with a £4 discharge grant and a halfpenny of his own; he went in search of his mother, but found that somebody else was living in the house. Three days later he came to the after-care centre, and asked for help in retrieving his clothes from home; he also said that he had been robbed of his discharge grant and overcoat at King's Cross station, that he hadn't eaten for two days and had no accommodation. The probation officer traced his mother's address through the housing department, but was told not to pass it on to Mr Vernon; he did, however, send a student along to collect the clothes. Damien was given £1 and a voucher for a hostel bed, and told to go to the Employment Exchange and Social Security office the next day; the probation officer commented that he did not think that Damien would stay in touch once the practical problems were solved.

Two days later, Damien came again, seemingly desperate for his shaving kit; however, it was another nineteen days before the probation officer was able to provide further information for him. The student had difficulty tracing the house because the housing department had given the wrong address; when at last he did so, there was no reply to his knock. Eventually, a telephone call was received from a niece of Damien's; she said that his mother was very old and frail, and she had been in a terrible state when Damien had gone to prison. The police had taken away some clothes, and there were no others left worth salvaging. She was insistent that Damien should not be told where his mother was now living, because they didn't want him to sponge off them.

When Damien came round to the office a week later, he was told the news. He felt that his sisters were being unfair to him, and were deliberately withholding the clothes. The niece never phoned again, and the probation officer found that the telephone number she had left was a false one. In the meantime, Damien was continuing to live at the hostel, and in the light of developments, the officer arranged for a letter to be provided for him to get help for clothes and shaving kit from Social Security: 'He is being very patient about the whole affair.'

He called twice more, and on one occasion the probation officer gave him a cup of tea, but it proved impossible to make further contact with the family, and it was felt that Damien would just have to accept the harsh truth that he was now on his own: 'He is obviously developing into a very lonely man, but without any expression of bitterness at all.'

Case example 3

Mick Murphy had a long record of offences, interspersed with periods of moderate stability in association with his family: he had experienced unemployment in the past, but usually found work as a labourer in the end. A rather inadequate, nervous man, he was regarded in the prison as a conformist to institutional routine; he expressed frequent anxiety about the health and welfare of his wife and son, and tended to involve the welfare officer in his problems more than average: 'He never seems satisfied with the continual attention that he receives.'

In May, Mick Murphy was granted parole; his wife had written in his support, and a former employer said that he was willing to take him back. He had been no trouble in prison, and was said to have provided useful information on one occasion to the staff (as a result of which he was given protection because of the risk of violence). The probation officer, Mr George, who had maintained contact and undertaken a good deal of supportive work with his wife during Mick's sentence, told her that he would be very strict with her husband because of the great responsibility involved in supervising parolees; Mrs Murphy was profuse in her gratitude for the help she'd received.

Mick came to the office straight from the prison in May, and was told about the probation officer's intended stringency. He then set off in search of a job. There was nothing at the Employment Exchange, and his former boss now said that he had nothing suitable after all; the possibility of a temporary job to tide him over came to nothing, and Mick had no luck with several other applications. Three weeks after his release, the probation officer 'spent roughly about an hour and a quarter telephoning fourteen firms before finally getting him an appointment for interview the next day'. Mick Murphy went off with Mr George's letter of introduction, but when he saw the probation officer the following week, he said that he hadn't taken the post because it paid less than he was getting from the Social Security, and he didn't think it was worth it. He was still looking around.

Both the probation officer and client then seemed to acquiesce in the situation and references to Mick's unemployment became rarer and briefer. Two months after release, the probation officer told him about a job in Leeds that he'd heard of and suggested that Mick should phone or call there; he did so but was told there were no vacancies – a fact which surprised the probation officer because the manager of the firm had told him that he had several. Mr George arranged for Mick's children to go on a summer holiday with a local charity.

Three months after discharge: 'Still no changes and still looking for a job. He remains cheerful.'

Four months after discharge: The probation officer was suggesting possible employers, but a dozen or more tentative hopes came to nothing, and one offer of work fell through because Mick's tax forms weren't in order.

At last, in October, Mick got a job as a builder's labourer. It gave him £2 more a week than Social Security was paying and was hard work, but he felt happy about it. It lasted six weeks, and nothing further was heard from him for over a month. His wife then phoned to say that he was ill in bed. Mick reported again the following week, and three weeks later his parole licence came to an end; he had, however, got himself a new job on a building site. He had worked for seven weeks during the nine months under supervision, but he had not committed any further offences.

Case example 4

Billy Miller was sentenced to borstal training three years ago for burglary. He was a good middle-of-the-road performer in an open institution, and was described as pleasant and intelligent but with a tendency to drop into bouts of self-pity and feelings of anti-authority. During his sentence, the probation officer, Mr Briscoe, maintained contact with Billy's wife Mary. He encouraged her to write to her husband, helped her through periods of deep depression, and gave practical assistance with regard to Social Security payments; the two themes which run through the records at this time are the feelings of confusion and near despair expressed by Mrs Miller, and the administrative headaches that continually arose over the question of help with clothing, vouchers for visiting her husband, and a grant to cover the cost of repairing a window following an apparent break-in. There were also large electricity arrears, and Mr Briscoe agreed to sort them out; shortly after this, contact was lost and 'Mrs Miller was rumoured to be living with friends'. It was suggested that she had embezzled money via Giro payments.

However, by the time Billy was released after serving eight months, Mary had returned; shortly afterwards, she gave birth to a second child, and more financial problems materialized. Then, when the baby was six weeks old, Mary left home. In his maternal role, Billy coped quite well. The probation officer advised him about the need for visits to the Health Clinic, and acted on his behalf to stave off the threat of an electricity cut-off because of the arrears outstanding. Three months after his release in April he took into the house a Mrs O'Shea – a nineteen-year-old immature girl, well known to the probation office. In May, Mary applied for custody, but, largely on the basis of the report prepared by Mr Briscoe, the application was adjourned *sine die*; the probation officer felt that the baby was being well cared for, while Mrs Miller was then of no fixed abode.

Mr Briscoe continued to act as something of a go-between where the Electricity Board and the Social Security were concerned. Trouble arose, for example, because an electricity man called five times to look at the meter, and on the last occasion Billy refused to let him in; the probation officer eventually got the Board to admit that the visits had been made as the result of an oversight.

In October, Billy was fined a total of £41 for an offence of joy-riding; at this time (about nine months after his release from borstal), the licencee was making no office calls, but the probation officer visited at intervals of six to eight weeks. Billy was not working, and had not done so since his coming home. The probation officer had had no success in encouraging him to seek a job, although he still felt that the low level of the family's income was a major source of stress. In April of the following year, a charge of schoolbreaking brought a suspended prison sentence to Billy.

For the next eight months Billy's position as guardian of his son became the prime consideration in the case. No further effort was made to persuade him to work, especially as his cohabitee, Mrs O'Shea, left him for her husband, first temporarily and then permanently. Mary started further proceedings for custody of their child in the Divorce Court, and Mr Briscoe found that his conclusions in the welfare report would be balanced differently this time. Mrs Miller now had good council accommodation, and Billy was on his own; in the light of these factors, the court agreed to grant custody to the baby's mother. Billy reacted bitterly; he felt the report had been critical of the care which he had exercised for nearly two years, and clearly thought his supervising officer had been unfair. It took two or three home visits before Mr Briscoe could record that 'he seemed to be in a pleasant frame of mind and the animosity between the writer and Billy has declined somewhat'.

The licence period ended shortly afterwards, while there was still some dispute over the legality of the custody decision, and while Billy Miller was expressing his determination to hold on to the baby. In fact, Mary abandoned her claim to the baby after she became pregnant again; the Social Services Department assumed rights of supervision, and the probation officer felt that much might depend on what kind of support they could offer in this instance. So far as the after-care order was concerned, he thought it was to Billy's credit that he had avoided turning to serious deviancy to solve his problems (although there had been two further convictions).

Conclusion

These four case examples illustrate four clear points about the work that the probation officer does with ex-prisoners:

1 The service that is on offer is superficially simple, though demanding in time and patience; in a case like Sam Bell's, the client's ability to use such a service is crucial to its value.

2 There are certain circumstances which the probation officer cannot change; Damien Vernon's family plight is sad and will become sadder, but the probation officer cannot intervene against the wishes of the other parties. It may be that improved residential facilities would be of help in such a case – but there could be no certainty that the client would respond to such an offer.

3 Despite an expressed determination to take a strong line with a parolee, the probation officer does not usually use his position to enforce a matter such as employment, but relies on the client acting on his own initiative.

4 The probation officer can sometimes find himself in a difficult role-conflict situation; having supported Billy Miller for two years, he found that he had to make a crucial recommendation to a Divorce Court indicating that the child should go to its mother. In such circumstances it is clear that the probation officer cannot separate his supervisory responsibilities from his allegiance to the agency and the court.

After-care is limited in what it can achieve in the community but it none the less can impose heavy strains on the working probation officer – strains which indeed may be aggravated by the very awareness of his own limitations.

2 Before release

A portrait of prisoners

Cartoonists create easily identifiable images to represent different groups in society: Bristow's desk-bound pen-pusher, Thelwell's middle-class child on its pony, Giles's extended family in a council house, and Osbert Lancaster's ladies on the fringes of cabinet politics. These are symbolic figures, and the closer one is to the reality, the more one recognizes both the truth and the error in such generalized presentations. But cartoonists have always relied as a body on two particular groups of men (always men) as providing them with symbolic reality in its purest form: the parson and the prisoner.

Moreover the cartoonist only reflects the symbolic use made of such groups by the media, by the joke-teller and perhaps by society as a whole. Why else should this news item be given front-page headlines in a large-circulation daily paper in the 1970s?

> The Rev. A. B., a 42-year-old vicar, married, with two children, has resigned from the ministry and left his parish. A married woman parishioner is also missing. The two were among six people who recently took part in a 48-hour fast in the town centre for a fund-raising effort. The rector said that members of the congregation were saddened. . . .

The break-up of two marriages has tragic personal implications, but, of itself, it is not news; even the claim that a vicar is a public figure is unconvincing, because marital separations within the medical profession, among teachers or Justices of the Peace would not attract the same attention. The parson is a symbolic representative of a certain style of behaviour, and because he is a symbol, his individuality, his identity as a person is often ignored – except when it contradicts the clarity of the image that we cling to.

It is the same (at the opposite end of the symbolic spectrum) with the prisoner. Our impression of him as a person is governed not only by the cartoonist's pen, but by the police identity photograph with its unshaven face and the staring eyes, or by the newspaper picture of a man being hustled into court covered with a blanket, or that in the Home Office handbook which shows him working in prison uniform but with his facial features photographically blurred. Once a man has been sent to prison (often long before conviction and sentence), he is no longer thought of as a person. Instead, he personalizes for the onlooker all that is bad, untrustworthy, violent and depraved in society – and perhaps in the onlooker himself. It is this symbolic and perhaps unconscious element in penology that renders its study at once both publicly appealing and intellectually difficult: the facts about men who commit offences, and the facts about the way that organized society reacts when they are caught, seem often to be inadequate to explain the prevalence and growth of criminal behaviour and the logic and purpose of society's response. Even the facts themselves are not so easily obtained as might be supposed. There is no better demonstration of the fact that society has clung to its view that all prisoners are basically alike, save only perhaps that they can be classified according to their grades of *badness*, than the discovery by the Estimates Committee in 1967 that no reliable evidence existed concerning the personal and social circumstances of the nation's prisoners at that time. Official documents record only administrative details, as, for example, the 1972 Departmental Report[1] which shows how the average population of prison establishments was made up during the year:

Prison (including remand centres):	%
awaiting trial or sentence	12
sentenced (adult)	64
sentenced (young prisoners)	4
non-criminal prisoners	1
Borstal	14
Detention centre	5
N = 38,328	

In 1969, the Home Office published a White Paper with the significant title of *People in prison*. Did this mean that prisoners were to be thought of henceforth as significant individuals with an identity of their own? Perhaps that was the intention, but any enquiring reader turning to the document with a view to discovering something about the system's inmates would be disappointed – at any rate, if it was the enforced inmates he was interested in. Five short paragraphs are devoted to 'the people in custody' and to the task of describing them;

reference is made to an appendix in which the ages, offences, number of previous convictions, and the number of previous institutional sentences are indicated (see pp. 17–19). An earlier version of the table referred to above is given and briefly discussed, and two facts are emphasized: most prisoners have been in custody before, and only one in five adult prisoners has to spend more than two years in custody. And that is all, even though the chapter is entitled 'Offenders in Custody'. For the rest, the reader is treated to occasional assertions which confirm his probable preconceptions (and this despite the more humane confession that 'there is no such person as the average offender. How should there be when all human beings are different? All generalizations about the characteristics of people in custody are therefore suspect.'[2]): 'There are dangerous and violent people in custody'[3]; '. . . if prisoners share a single common factor it is their propensity to attract problems to themselves'.[4]

The Home Office profile of the prison population

These five tables are broadly based on the data reproduced in the appendix to *People in prison*.[5] The 1967 and 1969 figures published in the White Paper are compared with more recent information. Tables 2.1 and 2.2 describe the sentenced adult male population in prison at a specified date; Tables 2.3–2.5 show the penal background of all sentenced adult male prisoners received during the calendar

Table 2.1 Analysis of the sentenced adult male population by present age

Age	March 1969 %	June 1972 %
21–4	26	29
25–9	21	25
30–9	31	28
40–9	15	13
50–9	5	5
60+	2	1
	100	101
	N = 20,698	24,188

years indicated. It seems that the prison population is becoming younger and marginally more experienced in terms of court appearances, convictions and institutional sentences. (Institutional experience is not strictly comparable because of the ending of Approved School sentences under the Children and Young Persons Act, 1969.)

Table 2.2 Analysis of the sentenced adult male population by type of offence

Offence	March 1969 %	June 1972 %
Burglary, attempted burglary	31	30
Theft	20	18
Violence against the person (except murder)	10	13
Robbery	8	7
Sex Offences	7	5
Fraud	6	6
Receiving	5	5
Taking and driving away, and other Highways Act offences	4	5
Murder	2	2
Other	7	8
	100	99
	N = 20,698	24,188

*Table 2.3 Sentenced adult male prisoners received into custody: number of previous proved offences**

No. of offences	1967 %	1972 %
0	8	7
1	6	4
2	6	5
3–5	21	19
6–10	29	32
11–20	22	26
20+	8	8
	100	101
	N = 31,270	25,259

* See footnote to Table 2.4.

*Table 2.4 Sentenced adult male prisoners: number of previous institutional sentences**

Number	1967 %	1972 %
0	28	27
1	15	16
2	12	13
3–5	23	24
6–10	15	13
11–20	6	5
20+	1	1
	100	99
	N = 31,270	25,259

* In respect of both these tables, the figures published in *People in prison* included men committed in default of payment of fines. Since 1970, the Home Office has not collected information on the previous history of persons so committed, and the proportions recorded for 1967 above have therefore been amended to make them comparable with those available for 1972; neither include the considerable number of receptions of fine defaulters (N = 11,109 in 1967 and 9,566 in 1972).

*Table 2.5 Number of adult male prisoners who have been previously in various types of institution**

Previous institutions	1967 %	1972 %
No previous institutional experience	28	27
Approved school	15	No inf.
Detention centre	9	17
Borstal training	22	28
Prison	69	63
[Suspended sentence	Not applicable	51]

* Excludes those committed to prison on default of payment of fines.

Since the publication of the White Paper, and possibly because of comments made by the 1969 Report of the House of Commons Estimates Committee (at a meeting of which the Director of Research admitted that not enough effort had been put into prison research), the Home Office Research Unit has conducted a detailed sample census of the prison population in south-east England, and work is proceeding on data analysis.

Reporting preliminary findings of the census, Dr Charlotte Banks has said that the sample comprised short- (37 per cent), medium- (40 per cent) and long-term (24 per cent) prisoners.[6] Although no statistics had yet been prepared on the long-term men, it was immediately clear that over half of all short-term and medium-term prisoners had been classified as either mentally abnormal or seriously maladjusted:

	Short-term %	*Medium-term %*
Mentally abnormal	16	23
Seriously maladjusted	38	43

Delay in publication is endemic to all such research, but until the full results are available, no-one has access to any reliable portrait of prisoners in Britain.

The experience of prison

The 1969 White Paper is noteworthy for the fact that it is essentially a well-intentioned and humane document and that it makes confessions of the system's weaknesses albeit by way of understatement: 'In some respects the conditions of a prisoner's daily life fall short of what society would currently approve.'[7] Nevertheless, some of the impressions created by *People in prison* and by successive reports of the work of the Prison Department need to be viewed alongside accounts given by those with a different experience of the daily routine.

People in prison refers back to 'the original basic elements of the well-ordered Victorian gaol – food, shelter, clothing, exercise (of a sort), religious services, and medical treatment', and comments that now there are, in addition, work, access to books, opportunities for education, and opportunities for social life and recreation within the institution:[8]

> The relationships in the daily contacts between members of the prison service and offenders in custody are generally good. (A visitor whose image of a prison has been formed by the harshness of its Victorian buildings, and by grim tales of prison life, is very often surprised by the relaxed atmosphere he finds inside the wall.) In the last few years . . . there has been a noticeable improvement in the atmosphere of our institutions.[9]

Certainly it is true that some of Britain's penal institutions are bright and airy places; a small but growing number of them are newly built, and the very newest have finally made the ultimate concession to the twentieth century by providing either individual lavatories in cells or allowing night access to communal facilities: there will, henceforth, be a handful of prisoners for whom slopping-out will be a thing of the past. But the impression, understandably though not necessarily wisely, given by the Home Office in its White Paper is only one view; that of the consumer or of the concerned observer may be different.

The prisoner's view

A large number of books have been written by or on behalf of people who have experienced prison at first hand, and yet the descriptions that they provide tend to be glossed over in many of the discussions about conditions in custody; certainly anybody reading autobiographical accounts of imprisonment would find it hard to reconcile them with some of the official claims about prison conditions. Ex-prisoners consistently emphasize the harshness, the depersonalization and the overbearing aimlessness of life in jail. Mention has been made of eleven aspects of prison life – some traditional, some more recent – that *People in prison* identified. What have other writers – mainly prisoners – to say about them?

(Two critical comments which can be made about the quotations that follow are recognized. First, many of them might seem to be invalid because they refer to conditions existing at various dates in the last two decades. Unfortunately the very nature of a prison sentence means that those who have experienced it can only write about it afterwards – perhaps long afterwards; but, in any case, although some things have changed – for example, in regard to women's clothing – the most recent autobiographical accounts suggest that, in most significant respects, the prisoners' everyday experiences are much as they would have been twenty years ago. Moreover, the accounts are not intended to represent a balanced judgment having maximum validity, but to reflect the opinions of people whose views are not normally juxtaposed with official and supposedly more objective descriptions of prison conditions.

Second, due recognition should be accorded to the fact that the opinions of people about such topics as institutional food or medical treatment in the community may frequently echo those voiced by the prisoners. Again, however, this is no reason for ignoring the comments of the men inside prisons, although it may serve to place their assertions in a broader perspective.)

Food There is conflict of opinion about meals in prison. Willetts was wholly critical of food in Holloway: 'The interminable bread soaked in water with a few dates thrown in, which, after a brief stay in the oven, was given to us as a Holloway bread pudding, and the unforsaking sense of hunger whose only alternative was the blown-out sensation that comes from living on bread and potatoes. . . .'[10] In an open prison to which she was later sent, she found the food much improved. This view was recently reiterated by a research worker in a women's open prison:[11] 'The vast majority found the food good and the conditions infinitely better than they had expected – some even referred to it, with giggles, as the (holiday) camp.' There is other evidence to suggest that menus have improved considerably since Willetts's experience, although there is inevitable difficulty in comparing the views of outside observers with those of the prisoners themselves. In 1973, Wilshaw visited Oxford and Kirkham Prisons, and found in both that the standard of cooking was higher than he had expected, although in Oxford the fact that the majority of men had to carry it back to their cells meant that 'it hardly matters what the food is like in these circumstances'.[12] The menu was varied and adequate, despite the fact that carbohydrates were 'well in evidence'; most diets were catered for. At Kirkham, the food was even better, much of it homegrown; 'the prison also supplied a Meals on Wheels service to the county'. And an even more favourable description of 1973 conditions was quoted by the *Daily Mail*: 'Britain's prisoners are eating twice as much fresh meat as the average person. And their diet is upsetting prison officers, who want prisoners' weekly ration cut down to the national average. . . .'[13]

Finally, the ambiguity is well summarized by a prisoner's judgment of the quality of meals in Strangeways Prison in 1973: 'On the whole the cleanliness and preparation of the food is poor. However no criticism can be made against the meat ration. This is a good allowance.'[14]

Shelter '. . . You're in this sort of dog-kennel because it's no bigger than that, with one bunk on top of the other and the third bed on the floor. You get three chamberpots, three washbowls, three tables, three chairs, three washstands, and you're normally in there from four in the evening till seven the next morning.'[15] '. . . You've got two little windows, no air, and in the winter you freeze and in the summer you sweat like a pig.'[16] In Strangeways, the drains are said to be frequently blocked, and the PROP report asserts that no disinfectant is issued.[17]

Clothing At one stage, a woman prisoner describes how she and her colleague 'were given bundles of the most extraordinary clothes . . . enormous black lace-up shoes, so ungainly that I thought I was going to fall over my own feet. . . . There is no system of giving size numbers to prison clothing and trying to give the women a suitable fit. Stockings, underwear and dresses seem to be distributed at random' thus transforming the women 'into clumsy and shapeless-looking criminals'.[18] However, women prisoners 'may now wear their own clothes. But men and boys have to wear prison uniform, including shoes which have often been worn before.'[19] Sometimes the clothes 'are issued in a dirty condition with food stains', and one prisoner claimed that he had not had a blanket change in sixteen months. An extra handkerchief was confiscated 'because I had not gained the necessary medical authority'.[20]

Ellis describes how borstal boys work hard to personalize their dress. Although 'they are all dressed alike', they put a great deal of 'thought and effort into being different. Those who work in the laundry, or who have friends there, will have their collars starched to Edwardian height. Others will take the buttons off their shirts and sew them on to their collar corners. They will taper their trousers, ink insignia on their denim jackets – such as sergeant's stripes, a swastika, their name, or even, pathetically, their number.'[21]

Exercise Peter Evans describes how every day at the appointed time the men in Strangeways go round and round 'under the eyes of prison officers, walking continuously, with their eyes fixed usually straight ahead or cast down . . .'.[22]

Religion 'Today is Sunday. . . . We have our Quaker meeting in the week (when it can be arranged) and so are not obliged to go to the Church of England service on Sunday mornings as most prisoners are.'[23] Few of the prisoners refer to any religious practice in prison, either positively or negatively.

Medical treatment '. . . the grim terror of illness, the helplessness of having to watch someone get worse without being able to do anything for them, knowing that they must wait until their ill-health was established beyond any shadow of a doubt before even the mildest form of treatment would be given. It would never do to treat anyone who might be putting it on.'[24] The same comments have been made more recently too: 'Methods of treatment are questionable.... The attitude of these doctors is that all prisoners are shamming',[25] and a number of detailed accounts have been reproduced in PROP and RAP literature.[26] Perhaps similar stories could be identified in the community, but Peter Scott's comment is wholly appropriate: 'Life was far worse aboard a destroyer, but the crew didn't think they were being punished.'[27]

Work '. . . Then out comes the knitting. At first I just couldn't believe it when other prisoners said this was going to be unpicked as soon as done. When I realised it was true, I could hardly make myself continue to knit – it seemed so completely demoralising'.[28]

'There are some 160–200 prisoners in Number 8 Mailbag Shop, repairing old and dirty mailbags thereby creating a large amount of dust. This is a vastly overcrowded workshop with no roof ventilation at all.' It is a new building 'and should comply with modern building regulations'.[29]

'Most prison work is degrading. Kitchen work, cleaning, laundry and so on are at least necessary to the running of any home, prison included. . . . Because of the chronic overcrowding, many prisoners are given no work at all.'[30] 'As far as can be ascertained, the majority of prisoners in Strangeways Prison would be earning less than 50p per 25-hours week.'[31]

Books 'One of the best ways to pass the time in the nick is to get armed with a library book', and O'Hara accordingly recommends prisoners to get well in with the library red-band by the standard procedure of supplying him with cigarettes.[32] Anne Turner's useful review of library services indicates some of the problems: poor accommodation, not enough money spent on books, too little choice, and, above all, inadequate liaison with the public library system. 'In prison, a good library should be regarded as a major need, not a minor one', said one prisoner, but a typical comment was: 'The books which are readable are strictly limited in supply. . . . I find myself using the library less and less.'[33] 'Educational books . . . are issued sometimes two weeks after being sent in.'[34]

Education and training 'We've got a French class. I go to it because my mates go. So we spend a couple of hours a week together. We've got no use for French. The teacher's a good sort, so we all enjoy the class. But that won't do for the [prison] commissioners: they've got to make a song and dance about it, and say they're reforming us through education. . . . I was told once of a prisoner who put down for music appreciation. There weren't any vacancies. So they stuck him in the shorthand class . . . and he couldn't write.

'Don't think I'm running down classes. I'm not. All I'm saying is we've got to be honest about them. They're not going to solve our problems when we go out even if a man does pass his City and Guilds and he gets a painter and decorator's job when he goes out. You'd probably find he's left the job within a couple of weeks anyway. No amount of certificates are going to change me into a good citizen when the psychiatrist says he hasn't a hope of doing it. But classes and training and correspondence courses all help. They give the prisoner an interest. . . . They help to make his time go quicker. So he feels less bitter about things. Anything that does that in these places is good.'[35]

The official view, of course, is very different. When opening the Prison Department's biggest educational block at Wetherby Borstal in 1973, a Home Office minister was enthusiastic about developments in this sector: prison education programmes had more than doubled during the preceding five years, and it was planned to offer inmates more opportunities 'to broaden their outlook and develop new interests and skills'. On the other hand, 'some long-term prisoners are given courses of instruction in trades such as brick-laying or plumbing; they are then given unrelated prison jobs'.[36]

Social life and recreation 'During the one hour in forty-eight of "smoking run" (for third stage good conduct men only) there was a long, low room with plenty of tables and chairs. Besides these there were ring-boards and chess-boards for men who played indoor games. Also there was a garden, with flower-beds and shrubberies, where a man could take a chair outside and enjoy a cigarette in peace and comfort.'[37] And in 1973, a prisoner in one large local prison commented to his visiting probation officer that, out of seventy-two hours including the weekend, he had spent sixty-nine locked up in his cell.

Relationships with the staff 'A man would eat his bread in four hungry bites and then be faced with the dismaying thought of no more food for 17 hours, while he could see screws calling at the kitchen on their way home to pick up parcels of his grub to supplement their own rations, the thieving bastards. . . . How did this man get into the uniform we loathed so much, the uniform all too often occupied by semi-literate brutes? We were accustomed to discipline screws who, because they were basically afraid and unsure of their ability to command a number of men among whom there were some very tough nuts, constantly assailed our ears with niggling and nagging shouts of "stop yer talking or yer'll be on report".'[38]

'. . . prison staff taking sides of ham, fruit, etc. home from the prison kitchen – our rations!'[39]

'Intimidation of prisoners by prison officers is an everyday occurrence.' 'Brutality and kicking of prisoners is known to occur, although generally this is confined to the solitary confinement cells which are separated from the rest of the wing so that witnesses are kept to nil.' 'I have observed petty thefts by several officers.' 'I have seen on several occasions prisoners who suffer from sudden epileptic fits completely ignored by prison officers who rendered absolutely no assistance.'[40] '. . . the general childlike treatment of prisoners by all prison staff. . . .'[41]

Of course, a natural reaction on the part of authority or of the reader may be to reject such personal comments as imply criticism of the system because of their inevitable one-sidedness. But they are not necessarily more biased or even more dishonest than official assertions which may reflect political good intentions rather than the facts, or which may stem from the limited perception of an occasional visitor to the institution rather than from the intensity of everyday personal experience. Certainly the reality of imprisonment is not changed by minor innovations within the traditional context of security, austerity and the imposition of a policy emphasizing the personal worthlessness of men and women who are treated essentially as objects. Even to improve the grim surroundings of our older prisons is not necessarily a gain if all else remains the same: simply to bring about physical changes seems 'like taking meticulous care over the icing of a cake that is soggy inside. Only those who have to eat it can know how mildewy it tastes.'[42]

Finally most of those who have written about prison as an experience emphasize the crisis of coming out, and the way in which the very period of imprisonment aggravates the problems which the man will face after his release:[43]

> Behind him . . . almost exactly six years of being in prison. Of getting up in the morning when the bell rang. Of performing trivial meaningless work day after day, week after week, month after month, for a wage less than the average schoolboy's pocket money. Of being clothed, fed, housed, sheltered, by number and by rote. Of obeying rules, keeping out of trouble, doing as he was told.

It is because society has gradually recognized the counter-productive nature of the prison experience, and in particular the problems that it was storing up for the inmates upon release, that it now employs prison welfare officers. What is their role? And what are their achievements?

The prison welfare service

In 1963 the recommendations of the ACTO report on *The organisation of after-care* plunged the probation service into that part of the penal system with which hitherto it had had only occasional or relatively distant contact, and the Government's decision to go even further and arrange for the employment of probation officers in penal institutions as welfare staff created an entirely new situation which was symbolized in the decision that henceforth the probation service was to be known officially as the probation and after-care service.

Because of its terms of reference, the ACTO report was primarily concerned with the concept of after-care, and its recommendations were specifically designed to achieve the smooth transition of prisoners back into the community. But with its assertion that 'within the penal institution it should be the conscious aim of the whole staff to promote the individual rehabilitation of each inmate' and with its explicit recognition of the potentially important role of professional social workers in the process, it was inevitable that the changes which followed its publication should create a fluid and at times difficult situation.

This fluidity was both reflected and increased in the policy statement from the Home Office[44] which defined the role of the newly created prison welfare service as being fourfold. The prison welfare officer was to be a social caseworker, the focal point of social work in the prison, the normal channel of communication on social problems with the outside world, and the planner of after-care.

The number of welfare officers in post (who were to be probation officers, employed by the local service, and seconded to the prison establishment where they would be responsible to the prison governor on all matters relating to their work) rose rapidly from 92 in 1966 to 294 in 1972, although the ratio of officers to prisoners improved less markedly because of the rise in the number of inmates during the same period. At the beginning of 1972, the ratio was 1 : 132, and the aim was said to be to reduce it to 1 : 100.[45] (In a study carried out in January 1970 by the National Association of Probation Officers,[46] welfare officers' caseloads ranged between 43 and 350, with an average of 153. When asked what they considered to be a viable caseload for the prison welfare officer, the average response worked out at 87. Annual turnover would of course be much higher than this, and one officer in a local prison was said to have been responsible for 300–500 men during 1969.)

Numerous assertions about the importance of the role to be played by welfare staff in prisons contributed to this growth, most notably those expressed by the Mountbatten Enquiry in December 1966 which recommended an increase in the size of the welfare service as one contribution towards raising prison morale and reducing the risk of escapes. Gradually, however, some of the limitations have been recognized, and in 1972 the Home Office announced that it was carrying out a general review of social work in prisons in the light of experience gained. The problems can be identified briefly in relation to the four roles defined in the 1967 Home Office Circular; they all involve the probation officer in the border area between the prison as a total institution and the community out of which prisoners have been taken and into which most of them will ultimately be returned.

1 The welfare officer as a social caseworker

The National Association of Probation Officers has discussed the problems of defining 'continuing casework',[47] and a representative of the service has described how, with large caseloads, 'it would take all one's time to get round the wing without looking at intensive work, although for one's own sanity as a caseworker one had to select a small number of five or ten [prisoners] with which one can do deep casework to satisfy one's own professional being'.[48] In the Home Office's Midlands Experiment, remarkable results have been reported following the introduction of regular casework (it could hardly be called intensive at less than an hour a week) for a randomly selected group of prisoners, by increasing the establishment of welfare officers in post.[49] Not only did the prisoners' attitudes towards the welfare staff show an improvement, but their post-release reconviction rates were markedly below those of a control group. Unfortunately, as with so many such experiments, it is not possible for the authors to say precisely what it was in the situation that led to improved performances following release, but if the validity of the finding were confirmed, its implications would be far-reaching indeed. If, by providing a personal casework service on a weekly basis, the probability of reconviction is reduced by 20 per cent in respect of all released prisoners, this would not only be a legitimate argument for aiming at a ratio of welfare officers to inmates more in the region of 1 : 50 or even 1 : 40 – that is to say, bringing it roughly in line with the average caseload size for probation officers in the community; it would also be an almost revolutionary breakthrough in the British correctional field. In all the talk about treatment and rehabilitation, it is not often openly recognized or admitted that the evidence of real behavioural impact within the penal system is minimal; but if a combination of casework and imprisonment could really be shown to represent a positive demonstration of effective social engineering, then the need to seek a theoretical understanding of the process and to explore its possible implications in other contexts would be pressing.

This is all the more so because the practice of casework – or the attempt to practise it – within penal institutions is in many respects inherently paradoxical. Almost all casework literature – especially that emanating from the USA – emphasizes the importance of the voluntary relationship in practice and refers to the essential element of respect for the individual. Despite Plant's critique of some of the underlying tenets of casework theory and his assertion that casework is ultimately anti-democratic in its assumption of worker superiority,[50] there is little doubt that many casework attitudes do run counter to the mood of the penal institution that the prisoner has learned to accept. In particular, perhaps, the concept of an individualized relationship – albeit a restricted one that falls far short of a democratic ideal – is so alien a notion within the setting of a total institution that it could assume an importance far in excess of that relating to any similar relationship in the wider community. Probably the significant element lies in its continuity up to the point of discharge and possibly beyond, and it is to this end that in recent years the notion of 'through-care' has been mooted as being preferable to after-care. Here, however, there is disagreement as to the extent to which the person responsible for through-care should be the home probation officer or the prison welfare officer; in both respects there are severe practical problems. In the former, geographical distance renders an ongoing relationship between prisoner and probation officer impossible in the majority of cases, especially in long-term sentences; in the latter, even assuming that the problems of workload could be resolved, the casework relationship would extend only to the point of discharge, and would be terminated at the very time of crisis which theory would suggest was when the need was likely to be most immediate. Shaw and Jarvis's paper, however, would seem to contradict this notion, in that no extraordinary attempt was made to ensure ongoing after-care other than that normally available; the impact of casework during the sentence stood in its own right as the major apparent determinant of post-release behaviour.[51]

One crucial question remains, however, although the researchers in the Midlands Experiment explored it in considerable detail.[52] Is casework in the prisons to be seen as a minor act of amelioration and contrast in an otherwise alien setting? Or is it to be an integral part of a wholly rehabilitative process? Whatever the hopes and wishes of politicians and administrators may be – and these should not perhaps be taken for granted – the practical probability is that regular casework with inmates is not only likely to continue to be the exception rather than the rule in prison establishments, but even given significant increases in welfare staff complements, practitioners will have to contend with the fact that the welfare officer is only one of a great many functional segments in the institution, that he is less in touch with most prisoners than is the discipline officer, and that he is still regarded with some suspicion or even hostility by prison officers whose primary responsibility is to maintain law and order within the institution and who rightly or wrongly identify much of what the welfare officer does as being likely to undermine their tenuous authority. It is not so much that prison officers themselves do not make individual relationships with prisoners; one of the findings in the Midlands Experiment was that, in normal conditions, prisoners are much more likely to name a discipline officer than a welfare officer as the person for whom they have the greatest sympathy and respect. The welfare officer is unlikely to be seen as a commonly approachable person.[53] But the separate development of the welfare service runs the risk of introducing a formal and functional separation of positive and negative roles in the institution which could have both a damaging effect on prison staff morale, and paradoxically lend emphasis to the controlling nature of the prison régime, the stability of which is almost certainly dependent first and foremost on the interacting relationships between inmates and discipline staff. It is quite possible that the occurrence of prison strikes and inmate rebellion is coincidental with the strengthening of the welfare service in prisons, the slight trend towards a recognition of the rights of prisoners as individuals, and the ambiguous role accorded to discipline officers in these developments. Sociologically it seems improbable that innovations of the kind achieved during the late 1960s and since can be made without affecting the overall balance of power and expectations in such a sensitive arena as a prison. The balance between casework and social control might well be critical.

2 *The welfare officer as the focal point for social work*

The NAPO report has highlighted the inevitable 'clash of interests and attitudes between the probation service and the prison service when the latter had to open its gates to accommodate the former'.[54] In place of workers employed by voluntary organizations with little status and less power, the prison employees have come to realize that the new policy has brought into the institutions representatives of a politically sensitive service with strong public support who are likely to exert an increasing influence on penal policy. With the arrival of welfare officers from the probation service, other workers in the prison setting have found that they were in danger of losing some of their traditional functions: not only prison officers, but assistant governors, chaplains and even medical officers began to wonder whether the welfare officer's nomination as 'the focal point for social work' would give him a status likely to usurp a small but increasingly important segment of their own work. The extent to which this is happening will vary from prison to prison, and perhaps the relatively rapid turnover among welfare officers will to some extent counter-balance the trend; but as the establishment size increases, and as problems of accommodation, clerical and ancillary staff are resolved, so the status and influence of the welfare officer is likely to grow.

Despite wide-ranging discussion about the need for continuing casework in prisons, the primary demands on the welfare officer are for the provision of welfare aid, as has again been shown in the

Midlands Study.[55] In one respect these demands may relate to the prisoner's links with the outside world – thus overlapping with the third of the prison welfare officer's roles – but they may also very often have to do with the life of the inmate in the institution. This involves the welfare officer in a way that is wholly appropriate to a casework commitment, in that it requires a psychosocial focus on the relationship between the client and his current social situation; but it must almost inevitably lead to elements of role-conflict for the welfare officer in so far as he may feel it necessary (as a caseworker) to try to intervene in the client's environment, i.e. the prison, or to discuss matters raised by the prisoner relating to other members of the prison staff in a way that might lead working colleagues to wonder whose side the welfare officer is on.

The probation service's perception of the problems involved in undertaking welfare work in prisons has been well expressed by the Chairman of the Principal Probation Officers' Conference. After emphasizing the need for the welfare officer to maintain the link between the prisoner and the community,[56] he implicitly acknowledges the tendency for the life of the institution to become dominant, not only for the offender but for the officer too:[57]

> I believe that from time to time [prison welfare officers] should be brought out of [institutions] to work in the community again to bring them back to the reality of the situation. My experience is that, over a number of years, like the rest of the prison staff, they become institution orientated and this is a bad thing for a social worker in any sort of situation.

Hence, there is a real conflict; the ideological commitment of the probation service is always to look beyond the prison walls, and to regard the sentence as an unfortunate interlude in a man's life which he must be helped to overcome. On the other hand, the notion of continuing treatment within the prison, the immediacy and exclusiveness of the prison experience in the inmate's mind, and the full-time commitment of all other members of the prison staff towards the custodial régime, all exert pressure on the welfare officer to identify with the institution. The more closely he works with the system, the more surely does he become a part of the closed community and the less valid is his claim to be the prisoner's link with the outside world. On the other hand, the relationship between the probation service and the prisons is a two-way process, and the future development of the newly-emergent welfare service will show not only the extent to which probation officers have adapted themselves to an institutional role in the correctional process, but also the extent to which the phenomenon of imprisonment remains unadulterated or alternatively evolves into a variety of semi-custodial forms of treatment.

3 The welfare officer as the normal channel of communication on social problems with the outside world

The extent to which this role overlaps with the last one depends entirely on the way in which the concept of prison welfare is defined. If, as has traditionally been the case, it tends to emphasize the prisoner's links with home and his problems on release, then the overlap might be complete, but it was argued in the last section that current trends indicate the development of a rather different welfare focus. Nevertheless, the welfare officer is still significant for the access that he has to outside social work agencies, including the prisoner's home probation officer, and it seems probable that he plays a functionally useful role on such matters as arranging for clothes to be stored, conveying news about the family situation to the prisoner, and obtaining relevant information about the prisoner's background from outside sources.

But once again the role, for all that it may be a helpful one, reflects a situation that appears to be changing, and that therefore gives rise to uncertainty. Put simply, it can be argued that if one of the aims of establishing a prison welfare service is to reduce the element of total isolation from the outside world that has traditionally characterized the prisoner's lot, then there are almost certainly more efficient, more constructive, and possibly cheaper ways in which this can be achieved; and that the alternatives are likely to be more in accord with the social work principles of raising the client's self-respect, encouraging his attempts at self-direction, and facilitating first-hand contacts with his responsibilities in the community. This is not to argue that in the absence of more radical reform, minor improvements in liaison are valueless; rather that their significance should not be exaggerated, nor should one lose sight of possibly better ways of achieving the same objectives. Talcott Parsons[58] argues that restricted links with the outside world are an understandable part of prison life, and hence that the use of employees (prison welfare officers) to monitor and organize communication is merely an extension of control, not a reduction: 'The most important aspect of deterrence is very generally blocking channels of communication; for example, the most important feature of imprisonment is preventing the prisoner from communicating with others except in ways and through channels his custodians can control.' Even the apparently forward-looking scheme whereby borstal inmates can telephone their parents only makes provision for 'monitored telephone calls'.[59]

If one of the primary objectives of the prison welfare service is to minimize the effects of a man's separation from his home community and from his family life, then it is obviously wholly anomalous to maintain the excessive restrictions that characterize prison life in regard to the inmate's personal contacts with the outside world. In the light of this, one might usefully speculate on the extent to which decisions in the Probation and After-care Department of the Home Office might increasingly determine some of the problems and the policies that have to be managed by the Prison Department. If it is true that the focus of concern in the probation service is on the supervision of offenders in the community, then the entry of probation officers to the prisons might yet prove to have been a major catalyst in the development or possibly the destruction of the prison system in the twentieth century; alternatively it might be argued that the Goverment's awareness of this possibility is one of the factors influencing the tendency towards increased central control over the probation service.

4 *The welfare officer as the planner of after-care*

It was with this role that the ACTO report was principally concerned' but it now appears that problems concerned specifically with after-care take up only a small part of the welfare officer's time, and that even some pre-discharge duties are of a kind which many officers think could better be handled by non-professionals: 'Prison staff should in all prisons take over the more purely welfare aspects of the prisoner's treatment during his sentence and on his discharge.'[60] One study[61] has demonstrated how short-sentence men are frequently missed altogether by the welfare service, although the problems that they present are often among the most severe, and it has been suggested that the movements of prisoners within the system often prevents them becoming properly known to the welfare service. Of the prisoners who were interviewed in the study, 20 per cent said that they had not heard of after-care and an additional 23 per cent that they had not heard of anything specific that the after-care service could help them with: 'It must therefore be concluded that information about after-care facilities had not been effectively communicated to over two-fifths of the prisoners.'[62] Moreover, of those who had heard of after-care, less than half (41 per cent) had been told about it within the month preceding discharge.[63] Despite some obvious exceptions, it is apparent from this study that in 1970 the welfare service was by no means fully operational as a pre-discharge preparation agency. It is true that the proportion of ex-prisoners attending probation offices for voluntary after-care has been rising gently, but as so often in regard to the provision of social work aid to offenders, the question must be asked: are good intentions and minor improvements enough? And are we not in danger of, first, deceiving ourselves into imagining that the recommendations of such bodies as the Advisory Council on the Treatment of Offenders have been effectively put into operation, and, then, of expressing disappointment at the poor response of prisoners to proffered aid. With preparation for after-care, as with other aspects of the work of the prison welfare service, more attention ought perhaps to be given to the consumer's view. More often than not he must still feel that only exceptionally does a prisoner receive maximum help and support from the probation and welfare services at the time of discharge. It is true that experiments in the provision of intensive care to discharged prisoners are now in train, but the real issue still hinges on the logic of providing social work aid in an essentially punitive and separatist institution.

It is now a very hackneyed quotation, although it is no less valid today than when it was first applied to the penal system, for despite the apparent social necessity of such an illogical system, it is still unlikely that one can 'train men for freedom in conditions of captivity'.[64]

> The crux of the matter seems to be: what is prison for? Once we have properly answered that question, if ever, we should then perhaps ask what can actually be done inside prison to achieve the prisoner's rehabilitation, because the day inevitably dawns when he comes out.[65]

In the absence of further clarification, the work of the prison welfare officer will continue to evolve in ways probably quite different from those envisaged by the Advisory Council when it discussed the organization of after-care in 1963.

3 Voluntary after-care

Prior to the 1963 ACTO report, the provision of voluntary after-care facilities had long been a responsibility of the Discharged Prisoners' Aid Societies, usually dependent on money received from charitable sources and on grants from public funds. Increasingly the reliance on government subsidy grew, and inevitably this rendered the societies vulnerable to central direction. Following the Maxwell Committee report in 1953, there was a switch of emphasis in the work of the societies from material aid on discharge to a policy of preparation for 'constructive after-care',[1] which in practice led to the appointment of the first prison welfare officers by the National Association of Discharged Prisoners' Aid Societies.

Following the 1963 ACTO report, voluntary after-care has played a steadily bigger and bigger part in the work of the probation service, as Table 3.1 shows.

Table 3.1 Voluntary after-care cases on the probation service's caseload at the end of each calendar year

Year	Number	Proportion of all after-care cases %	Proportion of total caseload %
1963	596	4·5	0·6
1964	897	5·9	0·9
1965	2,580	13·9	2·3
1966	3,942	19·1	3·4
1967	5,395	23·7	4·5
1968	5,490	22·0	4·5
1969	6,566	24·5	5·1
1970	8,197	27·3	6·1
1971	9,288	29·1	7·2

Source: Annual probation and after-care statistics, Home Office, London.

The recommendations of the report were generally implemented, and a mark of the importance accorded to the service's new responsibilities was the creation of a special division in the new Probation and After-care Department in the Home Office to plan for all the changes expected (October 1964). Some men who leave prison are subject to statutory after-care on licence, but the vast majority are not: they comprise all men and women aged 21 or over who are sentenced to prison for other than life sentences and who are ineligible, unsuccessful in their application, or who do not choose to apply, for parole. Inevitably, therefore, they tend to be either the relatively bad risks or those who have been given sentences of less than eighteen months.

Among recent developments in this area have been the opening and establishment of specialist after-care units in some major urban areas, the creation of a special fund by the Government to subsidize the capital costs of providing hostel accommodation for homeless ex-prisoners and the corresponding increase in the availability of such hostels, and the use by probation officers of voluntary associates in an attempt to increase the amount and intensity of work possible with men both before and after their release. A limited amount of family casework has been attempted with the wives of men in prison, and some special Wives Groups have been set up near local prisons. In addition a surprising amount of research has been undertaken both in the Home Office and elsewhere, as a result of which it is possible to form a relatively clear picture of the problems and possibilities inherent in the present structure of voluntary after-care.

Although the proportion of voluntary after-care clients on the caseload of the probation service has been rising, the proportion of prisoners actually opting for after-care in any shape or form is still only a minority of those released. Estimates have varied, but one probably reliable figure[2] records that 42 per cent of the men released from fourteen prisons called at a probation office or at an after-care unit shortly after discharge. There was a significant difference in attendance between those who had expressed an intention of taking up the offer of after-care (72 per cent actually went) and those who had been doubtful (39 per cent) or who had indicated that they would not go for help (21 per cent none the less did so). It is possible that these figures exaggerate normal usage because the research interviews themselves may well have influenced the behaviour of the prisoners, as in many cases the fifteen-minute research interview shortly before discharge was focused more on the availability of after-care than were many of the men's routine contacts with the prison welfare staff, and some men claimed that they did not previously know anything about the after-care service available.

The nature of the typical after-care relationship is highlighted by the fact that 40 per cent of all those who came to a probation office in 1971 for after-care attended for one interview only and did not return. A further 15 per cent came for less than one month. Table 3.2, however, suggests that there might be some cause for satisfaction, perhaps, in the fact that the proportion of men staying for a longer period has been rising slowly: the proportion of those attending for three months and over, for example, has risen from 18 per cent in 1965 to 26 per cent in 1971.

Table 3.2 The work of the probation service in voluntary after-care

	1965	1968	1971
Enquiries or contacts made by probation officer before release	7,484	17,703	30,912
Persons befriended after release	12,068	22,030	24,556
Length of contact:	%	%	%
one interview only	46	43	40
less than 1 month	20	17	15
over 1 and under 3 months	16	17	19
over 3 and under 6 months	9	11	12
over 6 months	9	12	14
Number of cases in which volunteers assisted	210	943	1,499

Source: Annual probation and after-care statistics, Home Office, London.

It seems probable that, unless the prison population begins to fall steadily, there will continue to be an increase in the numbers of men taking advantage of available after-care facilities, if only on a short-term basis; moreover, there seems to be some evidence that an improvement in communication about after-care in the prisons – which would presumably come about in the event of an increase in the establishment of prison welfare officers – might lead to a higher take-up rate among ex-prisoners. But the extent to which voluntary clients of the after-care service will make more long-term demands on probation officers is much more doubtful; presumably it depends entirely on the nature, extent and quality of the service offered, and the way it is viewed by the potential clients. What then is the nature of the after-care relationship and how successful has the probation service been in providing for the needs of ex-prisoners?

One especially useful Home Office research report[3] goes a long way towards describing in detail both the typical client of the after-care service and the difficulties involved in meeting his needs. Although some of the clients were relatively capable of managing their own affairs, and came wanting precise guidance or advice, these seemed to form only a small minority of the callers at the specialized after-care units in city centres. The typical after-care client called without any advance arrangements being made, and was unlikely to have been seen by a probation officer while in prison:[4]

> Most of the clients, apart from being impecunious ex-prisoners, manifested their needs and problems on three distinct levels which were in constant interaction with each other:
>
> 1 The most salient features of their social situation were that they were homeless, unattached, unemployed and sometimes unemployable.
>
> 2 Their ability to support themselves was seriously impaired as the result of one or more of the following conditions: addiction to alcohol or drugs, physical ill-health and sometimes disabilities, mental illness, and behaviour disorders.
>
> 3 These symptoms in their turn arose from a disturbance of personality of varying severity.

Silberman and Chapman summarize in diagrammatic form the problems involved in undertaking casework with such men (see Figure 2, p. 40).

There was an almost total lack of reliable information about the ex-prisoners, thus preventing any skilled diagnosis. The clients generally came to the units with pressing material needs for money, for work and for accommodation;[5] hence the focus of their requests was on the here-and-now, and there was little or no point in gathering lengthy social histories, especially as experience had taught the workers that the majority of the clients would be unlikely to become ongoing cases. As a result, the authors argue that 'the negotiations

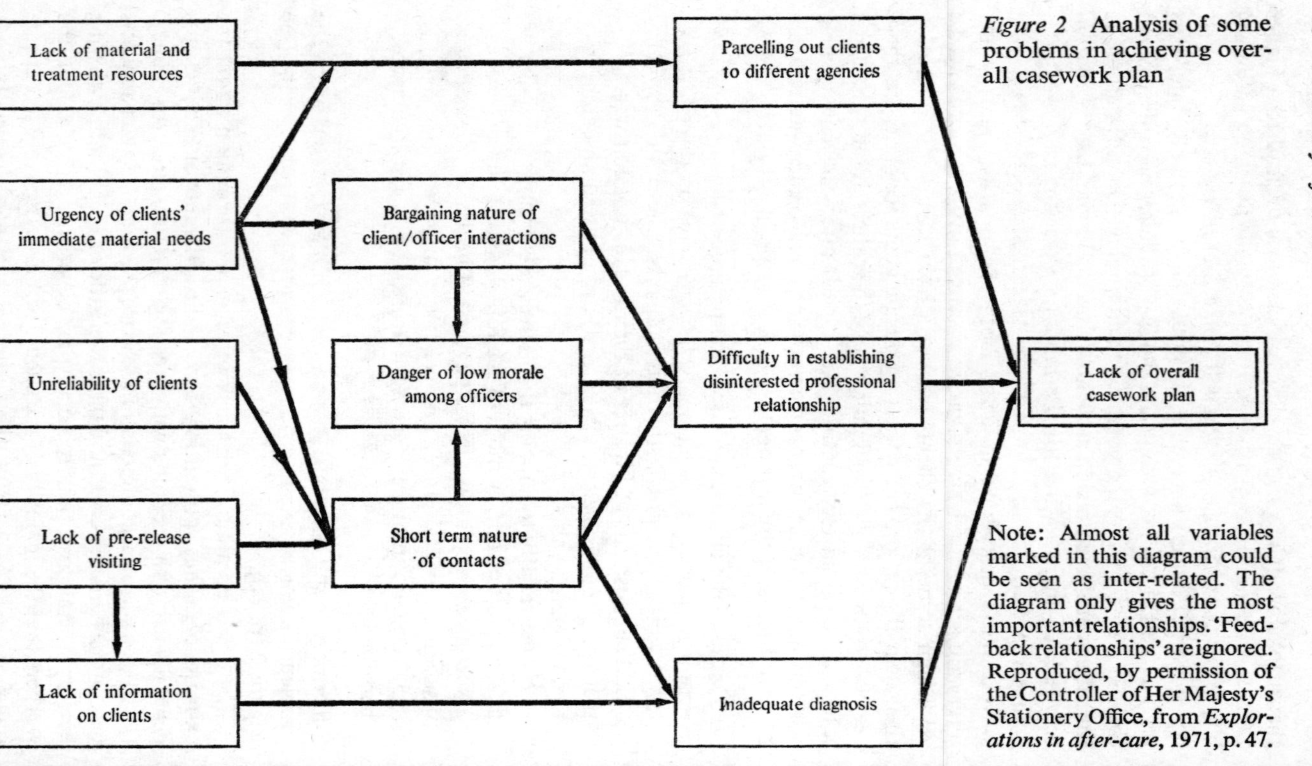

Figure 2 Analysis of some problems in achieving overall casework plan

Note: Almost all variables marked in this diagram could be seen as inter-related. The diagram only gives the most important relationships. 'Feedback relationships' are ignored. Reproduced, by permission of the Controller of Her Majesty's Stationery Office, from *Explorations in after-care*, 1971, p. 47.

between the probation officers and the clients of after-care were essentially of a bargaining type', because the officers had only very limited access to direct material aid (although their ability to refer needy clients to other agencies could itself be seen as a valuable commodity in some cases). For many probation officers, the crude pattern of bargaining and referral-out seemed to go against the grain of their casework training and professional commitment, led at times to a low level of office morale, and tended to preclude the establishment of a valid casework relationship in all but a tiny minority of instances.

There seemed to be a basic conflict of expectations between the nature of the agency as its staff would have preferred it to be and the felt needs of the clients:[6]

> As a casework agency, the unit would have liked to help its clients by concentrating effort on the underlying problems and the provision of the material means required for their treatment or amelioration, whereas in fact the treatment of basic problems was left more or less in abeyance while much effort was spent in deciding on the allocation of inadequate means for day to day ends. In so far as his basic problems were concerned the client of after-care remained unsupported.

Responding to the needs of the ex-prisoner

The description emerging from the work of Silberman and Chapman may appear to present a rather jaundiced view in contrast to the picture built up in official reports during the 1960s, in which heavy emphasis was laid on the potential value of a professional social work service to the ex-prisoner; indeed, one of the reasons for the low morale among the officers concerned may well have been their awareness of the extent to which their routine work and its apparent effects varied from that which those in authority had earlier anticipated. It is of course true that instances can be highlighted in which ongoing help was given and appreciated; the 14 per cent of ex-prisoners who, in 1971, *did* keep coming for six months or more on a voluntary basis is a not insignificant minority. It can be argued also that, ultimately it *is* the responsibility of the prospective recipient of aid to make such use as he or she can of that which is made available; in particular, it is foolish to hold the probation officer wholly responsible for any failure to make much impact on clients who come to him with a lifetime of problems behind them.

Nevertheless, the modal pattern is clear and is not encouraging. There is a recognizable gap between the needs which ex-prisoners perceive as being primary and the resources which the social aid agencies in general and the probation service in particular have at their disposal:[7]

> The clients of after-care seemed frequently unable to manage their social security grants. They reported to the after-care units with a variety of needs which could be broadly classified under the following headings: immediate practical needs, such as money and clothing; accommodation requirements; employment problems; legal problems, non-payment of debts and domestic problems; miscellaneous difficulties.

So far as financial support is concerned, the probation service has inherited from the Discharged Prisoners' Aid Societies the task of providing for the immediate post-release period, and there is little doubt that, in many cases, the working relationship between prisons, probation officers and the DHSS (who pay supplementary benefits) has improved in recent years. This is not to say that all is satisfactory. In July 1973, a Conservative MP was reported as expressing doubts about the quality of co-ordination between the Home Office and the DHSS. Particular difficulties appear to arise over the additional discharge grant (on top of the basic allowance) which can be claimed from Social Security as payment for lodgings; it is paid to only 10 per cent of those due for release, although a much larger proportion get into difficulties in securing accommodation (this provision was abolished in 1974). Probation officers themselves do not have ready access to large funds for cash grants, but they can provide for some basic needs like clothing, fares, food, tools, rent and occasionally for the partial repayment of accumulated debts. However, the main role of the probation officer is to refer the client to another agency, often with an introductory letter or an advance telephone call; occasionally he will even accompany the client and help him make his request. It is widely believed among clients that the visible support of the probation officer at such a time can lead to more probable or more generous cash aid from the appropriate source, and there is some research evidence to support the belief.

Many have argued that much more generous financial aid on discharge is a self-evident need for ex-prisoners, and Taggart[8] suggests that the conceptual case for income maintenance following release is compelling because of the adjustment problems that ex-prisoners face, because they generally have few resources to fall back on, and because in the absence of funds it would seem likely that many might turn to the skill they know best – crime. However, Oliver[9] has reported an experiment in which 250 offenders were given an average of $1,000 on discharge, but as a result were not noticeably more employable or less likely to re-offend. In spite of such negative empirical findings, Oliver none the less argues that most counsellors would still prefer to see an increase in the size of the discharge grant; but Taggart understandably comments that the research results make it more difficult to support the claim that income maintenance is worthwhile:[10]

> It is unlikely that society will allocate a scarce resource to this aspect of corrections unless there are demonstrated results in terms of quantitative or qualitative improvements in employment and reductions in recidivism. As yet, the conceptual benefits of income maintenance during post-release have not been demonstrated.

Taggart's is a simple reductivist argument: if additional payments on release from prison do not produce improved 'results' in the measurable terms of a lower reconviction rate, then their legitimacy is questionable; but, as with all forms of social work support, this may represent too narrow an approach. The problems of accommodation and employment will be examined separately in later chapters, but two contrasting case examples indicate the dangerous naïvety of failing to take into account the widely different levels of coping at a personal level when considering appropriate after-care strategies. The resources available and the response to be made by the worker may not only need to be quite different in degree, but also in terms of the anticipated outcome. In the case examples that follow, the service needed for Bernard Varley is utterly distinct from that which the probation officer patiently tries to provide for Martha Mopp; it is important to recognize the probation officer's doubts as to whether he was even justified in spending time with Mr Varley. Perhaps the ultimate paradox of social work is that the client who seems least capable of using the help given or least likely to improve his situation in response to external support is nevertheless the rightful recipient of the most skilled and the most patient personal service that society can offer.

Case example 1

Bernard Varley committed an assault on a Spaniard while he was serving with the Royal Signals in Gibraltar; he was sentenced to eight months' imprisonment, which he served in three British prisons. Aged 20, he is said to have had a happy upbringing and returned to his parents on discharge; rather to everyone's surprise, he asked for after-care because he thought the probation service could help him to settle down.

Although said by some to be outspoken and arrogant, the probation officer found him pleasant enough when he visited him in an East Anglian open prison a week before discharge; they had a 'general discussion', and it was arranged that Bernard would call in to see Mr Tripp on the day of his release. Apart from the prison visit, pre-release work by the probation officer involved several exchanges of correspondence and telephone calls with prison welfare departments, two home visits to Bernard's mother, and a telephone conversation with her.

When Bernard came to the office, Mr Tripp gave him letters of introduction to the Employment and Social Security agencies; after a short holiday, Bernard quickly got a factory job and settled in well. During the next five months, he called into the office four times and the probation officer made two home visits; conversation covered current developments at work and in the home. For example: 'Father is currently sleeping downstairs having been released from hospital on Wednesday of last week after having a hernia operation; says that he still feels a little sore but is getting stronger every day. Learned that Bernard has now changed his job and is back in plastering. He is getting engaged in March. Everything seems to be going along quite well, and there are no problems.'

At the outset of the case, the probation officer commented that Bernard had an apparently good relationship with his family, 'and one wonders why he considered it necessary to opt for after-care'; and in the final summary, he again indicated that after-care had not been needed in this case. However, 'Bernard seemed to enjoy his visits'.

Case example 2

Martha Mopp, now aged 57, is the sort of person that people tend to refer to, somewhat euphemistically perhaps, as a well-known local character. Her history is liberally embroidered with psychiatric reports, court appearances, incidents with the neighbours, and bouts of heavy drinking. Her appearance is somewhat bedraggled, she has been married twice, has eight children all of whom were taken into care by the local authority, and she seems unlikely ever to be much different.

Five years ago, she appeared in court for her usual offence – breaking windows, after she had drunk too much white wine. The probation officer commented that prison had been no deterrent in the past, and that, as it was twenty years since she'd had a probation order, the court might have another try 'to see if Martha could . . . modify her behaviour within society'. The court agreed, but less than a month later the lady probation officer was awoken at 12.30 a.m. by the police because Martha had broken another window and they weren't prepared to keep her in the police station overnight. The police held the probation officer responsible, and she took Martha to a welfare hostel seven miles away. For that offence, Martha was committed to a psychiatric hospital, where she stayed for nearly four years; during this time, whenever she was released on parole she drank wine or whisky and broke windows. Eventually, following a further such incident, she appeared in court again, and a report was prepared by the probation officer on court duty. The hospital where she had previously stayed would not readmit her – they said they had more urgent cases on their waiting list, and that Martha was in need of more control than they could exercise. No hostel places appeared to be available, and the case highlighted the lack of any specialized institutions for women like Martha Mopp; a firm recommendation was made against probation. In the event, Martha was sentenced to six months' imprisonment.

In less than a month Mrs Crockett, the probation officer who had helped her in the past, but who had expressed doubts about the viability of supervision, was none the less being drawn into discharge plans. Martha thought that an uncle of hers might be able to offer her accommodation, but Mrs Crockett discovered that he had died three years earlier; instead she began negotiations with the local Social Services Department to see if they could find Martha a place in a hostel.

When Mrs Crockett went to visit her in prison, Martha said she was going to be a good girl this time, and expressed gratitude for the probation officer's help: 'I've nobody else'.

On her release, Martha arrived at the office with three suitcases.

'The whole morning was spent fruitlessly searching for accommodation, during the course of which Martha was bitten by a dog' and they all had to go to the doctor's. In the afternoon, they went to the Social Security, but Martha wasn't eligible for benefit because she had £41 in savings. The next day, Martha called to say she was staying with a family she had known before; this lasted a month, after which she moved in with a former cohabitee who had a single room in a local hostel. She then broke a leg, and went to hospital followed by a fortnight's convalescence: in a picture postcard to the probation officer, she said that she liked the food, but the sea air and water made her arms and body itch. . . .

When she returned it was hoped that she would move into a specially designated flat made available by the local authority Housing Department; Mrs Crockett became aware of this possible solution through a colleague who sat on a Community Involvement Council which had established links with the Housing Committee. Whether the opportunity of independence and responsibility would prove to be too much for Martha, who could say? But it seemed important that an effort was being made.

Work with wives and families

Not all men in prison are or will be homeless, of course, and a significant number are married with families in the outside world, to whom they hope to return on release. Pauline Morris's study (1965) provides a detailed picture of the plight of prisoners' wives, and although it is conceivable that some improvement may have occurred in succeeding years, such evidence as there is is not encouraging. Of wives living with their husbands at the time of their arrest, 86 per cent had children to care for, and most were suffering from acute poverty; debts and other money problems were preponderant, but half the sample studied by Morris also showed symptoms of physical or mental illness. The amount of contact with helping agencies was very limited – mainly through the women's ignorance of what might be available. Morris found clear evidence of gaps in the welfare provisions and in after-care arrangements, but it was not possible to conclude that filling the gaps would do more than put a humanitarian gloss on an inevitably damaging event in the family's life. In an intensive examination of fifty wives living near London, Morris found that, on the man's release, the marital relationship tended to continue from where it left off; in spite of material problems, the wives generally managed to survive and afterwards to resurrect the pattern of life to which they had formerly been accustomed.

Morris incidentally emphasized the plight of civil debtors whose prison sentence seemed to serve no useful purpose whatever, and where financial management was often the prime problem; it is significant that in a recent account of the workings of the prison welfare service, it is reported that prison welfare officers are unclear as to their role and duty *vis-à-vis* civil prisoners. Although the time that debtors spend in prison is generally short, there is a manifestly unmet need for guidance and help in the management of their affairs which appears to be no nearer satisfactory handling now than it was ten years ago.[11]

Casework's rediscovery of a potential family-focus during the 1960s, and the greater willingness of workers to experiment have, however, combined in recent years with Morris's revelations to produce a number of new initiatives in this area.

In Nottingham, a prisoners' families project was launched in 1970 with the aim of providing a professional casework service for the families of men in custody.[12] The wife is identified as the client: 'Husbands would be informed that help would be extended to their families rather than be asked to make a decision about it.' Families are visited at regular intervals during the man's sentence, and a forceful approach is adopted:

> An unusual feature will lie in the persistence of the attempt to give help. Refusal to take it will of course have to be accepted, but periodically the offer will be renewed, instead of the assumption being made that refusal at a particular moment means all-time refusal.

Monger and Pendleton thus identify what they consider to be one of the most vital questions in casework: how to improve the degree of co-operation by the prisoner and his family during the period of after-care.

The Prisoners' Wives Service, running in Birmingham, London, and elsewhere, is in sharp contrast to the Nottingham project. Founded in 1965, it depends mainly on the provision of a meeting room near the prison in which the wives can join together in groups. These act as a support service for women who feel totally bereft of all aid; they give information when it is needed, and offer a social situation in which the prisoner's wife can feel less of a social outcast.

In Birmingham, a Families Centre is staffed every afternoon by volunteers who provide tea, talk and look after the children while wives make their visits; but the probation service claims that the material base has proved to be only the foundation on which long-term rehabilitative work can be built.[13]

Morris's interviews with the wives of prisoners indicated a general level of dissatisfaction with the work of both statutory and voluntary welfare agencies, although 'probation officers tended to be well thought of, as did the NSPCC'.[14] Both in regard to material aid and social support, Morris's study of the scene in the early 1960s led her to criticize welfare facilities at that time, and in particular to argue that 'there is virtually no attempt made at present to enable the family to be dealt with as a complete unit, to include the prisoner'.[15] Since then, no further large-scale studies have been published regarding the plight of prisoners' wives, although the Nottingham project is being monitored, and the Birmingham work overlaps with the Home Office's Midlands Experiment in after-care.

Welfare of prisoners' wives and families is a self-evident good cause, but many of the problems are similar to those of all one-parent families – a group now emergent as one of the most under-privileged classes of our contemporary society. There are undoubtedly special problems deriving from the stigma of prison and the need to prepare wives for their husbands' release; but one cannot but still feel, as Morris found, that material needs must be first and foremost in the minds of most prisoners' wives.[16] It is to be hoped that any future examination of family casework or group-work in this sector records the extent to which the social worker was able or unable to ensure that the clients received an income sufficient for their needs.

One of the most widely noted developments in after-care during the 1960s has been the use of voluntary associates to aid the probation service in its work. Such a policy has several built-in attractions: at first sight, it seems likely to cost nothing or at most to involve only nominal expenditure; second, if cases requiring relatively straightforward supervision could be delegated to voluntary workers, the skilled staff's time could perhaps be more profitably used where their expertise was most needed; and third, it appears to be a way of embodying the notion of community responsibility for offenders – an idea that appeals to penal reformers and politicians alike. The first two attractions are now, however, felt to be largely illusory.

Even if a scheme can be introduced with little budgetary allowance, it is widely recognized that anything in the nature of an adequate commitment to the use of voluntary associates can be extremely expensive in terms of professional staff time. Hugh Barr's description (1971) of the ambitious training programme launched by Teamwork Associates in London, demonstrates how much money could be spent by probation areas if they were determined to do the job properly, and also shows what input is required for the disappointingly small output in terms of satisfactory associates who stay the course long enough to repay the service's initial investment.

The third attraction is based on false assumptions about the sort of person generally willing to volunteer, and while it is now true that most probation areas have a significant number of associates in post, many of them undertaking valued work with probation officers, it is more often the case that these represent would-be social workers or self-perceived social leaders rather than the originally conceived man in the street who recognizes his *alter ego* in the face of the offender. If voluntary associates do demonstrate an aspect of community responsibility, they none the less represent a highly selective and easily recognizable sub-group within the community: 'The volunteers vary enormously in personality but are almost all middle-class and professional women.'[17]

Goldberg's study of the elderly (1971) came up with similar conclusions regarding the disappointing outcome when volunteer visitors were used to provide company for the old; the wastage rate was very high, and the positive results achieved seemed disappointingly slight.

Table 3.2 (p. 38) shows how the use of voluntary associates has increased following the publicity of recent years. One major problem, often referred to within the service, lies in finding suitable jobs for associates to do, that is, suitable in that they are actually useful and not merely superfluous creations with a view to keeping the volunteer busy: jobs which satisfy the associate's own perception of what he thinks he ought to be doing, but yet jobs which retain an adequate distinction between the work of the amateur associate and the professional social worker. An added complexity in the role-relationship involved must follow from any extensive use of ex-offenders as associates as is now commonly done in some American states, and which is beginning to be seen in Great Britain.

The recommended use of voluntary associates and the need to clarify their role *vis-à-vis* the professional cannot be divorced from an understanding of the normal aspirations of the probation service within the penal system or indeed from the career ambitions of probation officers in wider society. One corollary of any extensive developments in this sphere is that the professional officer might gradually assume a managerial role while volunteers would be seen as one of a range of resources to be employed for the benefit of the offender under supervision; occasionally the supervising officer may be expected to undertake skilled casework functions in difficult cases, or specialist officers might be allocated to intensive treatment tasks. However, if this meant that the *general care* role – crucial as it is to the whole pattern of social work – were to be relegated to a more marginal position in the professional spectrum, then this must have important and possibly damaging repercussions for casework practice.

Nor must scepticism about the use of voluntary associates be ignored, especially where it comes from those who are intended to be helped by such schemes. On voluntary visitors to prisons, two comments are typical from the literature: prison visitors – 'a waste of time, unless they give you cigarettes'.[18] 'What's the use of people like this? What do they hope to achieve? In his case [a prison visitor], only some sort of self-satisfaction, a feeling he was doing good in the world by giving up a bit of time to convicts – but nothing for them at all, that never came into it.'[19]

The same reaction must be reflected in the figure quoted by Lacey (1964) to the effect that 90 per cent of relationships between ex-prisoners and voluntary associates end soon after discharge because the offender rejects the relationship. Barr's work obtained more encouraging results than this, although it was still found that half of the terminated cases lasted less than three months.

In view of the great enthusiasm for the use of volunteers in social service, the heavy reinforcement given by the Seebohm and Aves reports,[20] and the continuing support for the idea in government circles, there would seem to be a clear need to explore in detail those cases in which the use of voluntary associates had fulfilled a useful function. In the absence of a more rigorous enquiry, the impression gained is that for a variety of reasons, volunteers are only rarely used in the probation service in such a way that their potential contribution comes up to the most optimistic expectations.

Conclusions

> Prisonization may be defined as the continuous and systematic destruction of the psyche in consequence of the experience of imprisonment, and the adoption of new attitudes and ways of behaving which are not only unsuited to life in the outside world but which may frequently make it impossible for the individual to act successfully in any normal social role.[21]

After-care is intended to undo the damage that prison has inflicted. Fortunately for society, the human individual is remarkably resilient, and many survive the rigours of a prison sentence relatively unscathed; for them after-care may be a useful provision at the time of release, but probably of little long-term use. For those who are damaged, or who were damaged before going to prison, it is sad but probable that community after-care is not going to undo easily or quickly the harm already done.

Nevertheless, the provisions available under the after-care scheme have been extended; they are more organized and more consistent in various parts of the country than at any time in the past. How much more can the probation service do? Outside of residential provision, the answer is 'probably very little'. The voluntary nature of the relationship is bound to restrict the probation officer's potential for involvement, and where the client actually appears to want help, the problems are often of such complexity and depth that we are taken out of the realm of after-care proper and into the question of how society as a whole should and could care for its inadequate adults – single or married. It is a problem that links up not only with the prisons – though they are probably the primary repository for such people – but also with the hospitals, the psychiatric service, the reception centres, and the voluntary bodies whose commitment in this sector of need is still high. In respect of no other group of men is it more important to clarify the aims and objectives of the social work profession, in which is included the probation service. Is it society's desire that the probation officer should work to meet these men's needs, whatever they may be, or is his primary aim that of social control – to contain deviant behaviour at whatever cost?

4 Release on licence

Background

In recent years, the number of men, women and children released from custody subject to supervision in the community has grown both absolutely and relative to other cases on the probation officer's workload. Only the number of approved schoolchildren has fallen, as a result of the transfer of responsibility for them from the probation service to the local authority social services departments. Since 1960 probation officers have become responsible for young men leaving detention centres who are now required to remain under supervision for a minimum of six and a maximum of twelve months; detention centre after-care accounts for about one-quarter of all statutory after-care cases and approximately 4 per cent of the probation caseload. Both borstal after care and prison licence

Table 4.1 Numbers under statutory after-care supervision at 31 December 1960 and 1970–2

	1960	1970	1971
Approved school after-care	2,892	2,866	1,444
Detention centre after-care	—	5,887	5,771
Borstal after-care	6,391	10,589	12,167
Prison licence	1,087	2,521	3,206
Total	10,370	21,863	22,588
Percentage of total case-load	12·4	16·3	17·3
Parole	—	1,600*	1,600*
Percentage of total case-load	—	1·2	1·2

* Approximate figures.

Sources: Annual probation and after-care statistics, Home Office, London. Annual reports of the Parole Board, HMSO, London.

numbers have risen as the number of men given custodial sentences has risen, although proportionately there has been little change in relation to the service's overall caseload during the decade. Many of the men subject to prison licence are 'young prisoners' (all prisoners who were under 21 at the date of sentence, except those committed in default) and are in many ways not dissimilar from the ex-borstal residents.

In 1968, the much-heralded parole scheme began to operate, but has never yet produced a national caseload in excess of 1,650: in other words, there is, at any one time, no more than one parolee under supervision to every two probation officers in post. However, the difference between this relatively small group of ex-prisoners and the others released on licence is held by many to be of great significance: whereas the latter group have served a sentence of normal span (albeit a variable one as with those in borstal or those serving a life sentence) and are subject to supervision as a predetermined part of their original sentence, the parolees have been specially selected for discharge in advance of their normal release date. In addition, they are unlike most other adult prisoners in that they have access to, and are required to maintain contact with, a specific probation officer. Nevertheless, the fact remains that, in volume, parolees account for only a small part of the total after-care workload.

The probation officer's objectives so far as the men newly released from penal institutions are concerned have been variously stated, but generally reduce to two core aims: (1) to reduce the probability of a client committing further offences – a preventive role; and (2) to rehabilitate the client.

The conceptual confusion inherent in these two aims will be discussed at length in Chapter 9, but a number of separate issues arise in respect of after-care that do not necessarily apply in any consideration of possible alternatives to imprisonment. First, there is the question of the relationship between the after-care officer and the institution, and the extent to which their respective influences on the client are in harmony. The evidence concerning the after-effects of institutions is ambiguous, but if one assumes that the aims of the borstal system to re-train its inmates are even partially achieved, then the probation officer's task in relation to borstal after-care is likely to be very different from that in respect of the rest of the prison system. In the former case, it can be argued that the training efforts made by the borstal staff would be wasted if they were not followed up efficiently in the community by the representative of the penal system responsible for after-care; so far as most prisoners are concerned, however, the efforts of the probation officer may be directed almost wholly at helping the ex-prisoner to overcome the negative effects of his recent conviction – to rehabilitate him as much from the effects of the custodial experience as from the repercussions of his own behaviour. In practice the contrast is never so clear-cut, but the situation illustrates the lack of clarity in our thinking about the precise function of an after-care licence: within the terms of a licence, the triangular relationship between the probation officer, the client and the institution might vary considerably. Two diagrams illustrate contrasting models, although they do not, of course, exhaust the range.

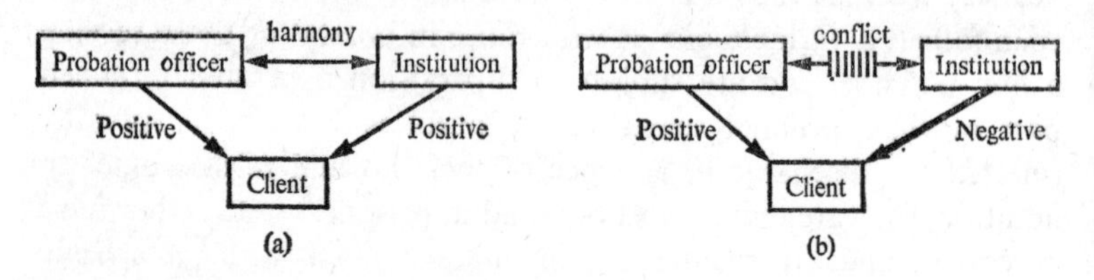

Figure 3 Relationship between probation officer, client and institution

In the first case (Figure 3a) the after-care officer in the community and the staff in the institution work together to change the client in predetermined and positive ways; in the second (Figure 3b), the institution's effect on the client is negative or counter-productive (whatever its intention may have been), and the officer finds himself in conflict with the institution because of his commitment to overcome the damage done in custody.

A different issue relates to parole, for although this involves the probation officer in a preventive and rehabilitative capacity, there is a third element too. A major plank in the public relations exercise undertaken by the Home Office since the inception of the parole scheme in April 1968, has been the insistence that early release carried with it responsibilities as well as privileges. Thus, close supervision by a probation officer is required not only to help the released prisoner but as a necessary reassurance to the public that its interests are being safeguarded. Whether it is a role that he would choose or not, the probation officer is nevertheless identified in some people's minds with the idea that he is policing the parolee after his release.

In this chapter, special consideration will be given to two of the groups of offenders noted in Table 4.1: parolees and ex-borstal boys. Out of a comparative analysis of these two groups, a number of contrasts emerge that highlight the paradoxes and the dilemmas confronting the probation service in its work with licencees.

The development of borstal after-care and parole

Borstals emerged from one of the earliest attempts to create a positive training element in the overwhelmingly negative reality that represented the prison system at the end of the nineteenth century, and the notion of post-release guidance has always been associated with the idea of borstal training. Even before the village of Borstal in Kent was selected for a special prison development, the Prison Commission (under its chairman, Sir Evelyn Ruggles-Brise) was trying to find better ways of handling young adult prisoners in London with a view to reforming them, and an Association of Visitors had been formed to offer friendship, support and supervision to the young men on release. It was an exact parallel to our present use of voluntary associates with discharged prisoners. *Plus ça change*. . .

In 1901 a part of the prison in Borstal was set aside for the special treatment of young prisoners selected from the metropolitan area, and in 1903 the initial commitment to the provision of after-care was confirmed with the creation of the Borstal Association to assist youths discharged from the prison (and later from the northern equivalent in Lincoln). In 1908 borstals were given statutory recognition, and there was introduced, 'in the form of the borstal licence, a new principle of vital importance to the future of after-care'.[1] The twin elements of support and control were written into the scheme from the start: the aim was rehabilitation, but the licencee must follow directions and advice or else run the risk of recall to the borstal institution. The arrangement remained virtually unchanged until the 1960s, but the involvement of the probation service became steadily more extensive, until in 1967, 'the probation and after-care service was made directly responsible for the supervision and after-care of borstal inmates'.[2] Largely because of resistance from the borstal staff there was, however, no attempt to appoint social workers in the borstals (except in the four girls' establishments), but some developments have been seen with the emergence and growth of active co-operation between institutional staff and the probation service, although organized links were rather slow and tentative until the 1970s.

Roger Hood (1965) has critically examined the decline in the positive commitment towards reform over the years, and the deterioration of the progressive hopes that were invested in the borstal system in the earliest days. Whereas it started by concentrating on a carefully chosen group of good risks, such young men are now effectively kept out of the custodial system altogether; borstal has become the receptacle for the hardened offender, the persistent probation failure, the graduate of the correctional process. There are relatively extensive varieties of borstal options open for training purposes, but frequent reference has been made to the fact that trades taught in the establishment are rarely carried over into the outside world after release. The high aspirations of Ruggles-Brise have foundered on the increasing individualization and humanity of the penal process as a whole.

If it is the aim of the system only to allow into the institutional treadmill the hardest of the hardened offenders, it follows that the custodial sector must in turn adapt itself in some way to handle such men. In order to do this, it seems probable that borstals may have to reconcile themselves to a high failure rate (over 60 per cent are reconvicted during the two years following discharge); but can they do this, and remain committed to a training programme? It seems unlikely, and certainly the trend has been towards a shorter sentence – increasingly similar to the six-month detention centre sentence – while detention centres contrarily have at the same time been adopting some of the constructive and individualized training elements traditionally associated with the borstals. (At the end of 1971, the average period spent in custody under a sentence of borstal training was nine and a half months.) Many inmates have tended to see both borstals and detention centres as equally punitive in effect if not in intent, and unless one dismisses the consumer's view altogether (which some penal administrators are perhaps only too ready to do), it must sadly be concluded that borstal has now become a means principally of removing serious or persistent offenders from the community for a period of time. Because of this, most offenders feel that they have served their sentence when the day comes to be released, and although there may be some appreciation of the probation officer's help at the time of discharge, the two-year period of after-care is all too frequently felt to be a second sentence. It is after all only akin to the probation orders which most borstal boys have already experienced, and in one sample of borstal inmates, 'more than half did not expect to obtain benefit from after-care supervision'.[3]

Parole was launched in April 1968 as a major penal innovation, but as Powell (1969) has shown, it was very much a part of the evolutionary trend in British penal affairs during the twentieth century. The notion of 'release on licence' had, as we have seen, originated in England and Wales with the Borstal scheme, but had also been extended to specific groups of adult prisoners: preventive detainees, corrective trainees and young prisoners. From 1948, the Central After-care Association assumed responsibility for adult ex-prisoners released on licence, and probation officers were increasingly involved in the provision of statutory supervision following discharge. Pre-release hostels were first opened in 1954 with a view to preparing selected inmates for life in the open community.

During the 1950s, the Home Secretary asked one of his advisory committees 'to consider the idea of compulsory supervision for ordinary ex-prisoners', and their largely positive recommendations were incorporated into the Criminal Justice Act 1961; this provided for the possibility of compulsory after-care for a large range of medium- and long-term prisoners, but because of the shortage of probation officers, this part of the Act never came into operation.

During the succeeding six years pressure for a scheme of parole mounted, and its inclusion in the Criminal Justice Act 1967 seems, in retrospect, to have been virtually inevitable. Groups in both the main political parties were arguing for parole as being an ideal way of combining restrictive control with supportive supervision in the community. In 1965 a White Paper, *The adult offender*, was published, and outlined almost the precise form in which the parole scheme was eventually adopted: the Home Secretary was empowered to release on licence any prisoner who had served at least one-third of his sentence or twelve months, whichever was the longer. Release on licence was to be restricted to those who were likely to respond to generous treatment and who were not regarded as a risk to the public. Licences would remain in force until the normal release date, i.e. upon completion of two-thirds of the original sentence.

The arguments which carried weight with both Conservative and Labour politicians and which led to almost unanimous agreement about the principle of release on licence were – as usual in contemporary discussion about the penal system – somewhat confused; they represented a combination of humane idealism, a simplistic view of human behaviour, and administrative concern about the pressure of numbers on the prison system. The idealists saw parole as being one means of reducing the punitive sanctions imposed by an inhumane corrective system: if society insists on retaining a largely negative form of penal control in its prisons, then one should not miss the opportunity of reducing – however slightly – the numbers of men subjected to the boredom and degradation of prison life. The White Paper's theme, 'You cannot train men for freedom in conditions of captivity', partially reflects this position, although it also implies that training in the community is one of the intentions of parole.

Not entirely in accord with this view was the argument that the lessons that a man might learn from his stay in prison would reach a peak of maximum impact and then recede; hence the need to get him out at the optimum point. This argument is based on little hard evidence, and in any case the parole scheme as introduced uses a statutorily determined earliest release date, and the likelihood of this coinciding with a hypothesized peak of conditioning is largely illusory. It must be concluded that the factors which ultimately carried weight were essentially administrative and political, despite the fact that officials went out of their way to deny that this was so. Parole should save money both in running costs and hopefully in capital development costs; careful selection procedures involve the minimum risk to the community in terms of recidivism, and the release of men must mean some relief on an increasingly overcrowded prison system. This last factor, which was clearly related to the economic arguments, was of particular relevance because the debates on the Bill coincided with the first awareness of the way in which the prison population had been rising during the 1960s; at the time of the Bill, a report was published which suggested that one of the aims of the scheme 'was to reduce the prison population by about 15 per cent'.[4]

The main controversy in debate centred on the recall procedures, and eventually the decision was accepted to involve the probation service in recommending recall, but to leave the ultimate responsibility with the Home Secretary, subject to confirmation by the Parole Board.

The release of a man into the community

The release of borstal inmates and of parolees is a planned process in both cases, but there are considerable differences between the

Figure 4 The pre-release process: borstal and parole

Borstal after-care	*Parole*
Sentence passed	Sentence passed
↓	↓
Contact with probation officer probably established. (Initiative taken either by the probation officer or the borstal.)	Contact with probation officer possibly established. (Initiative taken either by the probation officer or the prison welfare officer.)
↓	↓
Release date known with fair precision, depending on the type of borstal and the behaviour of the resident. After-care taken for granted, though it may be resented later.	Earliest date of release (after two-thirds sentence) known exactly. Possibility of selection for parole not known in any individual case, though allocation to different prisons, and advice by inmates and staff will give a fair indication of probable chances.
↓	↓
The borstal routine, while probably not as effective as many might hope, absorbs the energies of most residents, and morale is generally higher than in other penal institutions. It is often said to be 'not as bad as had been expected'.	The uncertainty of selection, and/or the actuality of rejection can cause institutional *malaise*, low morale and unrest. Prisoners rarely have a good word to say about their experiences inside.
↓	↓
Preparation for release, the concern of the housemasters, home leave, and the interest of the probation officer tend to produce a positive expectation of after-care. Self-respect often benefits.	The selection process is lengthy, time-consuming and bureaucratic, and the inmate has little feeling of participation; it confirms rather than counteracts his self-perception as object.
↓	↓
The actuality of release is often an anticlimax; residential staff tend to be critical of the failure of the probation service to carry on the work begun inside; previous preparations seem to have little relevance for life outside, and after-care is quickly seen as an unwelcome imposition. Failure rate is high, if only because of the high-risk men involved.	Release comes as a great relief. Because of the political importance of parole, probation officers tend to give a good deal of help in the first few days. Parolees respond quickly on the whole, and success rates are high if only because of the care with which men are selected for discharge on licence.

situations which affect the staff in the institution, the probation service and the inmates, and which further influence the perception of each process by politicians and the public. The chronological order of the process is indicated in Figure 4 which highlights the contrasting elements.

1 The opportunity for parole is a privilege which is available only on the basis of selection, whereas after-care for borstal residents is a condition of the original sentence; its start may be delayed to a restricted extent as a result of bad behaviour or the knowledge of difficult circumstances awaiting the inmate on release.

2 Parole is built up into a major reward within the prison sub-culture, and becomes a part of the internal folk-lore in the institution. In spite of gestures by the establishment to explain how and when parole is given, it is inevitable that the inmates themselves will have their own interpretation of reasons for selection, and that this in turn will affect the atmosphere of individual prisons. In particular, parole rates from different jails vary enormously, so that movement within the prison system is naturally interpreted as providing an indication of the probability of parole. In other words, the prospect of parole is a major new element in prison life, whereas borstal after-care is seen as a normal stage in the penal process that will affect everybody equally.

3 Parole is interpreted as a lessening of the sentence, whereas borstal after-care is often perceived as an unwelcome addition after a man has already done his time.

4 The basis of selection for parole, however rational it may be in the eyes of the Parole Board, the local review committees, the Home Office, or external observers, is unlikely to coincide with the prisoner's view of fair play, and in particular the inevitable emphasis on the value of a relatively stable environment outside must seem to favour the more socially privileged prisoners irrespective of the nature or seriousness of the crime committed. Release from borstal, on the other hand, is geared much more specifically to inmate behaviour, and such variations as occur are more easily understood – even if resented – by most residents.

5 Determined efforts are made in most borstals to prepare a resident for release: discussion groups may be held at which resident staff and invited outsiders talk with the inmates about their plans and expectations; the very régime in a borstal is geared hopefully towards the learning of skills which will benefit the men on release (although research has shown how rarely this proves to have been the case); direct links between the borstal staff and the prospective after-care officer are established during residence and probation officers are in some cases encouraged to visit the men in their

institution; the inmates are granted five days' home leave shortly before the end of their captivity to put down tentative roots again, look for jobs, and visit their probation officer. The focus of the sentence is towards re-training and release, even though many residents might question the extent to which this focus is achieved in some borstals.

In parole, on the other hand, the philosophy of prison predominates. After-care arrangements are in the hands of the prison welfare staff who represent only a minute part of the institution, and containment within the boundaries of the prison is the principal focus. The preparations for parole are dominated by the selection process in which the prisoner is a unit to be investigated rather than a person to be helped. If the investigation (the purpose of which is primarily to allay the public's suspicions and to keep the effective reconviction rates as low as possible) indicates eligibility for parole, little further preparation is undertaken; indeed, the space of time between recommendation and release is usually quite short. (One organization working with white-collar parolees reports that mostly they get three to four weeks' notice 'which is nowhere near long enough for us to get them placed prior to release'. Pre-discharge planning is quite inadequate in many cases, with the result that an unnecessary number of parolees are forced to accept Social Security benefits because of the time it takes to find them an appropriate job.[5]) Arrangements for the prisoner to be received by the probation service are made by the Home Office, rather than by the prison, and the parolee duly arrives at the office reception desk to begin his licence.

6 In recidivist terms, the quality of parolees is immeasurably better than the quality of borstal after-care men, with the actual reconviction rate of parolees over a two-year period being a quarter that of borstal residents.[6] But paradoxically, it is the parolees that have caused public apprehension, it is the parolee licence breakers who make the biggest headlines, and it is the inauguration of the parole scheme which has led some politicians and administrators to imagine that the probation service in the 1970s is being asked to supervise tougher and more dangerous cases than has previously been the case.

Thus there are major differences in the type of sentence served, in the process of selection for supervision, in preparation for release, in the attitude among inmates towards after-care, and in the type of men making up the released workload. But following release, both parolees and ex-borstal residents become ordinary clients of the probation service, and there is evidence to indicate that they are viewed by the officers in much the same way as are other statutory clients, and in much the same way as each other.

Probation practice

How much supervision?

Both parole and borstal after-care have recently been studied for their treatment content.[7] Probation officers see parolees on average twice a month during the period on licence; most contacts take place in the office, but home visits are paid approximately every two or three months. Of course, there is wide variation between individual cases: some parolees are in touch with their probation officer on an almost daily basis during periods of crisis, but others may go a month or more without reporting; moreover, the average figure masks the fact that the frequency of contact is greater when the licence is new than it is later on. Nevertheless, the basic situation is self-evident: probation officers generally find that most parolees require little more help or supervision than they are accustomed to giving the average probationer. Smith[8] has quoted Home Office figures which indicate that probationers under supervision for one year are seen about once every three weeks; however, it is known that the frequency of contact declines during the course of a probation order, so that the incidence of interviews is greater during the first six months – probably about once a fortnight. In view of the fact that most parole cases are under supervision for less than a year, it would appear that the pattern of contacts is very similar to that employed in probation. Despite the fact that even after five years parole was still very much in the public eye, the conclusion must be that the probation service has absorbed an allegedly radical innovation into the fabric of its daily routine. Although the public may regard parole as something special, and although it may indeed be based on a penal idea new to this country in quantitative terms, the probation service treats its parolees much as it treats its other supervised clients.

Although most borstal inmates have previously been on probation, they will not necessarily be supervised by an officer already known to them: Bottoms and McClintock[9] report that only 38 per cent of their sample had previously met their after-care officer. However, before their release from the institution, most borstal residents return home for a period of five days' leave, and during this time they have a chance to see the officer who will be responsible for their after-care.

In the Dover study, no mean contact figure is quoted, but data are provided to indicate the average number of interviews that probation officers had with inmates during the total period of after-care in the community:

Average number of interviews	*Proportion of inmates*
	%
Less than one a month	25
1 and less than 2 a month	48
2 and less than 4 a month	22
4 or more a month	2
No information	3

The proportion of ex-inmates who saw their after-care officer even fortnightly was thus less than a quarter.[10] However, the relatively low incidence of contact was due only partly to pressures on the time of the officers, for 25 per cent of the cases were completely out of touch with their supervisor for periods of time ranging from a week or two, to eight or nine months; during these periods, the officers had no knowledge of their clients' whereabouts, and could not therefore carry out any treatment plan.

As with parolees, home visits were much less frequent than office interviews although contact with relatives or close friends was made in most cases.

What kind of supervision?

The nature of the supervision given by probation officers is determined for parolees and for ex-borstal men by the intensity of the problems awaiting them on their release, by the length of time that they remain under supervision, and by the attitude of individual probation officers towards their needs and circumstances.

The parolees Whatever preparations the probation officer might have made before a licencee's release, and whatever home enquiries he might have carried out then, probation officers frequently had no contact with the parolee's family during the licence period. The after-care task was heavily focused on the office interview situation, although an active role was played in establishing contact with other helping agencies – especially those concerned with money or work. Officers contacted the Supplementary Benefits office, the Employment Exchange and potential employers in a significant minority of cases. In isolated instances, help might also be sought from agencies like the housing department of the local authority or from voluntary organizations.

The Home Office[11] has recognized that, despite some differences, the basic aims of supervision in parole are essentially the same as those in other statutory situations, and a willingness by officers to take an active line in intervention will therefore only rarely be displayed. For the most part, parolees will be expected to fend for themselves, and because of the selection policy, the majority of them will be perfectly capable of doing so. However, Powell has highlighted the service's feelings of dissatisfaction with the short duration of parole that applies in the majority of cases.[12] On the one hand, officers argue that they do not have enough time to diagnose and treat their clients, and on the other, they feel that parolees on licence for only a few weeks tend to go 'through the motions' of responding to supervision. These assertions suggest that the probation officers' tendency to absorb parole into their normal pattern of working may have precluded some from adjusting their treatment methods to the time available; in particular, it would seem to be unwise to think in ambitious terms about treatment programmes, and might be more realistic to consider the applicability of crisis theory to the period following release, and to agree a specific contract with the licencee relating to the feasible aims of the treatment relationship.

Borstal release Complaints about time restrictions do not apply in borstal after-care; all licencees are subject to supervision for a period of two years. In theory, the fact that they are probably already known to the probation service, can be visited in the institution, and must report to their after-care officer during home leave, means that there is ample opportunity for detailed diagnosis prior to the licence period. In so far as this is done, there is nevertheless ample evidence from Bottoms and McClintock to show that the treatment response is in a relatively low key: in almost half of the cases officers reported at the end of the first year's work that their approach had been characterized by an application of low support and low control; their self-perceived role was that of offering to two-thirds of ex-borstal inmates either supportive supervision or general counselling; intensive casework was given to only one in ten, while directive supervision was even rarer. This analysis accurately reflects the assessment of one borstal governor who writes of his attempts to increase the institution's involvement with the probation and after-care service: the aim is to provide the trainee with an opportunity 'to explore more realistically the function of the supervising officer. All too often trainees regard probation officers as people who "ought" to do things for them: they "ought to get me a job"; they "ought to find me lodgings". We need to change this to the reality of showing the probation officers as people who help and assist trainees to do things for themselves.'[13]

The problems faced by ex-borstal inmates tend to be fairly severe, however, and the contrast between the intensive training programme in the institution and the permissive supervision generally on offer highlights the lack of integration between the two parts of the sentence. Moreover, although those who had previously suffered serious social problems were most likely to suffer similarly after their release, the provision of intensive after-care was only marginally linked to those in greatest need of support or control. Indeed,[14]

> there were considerable variations in the type of after-care supervision given, which perhaps suggests that after-care arrangements are primarily a matter of the preference of the individual after-care officer and that a more effective system might be developed if after-care staff collaborated more closely with those in the institution.

However, reference to the apparent need for a planned strategic approach to after-care because of the failure of the borstal sentence itself to bring about much improvement in family life, employment, or leisure-time activities, takes the discussion away from the traditional notion of after-care as we understand it. In Britain borstal inmates and prisoners both serve their sentence and then come out; probation officers, with caseloads ranging from forty-five to sixty, and required to spend a fifth of their time preparing social enquiry reports for the courts,[15] are simply not in a position to provide *treatment* in a positive sense. Rather should we be looking to alternatives which integrate residential and non-residential treatment, like that described by Palmer (1973): recidivist youths in the Californian Community Treatment Project receive intensive treatment in the community rather than borstal-style incarceration. The supervising officer has a caseload of twelve, and supervision extends for two or three years; extra facilities available include group homes, family-centred treatment, a school programme and recreational activities. The youths going through the project during the 1960s did either as well or better than those given the standard institution-plus-after-care allocation. There are indications that the Home Office in Britain is increasingly prepared to experiment with penal alternatives, but it would seem that it will need to be vastly more ambitious than was possible in the Dover borstal project, where the experimental régime – modest enough in all conscience – simply reverted to conventional type because of staff changes, externally-imposed administrative decisions, and the unshakeable influence of the central bureaucracy.[16]

In the meantime, patterns of conventional after-care are fairly consistent and well documented. Of course, the treatment given to ex-prisoners and to ex-borstal inmates can vary from total non-contact to maximum-possible-input. There will be exceptional cases where special measures are taken to meet special circumstances, or where the probation service seriously fails to meet even its minimum responsibilities, but for the most part, supervision follows a clear pattern:

1 immediate contact on release;
2 intensive help with environmental problems (work, accommodation, money, clothes), if needed;
3 the offer of personal support through office interviews; rare home visits; plus occasional special efforts in response to the client's request;
4 diminishing frequency of contact during the period under supervision;
5 in the event of a crisis or a breakdown, immediate increase in contact and possible reversion to 2;
6 throughout the period, administrative records will be kept; reports will be made to central agencies regarding progress;
7 recall for reasons other than the commission of a further offence is rare.

Three case histories

The three case histories that follow do not, in any strict sense, purport to be representative. They are, however, illustrative of the kind of men who fall within the mainstream of parole and borstal after-care, and both reflect the problems (or lack of problems) that are presented to the supervising probation officer.

Borstal after-care

The case of Peter Battista is a good illustration of the complex social and personality problems that can be expected with ex-borstal inmates, and of the relatively passive approach to supervision that characterizes the average probation officer's work during much of the licence period. Technically a failure (because of the court appearance) Peter nevertheless ended up out of work but apparently more settled than before.

Peter Battista is the younger son of Italian parents who emigrated to Britain twenty years ago; Italian is the family language, but the urban north is the only culture that Peter has ever known. Family life is now dominated by the conflict between father and son, and Peter has appeared in court eight times in two years. Apart from a spell in detention centre, every effort has been made to maintain him in the community: discharges, fines, probation orders and suspended sentences have all been used. Both Peter and his father are critical of the failure of his probation officer to provide practical assistance, however, and for two months prior to the borstal sentence, Peter was living rough. During this time he called in home and stole jewellery from his mother to give to a friend. 'It would appear from this', commented the probation officer to the court, 'that he has little sense of obligation or gratitude and in the circumstances, it is respectfully suggested that he may benefit from a period of borstal training.'

Despite poor prognosis at reception, it was thought that Peter was 'worth a chance in open conditions'. He was known for his emotional sensitivity – especially when family problems were mentioned – and the diagnosis makes an inevitable reference to his Italian blood. He seemed to be quite liked by the borstal staff, but they were rather baffled as to how he might best be helped. He tended to drift in the institution much as he had done outside; he was described as immature and fiery-tempered, and the Governor said that he had adopted a rather contemptuous attitude towards training and staff. 'He leaves one's office having promised better things and five minutes later is found skylarking around and behaving childishly.' The borstal staff felt that they had achieved little, and thought that his chances of avoiding further custody were slim.

Before his borstal sentence, Peter had in effect left home, and for a time he insisted that he would not return there. After the probation officer had found that his married brother could not house him, however, it was fixed that he should none the less go back to his parents. While these arrangements were being made, the probation officer – a different one from that earlier involved – had to withstand attacks by both Mr Battista and Peter regarding the inefficiency and impotence of the probation service. Peter was also openly critical of his borstal training which, he said, had been a waste of time; he'd learnt nothing from his plumbing course. While Peter was out on home leave, he visited the probation officer in the office and was visited at home too; on this latter occasion, it was Peter's father who did all the shouting – a volatile person, but 'all his words seem to go over Peter's head – no doubt he's used to it'.

After his release, Peter came in to see the officer four hours late; he'd been drinking and was rather cocky. It was too late in the day to do anything about money or jobs, but the officer said that Peter must set about it the next day. During the following month, Peter reported once, but was otherwise elusive; when Mr Honeyman, the probation officer, met him in the street one day, Peter said that he couldn't come to report in the day-time because he was busy looking for work, and couldn't come in the evenings because he saw his girlfriend then. Mr Honeyman said this was unsatisfactory, and Peter would have to try harder. In his initial assessment, the probation officer thought that Peter had a chip on his shoulder as well as 'an authoritarian problem'. His strategy for treatment was to get him into regular work and to gain his trust 'and so break through the barrier of suspicion that seems to exist with authority figures'.

By the time five weeks had passed since his release from the borstal, Peter had achieved the first of the probation officer's aims: he had a job as a building site labourer, but there were still difficulties about getting him to report regularly. Moreover, at about this time he got involved in a pub brawl, which left him with a gashed face and a £5 fine; the probation officer was not surprised because he thought that his arrogant manner meant that 'it was only a matter of time before he got what he was obviously asking for'.

After the fight, Mr Honeyman made two home visits in search of Peter, and again laid down the law when he next saw him in the office. At about the time he appeared in court, Peter got the sack and became very despondent: 'He said he could see himself doing a "job" and going back inside.' Mr Honeyman pointed out that this would solve nothing, but confessed that he thought a further offence quite probable. 'Battista is a bumptious, feckless young man who probably sees himself as something of a big shot, but unfortunately he is unable to live up to these expectations.' Peter was told to report again in a week's time. Shortly after this, he was given a factory post, and the probation officer noticed quite a marked improvement in his response – more co-operative, less truculent; he thought he need now see him only at monthly intervals.

Meanwhile, Peter met up with a girlfriend, moved out of his parents' home, and into a flat with the girl. He was relieved when the probation officer did not react negatively, and four months later he got married. No further offences were recorded during the next eight months, although progress was rather mixed: Peter had an accident at work in which he was badly burned; he had difficulty standing up, and did not return to work. His wife gave birth to a baby, and they all moved in with Peter's in-laws.

By this stage, the probation officer felt that the chip on Peter's shoulders had become much smaller. 'No real problems seem evident. . . .'

Parole

Two quite different cases illustrate the role of a probation officer with parolees. In the first case, Richard Meek presented no problems at all, but the probation officer was actively involved during the sentence and immediately following release in trying to overcome the feelings of stress and depression that affected both the client and his wife. In respect of Jerome Farthing, we see a situation commonly experienced in the probation service: that of a highly competent person, convicted of a large-scale deception, and, following his release from prison, going straight with a degree of self-assurance that seems to the officer somehow inappropriate. On the surface, there could be no better example of a successful pattern of rehabilitation, and yet, almost alone among those who have dealt with him in the correctional system, the probation officer cannot conceal his hesitancy. The parolee is clearly hard working, but is he honest? Is his operating area, in any case, one in which the border-line between honesty and deception is uncertain? And how does the probation officer feel about the apparent ease with which this ex-offender can boost his earnings so quickly to the supertax level? Whatever the answers to these questions, the Farthing case is one in which the probation officer appears to play even less of an active role than is the case with most parolees; the initiative rests very considerably with the client.

Case example 1

A couple of years ago, Richard Meek's wife, Mary, went out for the evening with two of her friends; after spending some time in a pub, she met one of Richard's friends, Jake Crockett, and walked home with him. While they talked, said Mary, they suddenly 'started kissing, it just happened'. Meanwhile Richard, who had been at home baby-sitting, began to wonder where his wife had got to, and came out to meet her. When he saw the necking couple, he hit out at Jake, and stabbed him twice with a penknife. At the Crown Court, the probation officer commented that 'supervision is not indicated' and expressed the view that many men might have acted similarly under such provocation. The judge, however, commented on the increasing frequency of 'this type of offence', and argued that 'it is not safe for people to walk the streets without being attacked by some hooligan or other.' Richard Meek was jailed for three years.

Following local policy, the probation officer provided a form of through-care in this case. He maintained contact with Richard's wife and met her on seven occasions over a twelve-month period; some discussions were also recorded with Richard's parents and in-laws. The officer, Mr Featherby, went to see Richard once; and the prison welfare officer saw him on reception and again at roughly quarterly intervals.

The officer's work at home consisted of giving advice regarding Social Security, and verbally supporting Mrs Meek in her determination to keep the house going in readiness for her husband's return. In the prison, the welfare officer did what he could to secure a place in one of the prison classes for Richard; this took some time because there was a waiting list when the request was first made, but eventually he was able to get him signed on for painting. The problem then was that the overcrowdedness of his cell (shared with two others) meant that he had difficulty in pursuing the hobby in his own time, of which there was of course a great deal.

In the prison, there was an impressive unanimity in the view that Richard would be an ideal subject for early release on licence: he had the promise of support on all sides from his family; there would be a job waiting for him; having regard to the circumstances of the offence, there was considerable sympathy for him; and, on top of that, he had conformed to the demands of the institution without any hint of reluctance. The local review committee considered the case, and their recommendation was duly backed by the Parole Board. Richard was released in due course, and Mr Featherby fixed him up with a job as a builder's labourer at a good wage. Richard bore no grudge against his sentence, and even said that perhaps he had needed prison because it had made him realize just how insignificant a person he was. A fortnight later Mr Featherby went to see Mrs Meek; she told him that Richard was very reluctant to go out anywhere for fear that he might be drawn into trouble; he was drinking only orange juice. The probation officer thought that both Richard and Mary were adopting a very mature attitude.

Mr Featherby remained in touch, but no problems arose. The post-release crisis was, in Richard's case, more psychological than environmental. At one stage he commented 'in many ways it would be easier to be back inside; you haven't got the frustrations of living. . . .'

Case example 2

Jerome Farthing is a middle-aged man who has worked hard to establish himself in a position of financial independence. During the 1960s, he set up a hire-purchase agency, but became the victim of a number of companies that went bankrupt. He took up employment in another hire-purchase firm, and as a direct result of the embarrassment he was in following his earlier deals, he started to embezzle money from the office. The police say that over £15,000 was involved, although Farthing disputes this; over 150 offences were taken into consideration. He was given three years.

There is no dispute over the offender's attitude once he was found out. The police reported that he had been very co-operative, and he several times expressed deep remorse. Mr Farthing sold up his home to pay back some of the debts, and said that he intended to pay the remainder after his release. Inside, he was a model prisoner; after the initial shock, he settled down to the sentence and was said to have adopted a 'mature' approach – he just wanted to get it over with. The library officer said that he worked extremely hard there and showed a keen interest in his work.

His wife stood by him, and worked a grocery stall in a market in preparation for him to take over after his release. The local rector visited him in prison, and wrote a letter to the Parole Board supporting the application for early release; the probation officer, too, commented on the fact that the matrimonial tie was a strong asset in this case.

Farthing's period on parole was characterized by his resumption of an active business life at an incredibly hectic pace; it was as if he was seeking expiation in the only way he knew how. Within a fortnight of his discharge, he was fully engaged in the grocery stall work, and had been offered his old job back in the hire-purchase business. The probation officer, who had earlier warned Mrs Farthing not to expect too much too soon because her husband might feel disorientated for a while was rather taken aback: 'For a man who has just come out of prison, he is very sure of himself and in view of his acceptance by his former colleagues, he may be in a position to start the same sort of crime which took him to prison again. . . . One feels that this man is plausible, and will have to be watched. . . .'

A slight hesitancy remains in the probation officer's comments throughout the nine-month licence period: the parolee is 'a smooth-talker and feels that parole is a matter of coming to the office, saying everything's all right and walking away again'. Then there is some concern about his running a street stall without local authority approval – an activity which Farthing sees as involving merely the risk of a fine to be regarded as a legitimate expense; and there is a recounted incident in which Farthing was buzzed by a police car at night, but got rid of them by his forceful and self-confident manner – a fact which the probation officer thought displayed 'an anti-authority attitude'.

At the same time, the record touches on Farthing's financial dealings which leave the probation officer feeling part awe-struck, part perplexed. His cut-price grocery stall earnings rose rapidly as he opened several new outlets during the year; at one point he was said to be making £300 profit a week, and he began to pay off his outstanding debts. On the other hand, a number of potential court actions were still in the offing, including one in which there was a possibility of bringing to light alleged corruption among local businessmen and councillors who had been involved in Farthing's case. The probation officer contemplated mentioning these matters 'in a relevant quarter', but apparently decided to leave well alone.

Mr Farthing settled back into the community with almost insolent ease. The probation officer, at the end of the period of supervision, felt that he had made little impression on his client's anti-authority feelings, and openly wondered whether he would offend again. He thought that the man's wife was perhaps the most positive element in a none the less doubtful situation.

Inside–outside relations

Most prisons and borstals are virtually closed systems, particularly so far as the convicted offender is concerned, but also to some extent in respect of the staff too. Inevitably the time of release involves a total switch from one world to another, and although all men and women become accustomed to having to adjust to major changes in the course of their lives, it is widely recognized that the move out of a sheltered or controlled institution into an open and possibly unstructured society is one of the most testing situations facing any person. Demobilization, leaving school or university, discharge from hospital, dismissal or resignation from a residential job: all these carry with them attendant problems. When the switch involves someone heavily stigmatized by society, someone only too aware of his own inadequacies, and possibly with little hope of receiving much support from family or friends, then the crisis that is inherent in such a situation is all the more intense. The problem is not made any the less if those who are responsible for the man before his release have little contact with or sympathy for those who will try to help him afterwards, or vice versa.

Parole

Prisoners due for parole spend most of their time either with other prisoners or with discipline officers, and only on rare occasions are they likely to find a prison officer with more than a vague knowledge of the work of the probation service. McWilliams and Davies (1971) discovered that hardly any prisoners had been advised about the availability of after-care by discipline staff despite their constant contact with them. The world outside is portrayed to prisoners either by visitors or by the restricted supply of letters allowed, or by prison officials mostly at white-collar level acting formally: governor grades, welfare staff, the chaplain, teachers. Among visitors from the 'real world' outside, and conceivably providing a valid link with the future too, there may be prison visitors, a probation officer or a voluntary associate from a probation office. No accurate estimate can be made about the degree of influence exerted by the latter group, but it certainly makes no significant impact on the majority of men due for general release, although most parolees will receive a pre-release visit from a probation officer.

It is the Parole Board which undertakes the effective job of linking a licencee's past with his future, and it may be significant that it is effectively a body divorced from (though obviously involving close links with) both prison and probation officer; each party makes its report to the Board, the man's inside response and outside circumstances are juxtaposed, and an independent decision is taken by the local review committee, the Parole Board and the Home Office. A huge volume of paper work, involving for every successful parole applicant over 52 man-hours' duty in the prisons alone,[17] culminates in the arrival of the parolee in the probation office with a strong probability that he will not see the inside of a prison again. Preparations there may have been and some officers inside may give him a few moments' thought after he has been discharged, but the fact remains that, in the eyes of most people and almost certainly in his own eyes, the impersonal system has simply accommodated him, contained him and finally returned him whence he came with only a token attempt to create some bridge between the inside and the outside world. Moreover, it is significant that even with parolees, as Powell has commented, there is frequently a wish on the client's part to have done with the past as quickly as possible. The relations between the inside and the outside are essentially restricted to formalities and to the conveying of information relevant to the subject's past and present circumstances. After his release, it is up to him, and to a limited extent his probation officer, to re-establish a base in the outside world. Perhaps it could not be otherwise.

Borstal after-care

Because of a feeling that weaknesses in internal–external relations were partly responsible for shortcomings in after-care arrangements, the administration at Everthorpe Borstal started an After-care Workshop to improve communications. Rutherford and Rogerson (1971) have described this 'attempt to bring some degree of relevance' into the situation. For the workshop, between six and ten probation officers visit the Borstal for two half-days, with an overnight stay in between; they have two formal sessions with staff and with about twenty trainees from their own area, and in addition have informal contacts in the course of the evening. Each workshop is set a task: to discuss the question, how can after-care be made to work? Discussion topics include mutual expectations, relationship pay-offs, individual and group meetings, and community resources.

Group structure is left deliberately open, and the ten workshops reported by Rutherford and Rogerson appeared to fall into three categories:

1 Academic seminars in which status relationships were unchallenged, feelings controlled, and even relations between the inside and the outside were stilted. 'The theme was for the trainee to come to terms with reality as perceived by POs and staff.'

2 Therapy groups, in which probation officers tended to take the initiative, offering theories, insight and advice to the trainees. 'There is little doubt that the therapy game was, in part at least, played as a defence against the uncomfortable task of looking at the issues, and in order to maintain the status differential which was threatened by the Workshop situation.'

3 Confrontation sessions. The usual method used was role reversal, and although participants found some difficulty in this, it did successfully expose status and power differentials to investigation; it also demonstrated the gaps between trainees' expectations of the after-care service and what probation officers felt they could provide in practice.

Rutherford and Rogerson report an attempt to evaluate the workshops by asking participants for their impressions. The findings indicate that all groups were positive in their appreciation of the opportunity provided for finding out about each other's area of activity, but that there was less evidence that the workshops had effectively led to any measurable improvement in the pre-release planning or post-release experience. Nevertheless the workshops opened up a series of working relationships which appeared to bring about a number of significant spin-offs: a greater willingness on the part of some probation officers to involve trainees in deciding the shape of the after-care relationship; a modest interest in the use of ex-trainees as voluntary associates and in other roles within probation departments; and, perhaps most impressively, the establishment both of after-care groups and of trainee self-help groups, with the initiative resting at least as much with the clients as with the workers. However, one Principal Probation Officer involved in the scheme has reported that it proved impossible to carry over the self-help groups from the institution to the after-care situation.[18]

It is all too easy to point to the limited achievements and shortcomings of such innovative efforts as that described by Rutherford and Rogerson, but the fact remains that, without such explorations, patterns of institutional treatment will only become atrophied and the barrier between the inside system and the outside community to which the trainees must ultimately return become more impenetrable. However, it is significant that in the course of their replies and reports, probation officers were much more inclined than either staff or trainees to question fundamental aspects of the borstal situation itself. One probation officer wrote:

> It may be time to re-think the whole borstal set-up, whether it would not be better to have much smaller local borstals. By removing these boys all we do is to leave in abeyance their problems until they are released.

Another officer from a major urban setting wrote:

> The situation appears chronic – with nothing in the borstal training seeming relevant to the problems of the lads themselves on entry – nor geared to their release and subsequent after-care. We feel the real focus should be on reorganising the borstal system.

> Of course,[19]

> for years the borstal system of training has taken pride in the interchanges which it encourages between institution and community. Visiting committees, volunteers, teachers and ministers come into the institution; borstal boys, reciprocally . . . attend schools, participate in community, club and church functions and in sports and games. In addition, they go camping and mountain climbing. . . .'

As Alper goes on to suggest, such partial community involvement inevitably prompts the question whether 'bold and imaginative administrative procedures' could not enable most of the treatment process to be located in the community.[20] But such community involvement is completely different from that to which the trainee will return, and for which the after-care agent is expected to carry some responsibility. It is not so much a matter of breaking down prison walls and of changing outdated attitudes, as being willing to recognize any elements of inconsistency and incompatibility between the custodial part of the sentence and the community-based period of after-care. Such comings-together which are facilitated in the Everthorpe Workshops may reduce areas of misunderstanding or they may harden entrenched attitudes. What they cannot do, any more than can parole, is to minimize the complexity of the personal and environmental problems presented by borstal residents on their return home; nor to overcome the dilemma posed by the fact that borstal sentences are essentially last resorts in the punitive scale for adolescent offenders, and that the success of trainees after release (if 'success' is what we are looking for) must depend on the primary effectiveness of the training programme rather than on the impact of the after-care supervision which is likely, in normal circumstances, to be little different from that previously provided for the same offenders on probation.

Evaluation of parole and after-care

In British research experience, there is virtually no tradition of random allocation to differential sentences or treatments for experimental purposes and, largely because of ethical objections to the idea of one man receiving a more punitive measure than another solely on the basis of organized chance, there is little likelihood of such an innovation being countenanced within the custodial sector (although it is now being used in studies of community supervision, where the ethical issues are less clear-cut because the alternatives are usually between one positive treatment-form and another possibly better form). There has therefore been no chance yet of producing evaluative evidence of the kind which approximates to that normally derived from the classical scientific model. Without random allocation it is impossible to assert with any great confidence that parole or after-care (or different kinds of parole or after-care) have been more or less successful than any other specified alternative facility.

Nevertheless, research workers find themselves – especially when they are employed within an administrative setting – increasingly expected to provide just such an evaluation, and a number of techniques have been developed which enable the research worker to claim that he can offer evaluative conclusions in respect of certain specified forms of treatment. In Britain, the most popular means of achieving this has been by the use of matching techniques,[21] but an alternative approach more highly developed in the USA is by making maximum use of sophisticated survey analysis techniques whereby experimental designs can often be simulated *ex post facto*.[22]

A quite separate area of evaluation is too important to ignore, although its significance tends to be undervalued in administrative circles. This is the research approach which seeks to monitor action programmes (whether experimental or not) by identifying their impact on the individuals involved, on patterns of social interaction, on organizational structures, and on the wider community outside the immediate range of the action. This type of research is particularly important in order to see whether the intended purposes of a programme are being achieved, not so much in terms of output (i.e. reducing reconviction rates) but rather whether it is reaching the target group for which it was intended, whether it is having unintended consequences for any parties involved, and whether the contents of the programme are being carried out as planned. If any findings in each of these three areas identified faults in the programme, there would be little value in any evaluation of output, especially if the results were negative.

Evaluation of output

The parole section within the Home Office Research Unit has developed a prediction formula for use in the selection of parolees which has also been employed in evaluating outcome. Such a prediction method is a variation on matching, in that it uses the same principles: that individuals are compared who are similar in a specified number of apparently relevant respects (in this case in respect of variables known to be related to reconviction rates) but who differ in regard to the dependent variable – whether or not they have been recommended for parole. The results from this study are said to be 'very encouraging'; indeed there appears to be evidence that the first batch of parolees performed markedly better than their prediction score would have led one to expect. 'The results now available suggest that parole has a marked short-term effect on offending during the licence period and a smaller effect on criminal behaviour during the two years following release.' The study is currently being repeated on a group of men released in a later – and possibly more typical – period.[23]

Unfortunately it is impossible to quote these results without reiterating the methodological problems inherent in the research approach. It can be summarized very simply: because parolees are not selected randomly, and because the reasons for non-selection have to do with things like inadequate environmental support, poor work record and intransigent attitudes, can one be sure that parolees and non-parolees with the same predicted probability of success are truly equally at risk? It would only need very slight differences in balance between the parolees and the non-parolees to produce quite marked contrasts in proportionate success rates. Only random selection for parole, followed by comparison within prediction scores, would ever provide truly conclusive evidence of the *positive* value of parole in reducing the probability of reconviction.

But of course parole does not need to claim such positive success in order to justify its existence. Even the very crude failure rate quoted by the Parole Board in its annual reports (6 per cent of all parolees had been recalled up to the end of 1971 and 8 per cent were recalled during 1972) is a useful indicator of the degree of confidence which Parliament and the public can feel in the scheme; they do not enable one to evaluate the scheme's impact, but they do evaluate the ability of parolees to steer clear of trouble during the time which they would, had they been serving their sentences before the introduction of parole, have spent in jail.

Whether parole actually reduces reconviction rates is open to debate. The basic facts are not, however, in dispute. About 90 per cent of parolees can be thought of as successes in the short term; only a tiny minority commit serious offences which they would not have committed at that time if they had been kept in prison to serve their full sentence.

The evaluative evidence from studies concerned with borstal after-care presents precisely similar problems. Hood's study of homeless borstal boys[24] used a 'before and after' method of comparing reconviction rates, and found that the success rate for boys released in 1957 (i.e. the recipients of the work of a specially created pre-discharge planning unit) was no better than that for boys released in 1953. In fact, there was an indication of a worsening response to supervision, though, of course, it would not be argued that this itself was a direct result of the creation of the planning unit. Hood concluded that Borstal After-Care was incorrect in assuming that poor results for homeless cases were due to poorly organized after-care. The introduction of long-term pre-discharge planning clearly failed to improve success rates. But although such a research approach is useful, it is not always possible, and in any case, it can still fail to take into account other simultaneous effects on the system quite unconnected with the specified innovation.

Cockett (1967) examined after-care results from seven borstals over a two-year period, and identified a 40 per cent success rate overall, which coincided almost precisely with the Mannheim–Wilkins prediction formula. His original hope had been to identify those borstals which attained success rates superior to those that might have been expected, having regard to the Mannheim–Wilkins scores. Although he found measurable differences between borstals, none of these exceeded what might have been expected by chance, although results in one institution 'came near to being significantly better than expected'.[25] Further analysis with 'refined' measures of success/failure did show significant differences, with the closed institutions performing markedly worse than the open ones. But Cockett counters this finding with the same argument as that referred to in relation to parole:[26]

> It has always been my contention that the allocation procedure [i.e. to open or closed borstals] takes account of quality features not covered by the Mannheim–Wilkins scale, so that, for example, even cases with the same Mannheim–Wilkins score are not necessarily comparable, although the features making for that are not objectively known so much as subjectively judged face to face with the individual and the facts of his case. How else indeed would it be decided whether to allocate to open or closed conditions?

Hence, the fact that the use of prediction formulae suggests a better success rate from open borstals after release is very far from being conclusive proof of their prospective impact on behaviour whilst subject to after-care; and, as the differences are in any case relatively slight, the impact of training as such would seem to be severely limited in reality.

Bottoms and McClintock studied failure rates in relation to different styles of after-care, and found that 'even when controlled on the prediction risk categories, there was no evidence to suggest that more intensive supervision produced better results'.[27] Moreover, when after-care was evaluated in respect of social adjustment rather than reconviction, again there was little indication of any success in improving results by various treatment innovations. 'The implications are of a need for a more critical appraisal of after-care as well as of further systematic study of any developments in institutional training methods.'[28]

Hence, such conclusions as can be drawn from the studies of

borstal after-care (as indeed from studies of borstal training before release) are largely negative. Compared with the high proportion of successes among parolees, failure rates among borstal trainees have been rising steadily over the years, and now approximate to 75 per cent over a three-year period. Moreover, the evaluative studies which have been attempted suggest that neither pre-discharge planning, an experimental casework régime, different kinds of traditional régime, nor intensive supervision after discharge (at least of the kind possible under the existing arrangements with the probation service) are likely to influence reconviction rates to any significant extent. Cockett suggests that, because most of the failures occur in the first nine months following discharge, 'any enhanced social attention and effort that might be devised for that part of the after-care could conceivably pay dividends'. The degree of attention and effort that might be required is unknown, however, and on the basis of American work, would probably need to be more intensive than is possible under community supervision; even the use of hostel accommodation might only delay the time when the borstal trainee has once again to face up to the unsheltered community with predictable results.[29]

Evaluation of content, target group and consequences

In both parole and borstal after-care, it has been shown that content of supervision is much like that of any other statutory case in the probation service; some offenders will receive relatively intensive treatment, others – especially as time goes by – may only be seen once every two or three weeks, or even less frequently. Preparation for release will also vary: for example, in one probation area half the borstal after-care clients had not had a pre-release visit in their institution, while in some cases officers had visited twice as well as maintaining contact with the home. But evaluation of this, as of parole supervision, depends very much on the alleged purposes of the activity, and it is argued that for the most part the reality of community supervision is that it offers crisis support for a short time in cases of need, provides continuing oversight, and fulfils the general requirement of maintaining an association between a convicted offender and the penal system for a specified period. To suggest that either parole or after-care has more ambitious aims – in particular that it is intended explicitly to control the client's behaviour, to undertake programmes of reform or even to provide a long-term service of social work support at an extensive level – is surely to confuse unrealistic expectations with actuality.

There is little doubt that parole policy has remained fairly consistent since its introduction, and that the relatively cautious selection of good-risk offenders for release on licence has conformed to political and public expectations, and to the notion that the rationale for parole is to give individual ex-prisoners the opportunity to make the most of their own situation, rather than to provide maximum community resources with a view to helping those most in need. The time for evaluating target groups will come as and when parole policy becomes more liberal, and higher-risk prisoners find themselves released before they have served two-thirds of their sentence; then it will be legitimate to ask whether additional facilities are needed, and if they are provided, whether they are being efficiently employed.

In a sense, this question is already relevant to borstal after-care, where there is no choice about licence on release: all borstal trainees receive after-care whether they want it or not, whether they are good, bad or medium risks, and whether they have independent skills or not. With borstal after-care, even more insistently than with probation, the appropriateness of the content for the target group must certainly be open to question. Bottoms and McClintock highlight some of the obvious shortcomings: the relatively low frequency of contact, especially when the whereabouts of the offender was unknown (which happened in as many as a quarter of the cases); the emphasis on office interviews; the high turnover of supervising officers (affecting 22 per cent of all cases examined in the study); the fact that intensive supervision was given to only one in ten clients; and that over two-thirds of the trainees were assessed by their officers as being either unco-operative or only passively co-operative. Altogether, as borstal staff seem to be aware, it is unlikely that after-care can fulfil in any way at all any of the more ambitious aims of community supervision without a radical review of its purpose and possibilities.

Remarkably little work has been carried out on the unintended consequences of penal legislation and policy, although there is clearly a rich field for exploration. Research is currently in progress to examine the effects of parole on prisoners who are rejected and on the prison régime as a whole; certainly there is a quantity of preliminary information which indicates that its impact has been considerable. Indeed, taken together with suspended sentences (which were introduced about the same time), one inevitable effect has been to increase the proportion of bad-risk and problem prisoners contained within the system, and it is significant that it is a similar change which has so impressed observers of the contemporary borstal scene:[30]

> Gone is that minority of really able youngsters who had somehow found their way into borstal; and in their absence we realise how much we in open camps had come to rely on them to set the tone, keep the place running and form a backbone for so many of the activities. Our traditional population of older mature lads with light records, little previous institutional experience, and good Mannheim-Wilkins prognosis has thinned, and in their places we are getting many more lads of greater criminal sophistication, lengthier and more varied treatment experience and poorer prediction.

The trend throughout the penal system is towards tighter classification systems, with the result that different sectors of the system receive increasingly homogeneous groups. Those (like the borstals and the top security prisons) who receive mainly hardened offenders, with the better risks steadily syphoned off, must inevitably feel the impact in terms of staff morale, inmate hostility, organizational changes, and the need to recognize what is and is not attainable with the allocated clientele. It seems probable that this trend will increasingly affect the probation service too, and it may find itself having to cope with similarly unanticipated consequences – especially in regard to its growing responsibilities in respect of statutory after-care and parole.

Current trends

If a penal innovation were to be judged by the amount of administrative attention it attracts, then parole would be counted a resounding success. The system of licensing has been developed within the framework of a decision-making system embracing the prisons, the probation service, many local dignitaries, the Home Office, and a growing number of nationally respected figures in the fields of criminology, corrections and the law. The superstructure has changed only slightly since its inception, although the Criminal Justice Act 1972 will enable devolutionary measures which, the Board have said, should facilitate a more liberal policy, and so extend the opportunity of parole to more offenders who repeatedly commit relatively minor offences against property. In respect of such insecure and inadequate recidivists, the Board has argued that 'mandatory support and supervision would be more in the public interest than prolonging their detention in prison followed by unconditional release'.[31]

In fact, there has been a very gentle trend in a liberal direction throughout the life of the parole scheme: since the scheme's first full year of operation (1969), the proportion of all cases dealt with who were finally recommended for parole has risen from 25 per cent to 30 per cent. But the Board has recently taken a relatively cautious line in claiming success for the scheme and, in 1973, argued that it was still too early to say that it had been 'effective in rehabilitating those who have been paroled so far'. However, whilst eschewing a total reliance on statistics, the Board none the less admitted that future developments would depend on the results of research evaluation:[32]

> We recognise that the prospect of reducing the repetition of crime was an important factor in the approval given to the system by Parliament. Any major advance [in the liberalization policy] should, in our opinion, await the production of more evidence to demonstrate the effectiveness of the system to date.

Whether the Home Office's own evaluation attempts will be adequate to overcome the methodological problems discussed earlier must then seem to be a major factor in predicting probable future trends, and is an indication of a new element in British social administration: the role of research in determining policy. For the present, however, the outlook for parole is not greatly different from its own recent history, although the Board has suggested that some thought might be given to the idea of arranging for more intensive supervision during the licence period.

But if parole was an innovation of the 1960s, and is now likely to consolidate its position and evolve only gradually, it appears probable that the borstal system will be a major target for reform during the 1970s. Elkin wrote in 1957 of the 'sense of enthusiasm and vocation' that characterized borstal life, and said that 'borstal training is an element in the penal system of which the Prison Commissioners can be justly proud'.[33] There has, however, been increasing disillusion with the vocational training element in borstals, and it seems likely that there will be a shift towards the provision of comprehensive local institutions catering for all young adult offenders. The aim will be to avoid as far as possible the dangers of institutionalization at an early age; to keep the young offender as close to his family as possible; to make much greater use of the probation service both inside and outside the residential setting; and to try to stimulate a two-way flow of contact between the offenders and the society without. One step in this direction has already been used experimentally in a number of centres: the employment of borstal boys in community service schemes, in which offenders have taken part in, for example, caring for autistic children, leading adventure playschemes and working in approved schools. Kelmanson (1973) has claimed that in one such scheme, out of 80 trainees there have been only two failures, but there would seem to be a need for fuller and more rigorous evaluation of the idea.

How the intended reforms will fare in the face of the high risk rate among borstal-eligible offenders will remain a crucial question for the future. At this stage, it is sufficient to note that there appears to be a greater willingness in the Home Office to experiment both in the custodial sector and in respect of borstal after-care facilities, and that this at least creates an opportunity for bringing about improvements in current provisions. How this is attempted, whether the efforts are appreciated by the youths intended to benefit, whether the innovations turn out to be as their originators hoped, and what effect they have on staff, residents and patterns of criminal behaviour . . . these will be the questions for research in the years to come. It may be that, by the end of the 1970s, the pattern of borstal training and after-care will have changed beyond recognition.

The principle of after-care examined

The volume of accumulating research data concerning both after-care and parole is relatively impressive. Parole in particular has been subject not only to a wholly disproportionate focus of interest among university investigators and commentators, but has also provided the first British example of a penal innovation being simultaneously monitored by a full-scale government research team. The interaction between research and administration is apparent, and demonstrates the potential for action/research within an establishment setting. More recently, and yet to bear significant fruit, the Home Office Research Unit has embarked on a programme of experimental evaluations including two concentrating specifically on borstal after-care.

As evidence accumulates about the penal process, our knowledge of its effectiveness should be impressive. And yet, the remarkable fact is that we know almost nothing about the validity or otherwise of our treatment objectives, and as a result, in after-care as elsewhere in the penal system, those objectives are undeniably confused. It can legitimately be argued that probation officers supervising ex-prisoners or ex-trainees are variously expected:

1 to complete the process of reform begun by the prison sentence;
2 to undo the damage inflicted on the individual by the prison sentence;
3 to undertake social support with the client's family with a view to minimizing the harmful effects of compulsory separation;
4 to represent the stern hand of authority;
5 to offer a non-judgmental, supportive service to a client in need;
6 to report misdemeanours in the relevant quarters, but not to report every single technical breach of the licence;
7 to give limited material aid where required; and
8 to intervene in the client's environment on suitable occasions.

The principle of after-care stands or falls by the existence of a proffered personal relationship. Too much concentration on its effectiveness in reducing crime rates or in repairing damage inflicted on a personality or social situation long ago can only spell doom for the primacy of the helping relationship. But if the administration insists on justifying either parole or after-care because of its effectiveness in reducing crime, then failure to prove this, or proof of a reverse relationship can only inflict irreparable damage on the essentially humanitarian concept of after-care. Limited aspirations may well be attainable, but penal administrators tend to persist in the larger view, and they must not be surprised if, in the future, the provision of what is essentially a social service is attacked because it is not fulfilling the correctional claims that have been made for it.

5 The homeless offender

There is nothing new about homelessness; but our perception of it as a problem has become heightened by an awareness of the greater comfort of the contrasting majority, and by the realization that some aspects of social policy appear to be aggravating rather than alleviating the difficulties of those involved. At a time when standards of accommodation for most men and women in privately owned and in rented property are higher than ever before, when Parker–Morris standards have raised the quality of council housing to unprecedented levels, and when the notion of a property-owning democracy is not a totally unrealistic political slogan, the persistence of vagrancy and drifting among single men and women seems not only perverse but unnecessary.

And yet homelessness not only does persist but appears to be increasing. In 1966, the Reading Report estimated that at least 5,000 homeless prisoners were discharged annually, but five years later a Home Office survey of prisoners' prospects on release[1] suggested that more than a quarter of those due for discharge had nowhere to go, while still others would be dependent on their ability to secure a place in a hostel or in lodgings. Other studies carried out within the probation service have put the proportion of those without prospects of accommodation even higher – between 39 and 44 per cent. One of these, covering East Anglia and South-East England, estimated that in these areas alone, there would be 4,630 ex-prisoners a year in need of help because of problems with accommodation.[2] Even allowing for the fact that some prisoners, left to their own devices, will resolve their difficulty without specialized support, it is nevertheless clear that the Reading Committee's expression of concern was timely, and that moreover, since its report was published, matters have become worse rather than better.

Although homelessness has been a matter of particular concern to those working with ex-prisoners, the after-care problem reflects a more general development, and it is doubtful whether there is validity in seeing it out of its wider contemporary context. There are at least four factors contributing to the lack of accommodation for single men and women.

First, there is a growing proportion of single men in the community (including those who are separated or divorced). Until recently, Britain contained a female majority among all adult age-groups,[3] but for a number of complex reasons (mainly to do with changing mortality rates), this is no longer the case: there is now a male surplus in every age-group up to 45–9. The trend is a recent one, but in the future – unless anything happens to interfere with the process – the fact that there is always an excess of males over females at conception means that British society will have to accommodate a growing proportion of single male adults. To the extent that some of these men exhibit problems of personal inadequacy or psychiatric disturbance, and to the extent that they are unaccustomed to fending for themselves domestically, these may well pose a social problem in residential terms; even if they present none of these characteristics, there is a possibility that the cultural norms of household management may well be challenged by the changed circumstances produced by the presence of surplus men in the community.

An additional factor, which may well be associated with this change in the balance of population, is the increased independence of married women, as a result of which some men (especially, perhaps, those sent to prison) may have less of a hold over their spouses, and therefore become more vulnerable to separation and the ensuing effects of social isolation, including loss of accommodation. Easier divorce laws, cheaper legal aid, and improved financial benefits for separated wives must also affect the security of some married men. Adams[4] puts the problem into a still broader perspective by noting that, between 1931 and 1971, the proportion of one-person households in the community rose from 7 per cent to 20 per cent, with the prospect of a further increase to at least 30 per cent in the future. Hence the most disadvantaged and inadequate homeless men must compete for scarce accommodation with the elderly, divorcees and a growing proportion of young people choosing to go it alone.

Third is the development of community care policies, especially in the field of mental health; the tendency to discharge psychiatric patients in order to avoid the risk of institutionalization is a well-intentioned (as well as an economic) approach to the treatment of disturbed people, but its success depends on the availability of adequate community resources to compensate for the termination of hospital care and to fulfil the need for support and sheltered accommodation among people not always apparently able to survive in a hostile environment. There is growing evidence that such resources are by no means widely available or accessible, and most commentators on the prison after-care scene are agreed that there is a considerable amount of overlap between the population of ex-prisoners and ex-psychiatric patients.[5]

Finally, urban redevelopment policies have had a disastrous but as yet largely uncharted effect on the availability of suitable accommodation for single people. In most of the big urban centres, demolition of the inner ring has led to the destruction of many large Victorian and Edwardian properties which have traditionally provided flats, bed-sitters, lodgings, and even hostels for a large number of relatively transient sections of the population – students, young married couples and lorry drivers as well as those who have experienced prison or mental hospital. Other aggravating factors include the reduction in the availability of private rented accommodation following the 1965 and 1968 Rent Acts, and the fall in the number of places available in common lodging houses. In London, between 1960 and 1972, the number of common lodging house beds declined from 6,405 to 4,708. Only rarely are alternative facilities made available, and even some of the traditional charities, like the Salvation Army, are upgrading parts of their hostel system and putting them out of reach of the most underprivileged groups. Local authority housing departments have, until recently, totally ignored the needs of single residents, but as time goes by, it would seem to be essential for councils to consider a wider range of tenants for municipal housing than has traditionally been the case. In the meantime single people, caught in the trap of homelessness, are drawn to the inner cities, *en route* for dereliction, where they search for new places of shelter to replace the demolished properties that have previously served for home. In October 1972, a headcount of the homeless sleeping out in London put the figure at about 1,500, but it is generally acknowledged that this was an underestimate; in any case, it is a higher figure than at any time since the early years of the century.[6]

Hence, the problem of the homeless ex-prisoner is not only (or perhaps even primarily) a penological problem. It is a problem of what society is doing and what it ought to do with one of its deviant minorities; and in particular it is a problem of whether the responsibility is that of the individual concerned or of society at large, and, if the latter, whether any proffered solutions truly resolve, contain or even only exacerbate the difficulty. The plight of the homeless ex-prisoner is not unique, but an examination of it throws light on some of the wider issues.

Going round in circles

The lack of accommodation represents both a basic social problem to which the probation officer as social worker must respond and a circumstance which *prima facie* must increase the probability of further offending and/or arrest. Two case examples illustrate the dilemmas and limitations of contemporary support available on release from prison – or in lieu of a custodial sentence; they both demonstrate the clear interaction between the lack of resources on offer, the weakness of the response made by the client, and the alternately supportive and hostile social systems within which the problem has to be contained. Both reflect the circular nature of the probation officer's involvement, and the fact that he stands to be called upon whether a probation order is made or a prison sentence imposed.

Case example 1

Patrick McGarry is a self-proclaimed professional thief with no home. After a life-time of offending, at 61 he shows little sign of a change of heart. For his latest court appearance (the theft of two tins of salmon, eighty razor blades and a shirt), a probation officer who knows him well, Mr Dingle, prepared a social enquiry report, and described him as friendly, co-operative and frank; in his final paragraph, Mr Dingle showed due recognition of the fact that Patrick deserved to go down for a long time, but cautiously hinted at a possible alternative: 'It is felt that, when he does eventually obtain his release, he might benefit by a renewed contact with the probation service.' The court picked up the somewhat ambiguous cue, and made a two-year probation order.

However, it was to be a different officer who was responsible for Patrick's supervision, and he clearly thought that the prospects were poor; Patrick's co-operative attitude was described as superficial, and the frankness disarming; 'He impresses as a likeable rogue.' (The officer also thought that the court had picked up the wrong cue from his colleague's report: 'Probation was certainly not recommended.') Immediately following the court appearance, the officer told Patrick to go and collect his belongings (including £1·68) from the police; after lunch, he returned smelling of rum. The probation officer phoned the Employment Exchange, but was told there was little hope of work for a man in his sixties; the local hostel 'had heard of Patrick McGarry' and wouldn't give him a bed (Patrick couldn't understand why), so the probation officer booked him in at the Salvation Army, and told him to come back the next day. Patrick asked for his bus-fare to town and got annoyed when this was refused; he said he would go out and do a job. He did not return, and three days later appeared in court again where he was sentenced to eight months' imprisonment for shoplifting.

Later from prison Patrick wrote to Mr Dingle, the officer who had written the earlier social enquiry report.

> Well as you can see I fell by the wayside again. I appreciate what you done for me. They gave me your report on me and to my estimates it was excellent, and I wish to thank you for my freedom. You were on leave, I went to your office and another gentlemen attended to me, and the only place he could advise was the Salvation Army hostel. I went there and got loused up, and I suppose you know what that means (destroy all clothes). . . . Since then I have been living in various places, empty houses, etcetera which were clean (I can not stand vermin). I explained everything to the magistrate. He said I had spent too long in prisons, did I like them. I said no, I love freedom. So he sent me down, and made me promise to contact you on my release. . . .

Mr Dingle then wrote to a probation colleague to see if a place could be found for Patrick on his release in a hostel for ex-prisoners which the probation service had recently opened. . . .

Case example 2

Cyril Hazel has a long criminal record mainly for theft and false pretences. Following his last release from prison eighteen months ago, the probation officer, Mr Belborough, helped him get fixed up with digs as well as with the Social Security and at the Employment Exchange; in addition he arranged for him to meet a voluntary worker on an informal basis in a pub on Friday nights. There was more help from the WRVS, and 50p from the petty cash. Soon, however, Cyril was thrown out of his digs for being drunk and for demanding a midnight meal; and later still it emerged that he had been round to the WRVS and Social Security trying to use an obviously forged note purporting to come from the probation officer. Mr Belborough pacified the officials, and fixed Cyril up in a local hostel; three months later, however, he was £15 in arrears with rent. Social Security helped him pay this, but two court appearances then produced total fines of £28. The probation officer became heavily involved in budgeting and organizing Cyril's finances; he was managing very well, with the co-operation of Social Security, and the rent and fines were brought reasonably up to date, when it emerged that Cyril had paid nothing for electricity for twelve months. In the meantime, he had set up home with a woman, and had had a further court appearance.

Mr Belborough continued to feel sympathetic towards Cyril, but was beginning to argue that he'd brought many of his troubles on himself. On one occasion, when the probation officer visited the flat he found Sal, the cohabitee, drinking cider, and Cyril out at the pub because 'he was far too busy to come and visit Mr Belborough'. 'One can only describe the conditions at the flat as atrocious and appalling. . . .'

At the next meeting, the fact that there were still rent, electricity and fines arrears outstanding led the probation officer to wonder whether Cyril wasn't beginning to prefer a prison sentence. 'He would be cleaner and better looked after if he were there. Cyril said that he felt that after-care had been a waste of time, nobody had done anything for him and everyone was against him.' The probation officer spelt out just what had been done on his behalf, and Cyril left.

He and Sal were being threatened with eviction from the flat, and within a matter of weeks, Cyril was back in prison. He wrote to Mr Belborough from Armley Prison asking for help with accommodation. . . .

When a homeless man appears before the magistrates for a relatively minor offence, what should they do? If the offender has little money, there is no point in fining him (although that does not stop the courts doing so at times); a conditional discharge is rarely appropriate for a hardened criminal who will almost certainly offend again within twelve months, so the options rest between probation, with or without a condition of residence in some specified accommodation, or prison, possibly suspended for a period. It is apparent that, in such a dilemma, much depends on the probation officer's report and on the recommendation that he makes; if the offender shows a glimmering of good intent and manages to convince the officer of his determination to make a go of it, a period under supervision might be suggested despite the low chance of success. Moreover, as is evident in the example of McGarry, courts are often only too eager to grasp at even a hint of a non-custodial recommendation, and to shift the burden of responsibility onto the shoulders of the probation service.

The truth is that the lack of a home in middle-age (or earlier, or later) is a major problem, and neither probation nor imprisonment are designed to resolve the problem. Probation provides an apparent opportunity for the social worker to act on his client's behalf, but he rarely has the time or resources, or possibly the inclination, to undertake the kind of work that would appear to be needed in many of the most persistent cases. Prison superficially resolves the problem, but only for a short time, and without any attempt (in normal circumstances) to extend the solution beyond the point of discharge; indeed, because it aggravates the alienation between the offender and society, it may even render the task of helping him after release all the harder.

It is because of this, and in recognition of the circularity of the problem, that so much attention has recently been given to the need for investment in full-scale accommodation for homeless ex-prisoners.[7]

Hostel provision

But what kind of hostel provision is needed? The danger in discussing ways of resolving problems of accommodation is to oversimplify both existing and prospective solutions. Some of the best descriptions of the wide range of facilities already available have been provided by W. A. Griffiths for the South West Regional Group Consultative Committee for After-Care Hostels.[8]

1 Commercial hostels

The commercial hostels are converted houses in central urban situations. They fit the traditional conception of a hostel 'and can be directly related to reception centres and the old casual wards of the workhouses'. The Church Army and the Salvation Army are the most prominent of the organizations involved. The hostels vary in size, but some accommodate well over a hundred residents; they tend to be short of recreational provision and space is restricted. Several of the larger hostels are reminiscent of the 1930s and of the paintings of L. S. Lowry: they seem to be populated by old, subnormal men in cloth caps, standing vacantly in silent groups or reading tattered newspapers and smoking dog-ends. An outsider is an immediate focal point of interest. There is no personal property, and very few residents seem to possess more than the clothes they stand up in. The larger hostels can sometimes give an overwhelming impression of caverns of dark brown paint with little spark of hope or vitality. . . . Without some goal it is inevitable that large groups of inadequate men will suffer progressive, depressive deterioration.

2 *Specialist hostels for ex-prisoners*

The development of these hostels is a phenomenon of the last fifteen years, and can be dated back to the opening of Norman House in London and the consequent description of its work in *Safe lodging* by Merfyn Turner. Such half-way houses are smaller than the commercial hostels, have a high staff–resident ratio and encourage a family atmosphere in which staff and residents mix on more or less informal terms. They have a highly selective admission policy, and appear to be most suitable for passive inadequates.

They place an enormous strain on the staff – physical, intellectual and emotional. For example, Diana Norman describes the work of the Bakers in the Langley House Trust. Men regarded June (Mrs Baker) as mother, sweetheart, sister: 'To try and blend all the roles while stopping some of the boys [*sic*] falling in love with her was like being a chameleon placed on a tartan background.'[9] After eighteen months, the Bakers were 'deathly tired', but they survived for another three years as warden and matron until they reached exhaustion point: 'The strain became too much.' Much the same point is made by Turner,[10] who describes how staff came to work in Norman House 'with great expectations but left dispirited, or dismayed, or resentful of the demands the community made upon them'. Well might Arthur Hague, the Home Office Adviser on voluntary work in after-care, be quoted as saying that 'it is the people with the religious motivation who keep the less attractive forms of voluntary social effort going',[11] for there can be no denying that the offering of intensive care in specialist hostels makes vocational demands on residential staff far in excess of those normally expected of professional social workers; it is a highly relevant factor to take into account when considering what kinds of provision the community can afford to offer homeless ex-prisoners.

3 *Communities*

The response of the 'communities' derives from their perception of the homeless man's criminality as 'part of a complex of vagrancy, unemployment, alcoholism, mental disorder and social isolation', and results in the offer of a kind of accommodation quite different from that available in the common lodging house or the small family-group hostel. Griffiths reported that one of the commercial hostels had a black list of one thousand men whom it would not accommodate (mainly because they had been violent or were bed-wetters), and he suggests that this indicates a desperate need for the kind of accommodation offered by the communities. A number of examples are given by Griffiths, but two will serve to identify the kind of service provided.

The House of St Martin is a small farming community. Its twenty men work the land with the guidance of the leader (or warden). Men are given considerable freedom to come or go and to find their own role within the group, doing what best they can. Very few demands are made upon them of the kind associated with the competitive world; for the most part residents are men who would not be acceptable to other hostels – derelict and battered people who view the misfortunes of prison, mental hospital, reception centre and road-side as arbitrary events in their damaged lives.[12]

The Simon Community is a national movement; the local branch offers overnight shelter for all who ask and runs a hostel of ten beds for vagrants with some desire to settle. Materially the derelict house is scruffy and tattered, with no pretence to formalism or the military tidiness of a reception centre. Yet it has a certain warmth and spontaneity, and perhaps leaves more room for human dignity than the bleak ordered austerity of certain commercial hostels. The basic Simon philosophy is that the bleakest and most unattractive social problems – vagrancy and skid-row alcoholism, the problems least amenable to bureaucratic or statutory help – can be helped by the enthusiasm of committed and idealistic people; the philosophy is open to abuse and various kinds of incompetence, but 'it is free from the corrosive cynicism and prejudice that can so dehumanise any involvement with the social derelict'.[13]

What kind of accommodation?

Turner has never claimed that the Norman House model would suit the needs of all offenders, and he has argued strongly that it is not able to help aggressive psychopaths or inadequate men who are too intellectually subnormal, damaged or disturbed in personality to profit from living at the house.[14] Moreover, he has identified how dependent this approach is on the personalities of the people who work there: 'We have never doubted that the role of the staff is central. Norman Houses are the wardens and their wives, and their assistants, who run them', and inevitably the working roles that are played are essentially those of a family – father, mother and oldest son.[15] But Griffiths[16] has commented on the more general limitations of the family model employed in the typical after-care hostel, particularly because of its inherent paternalism and the impossibility of providing adequate scope for the residents to 'grow up' in the way that children do in their family of origin:[17]

> The tension of a darkened television room in an after-care hostel is almost unique. When the programme is sexually stimulating, men grip the arms of their chairs and are riveted to the screen. They are unable to integrate a host of conflicting emotions: the genital drives of adult bodies war with the infantile emotions roused by the promise of family. Only drunkenness or aggression can satisfy the conflict; Charlie's act of indecent exposure is a moment of catharsis.

Such hostels appear to be an inadequate substitute for normality, and yet who is to define what *is* normality for the homeless single man? The specialized after-care hostel, on the family model, seems likely to become yet more common: 'The investment of money and effort is too substantial to permit otherwise. And for some workers the family concept may be the only comprehensible one: it expresses care and involvement.'[18] In so far as the homeless ex-prisoner is defined as being *in need of* care, then society – both in its official and its voluntary guises – seems likely to respond accordingly, with a form of paternalism and maternalism offered as a straight option to the institutional impersonality of the prison cell, the doss-house or the hospital. It may be, as Griffiths suggests, that anarchic alternatives are too threatening or too intellectually demanding to those willing to work in such settings. And yet at a time when many people are recognizing that the nuclear family is only one of many alternative forms of social living, and are exploring other ideas in therapeutic groups, communes and more flexible domestic communities, it would seem to be possibly short sighted to think only of a traditional family model for use in hostel situations.

Sinclair (1971) has carried out a detailed study of probation hostels which serves to warn against the assumption that all such places are essentially the same; he found wide variations (not least in the reconviction rates), and although all conformed to the basic family model, their differential impact was marked. He argues that, although the warden as a factor in the hostel régime cannot be discounted, there are many other elements which help to determine atmosphere, achievement and outcome: thus, even in a paternalistic régime, it would be wrong to deny altogether the concept of community. By placing ex-prisoners in specialized accommodation, we are directing them into a social situation, the nature of which we only partially comprehend, the implications of which are confused and unpredictable, and the purpose of which is imprecise. Simply to talk of putting a roof over a man's head or of subjecting him to a beneficent influence are clearly gross oversimplifications, but it would be easier to understand what we were doing if we were clear first of all about our intentions.

Sinclair and Snow (1971) carried out a national survey of after-care hostels, and commented particularly on the ambiguity of their aims; they emphasize the critical distinction between three functions – the provision of immediate aid, the containment of offending behaviour, and rehabilitation.

1 Crisis accommodation

Release from prison is a crisis in the sense that it involves a sudden transfer from one cultural setting to another; in addition, it may contain within it elements of other crises arising out of the lack of accommodation, work and money. In many respects, it is to meet such needs as these that hostels are most frequently called upon, and traditionally, probation officers have been able to refer men in need of a bed to Salvation Army or Church Army hostels, reception centres or other large institutions.

Many of the specialist after-care hostels now take homeless men either straight from prison by prior arrangement, or at the immediate request of the probation officer. However, Sinclair and Snow's study showed that in a total of fifteen hostels examined, 15 per cent of the intake left within a week, 43 per cent within a month, and 64 per cent within two months; the authors conclude that 'for the majority of residents, then, the hostel was very literally a halfway house' – clearly meeting a felt need, but leaving doubts about what happened to those who passed through it and then moved on.[19]

2 *Containment*

There is no evidence that after-care hostels reduce the probability of reconviction. In the Home Office study it had been thought that 'residents were not likely to become unsettled in the early weeks of freedom' and hostel wardens had reported that reconvictions during the early period after release from prison were few;[20] the statistics, however, contradicted these expectations, and revealed a disappointingly high level of failure (25 per cent) during the first three months in residence – a reconviction rate more marked than that found in other studies. Of course, without an experimental study, it is not possible to assert that the reconviction rates either would or would not have been worse had the offenders been without the 'advantage' of hostel accommodation, but the danger of making too easy assumptions about hostel effectiveness is referred to by the authors:

> It is conceivable that the stresses of a hostel may trigger off some men into committing offences and there was in fact some slight evidence in earlier probation hostel research[21] that probation hostels had this effect on offenders who moved from home to home. . . . No one can fully understand the emotions which the quasi-family situation of a hostel may arouse in a disturbed person, nor what feelings of guilt or regret he is likely to have when he leaves it.

Nevertheless hostels do tend to be seen as a cheaper and more humane alternative to prison, and as such they become subject to expectations that it appears unlikely they can fulfil. 'At first sight,' say Sinclair and Snow, 'the philosophy behind the Reading Report (which stimulated much of the growth in hostel places during the 1960s and since) is one of containment.' But the argument that 'hostels are needed to overcome homelessness because homelessness causes crime' – though politically attractive – almost certainly oversimplifies the nature of cause-and-effect. First, the very state of homelessness may itself be an indication of 'the difficulty the offender has in adjusting to any ordered life',[22] so that attempts to provide him with a substitute home might be frustrated by the individual's own reaction to those attempts; and second, as we have already argued, the inevitably complex nature of the personality of the homeless individual means that the provision of accommodation is very unlikely to meet his needs – especially if it is dependent on either statutory restrictions or the willingness of voluntary workers or employees to play an active part in setting it up. One cannot assume that the 'accidental' provision of hostel accommodation will in any sense whatever coincide with what the homeless person believes he requires. Only when assumptions are made about the need for the homeless to take what is offered and be grateful for it can arbitrarily designed hostels be justified, and these then become essentially half-way houses for use until the resident can find something more to his liking.

3 *Rehabilitation*

Many of the reasons why containment is an unrealistic objective for after-care hostels apply similarly to the notion of rehabilitation. It is true that all hostels are probably successful in both containing and rehabilitating isolated individuals, but in general the length of stay is too short, the atmosphere too ambiguous, and the provision of specialist skills too rare: 'Rehabilitation, if it is possible, is likely to be costly and to take a long time.'[23]

The problem of costs is undoubtedly a major difficulty, and because after-care hostels are not offered as an alternative to a custodial sentence, but as a post-release facility, the justification of expenditure in extending the present system depends more on arguments about social need than about containment or rehabilitation.

An indication of the kind of money involved in providing hostel places for ex-prisoners is given in the Expenditure Committee's report.[24] In 1971, there were approximately 100 after-care hostels in England and Wales, providing 1,100 places for offenders. Of these, 178 places had been provided in 17 hostels with the aid of a capital grant from the Bridgehead Housing Association, a Home

Office sponsored body which provides funds for voluntary associations to purchase and equip premises. These places had been established at a cost of £378 each, plus the administrative cost of the Bridgehead Association, which in 1970–1 worked out at roughly £74 per place established in that year. In addition, the Home Office makes an annual cash grant of up to £150 per place to match the voluntary association's own contribution to running costs; it is assumed that residents contribute from their earnings only 20 per cent of the costs. The Home Office grant rises to a possible £250 per place per year for specialist hostels requiring extra care (e.g. hostels for alcoholics, drug addicts, etc.).

Even with such a contribution from central government funds, the Home Office stressed that 'it is not to be expected that the momentum will easily be sustained'. Nevertheless, the Expenditure Committee asserted, 'If the after-care hostels play a valuable role in the rehabilitation of the offender [*sic*], they ought to be provided in greater numbers. We recommend that the provision of new after-care hostels should be accelerated.' The Home Office responded somewhat cautiously by commenting on the need to guard against over-provision, but nevertheless noted that the Criminal Justice Act 1972 would confer the power on probation and after-care committees to set up their own hostels if they thought it necessary. (In 1973 the National Association of Probation Officers commented on the fact that few committees had taken any action in this respect.) In the Prison Department Report 1972, it was reported that the number of hostel places for ex-prisoners had risen to 1,500 in some 150 hostels, with the total growing at the rate of 200 places a year. Reference was also made to promising experiments 'with the provision of social support work for landladies willing to accommodate offenders'.

It is, perhaps, only when factors of cost become significant, that the validity of arguments about 'rehabilitation' loom large; more generally it is convenient to act on the assumption that anything is better than nothing in an area of obvious social need, and when early hopes are confounded one innovation is replaced by another. But now that the evidence about the difficulties of producing true treatment effects in penal systems is accumulating, it may become more important to argue that such facilities as hostel or lodgings accommodation should be provided as a humane obligation on society rather than as a means of reducing recidivism or of 'changing' the offender into a different kind of person.

The accommodation continuum

However, as so often in social administration, the desire to do good is no substitute for rational thinking and a critical awareness of social reality – more particularly because that very desire can sometimes lead social reformers into more complex schemes than are really needed. There has in recent years been a great upsurge of interest in providing for the needs of the homeless which has only been matched by the contrary forces aggravating the problem. It is entirely worthy that government committees, professional social work organizations, statutory services, academics and voluntary agencies should seek to meet the unmet needs:[25]

> If it is agreed [*sic*] that homelessness is an important factor making an ex-prisoner more likely to be convicted and imprisoned again, then any country that wishes to reduce crime and the prison population must tackle seriously the question of the homeless prisoner.

By this, Walmsley means that accommodation must be seen in the context of after-care as a whole, offered in a highly systematized fashion according to diagnosed 'need', and hopefully, designed in such a way that it could reduce demand on the custodial sector in the penal system. To this end, he outlines a continuum of different types of accommodation on the market, or 'a series of steps from the institutional experience of prison to complete independence' with most homeless men needing to set foot on at least one step, but men with a home to go to being able to leap the whole flight.[26] The continuum is identified:

1 The sheltered caring community for the elderly and the severely institutionalized.
2 The hostel providing long-term support, while the resident goes out to work.
3 Various types of halfway house, providing either close family support, hostel-type support or group support.
4 Open-family support hostels, with less involvement between warden, wife and residents.
5 Non-resident support settings: bed-sitters or rooms for the residents.
6 Supported lodgings.
7 Unsupported lodgings.

In addition, Walmsley indicates that, apart from the continuum, there is a need for specialist hostels – for alcoholics, drug abusers, and in particular to meet the demand for short-term, multi-purpose accommodation prior to full diagnosis and referral:[27]

> Lady Reading's committee made this the most urgent proposal because not every offender will have been classified as to his needs before he leaves prison and the probation service often needs a hostel where offenders under its care can be lodged, usually for temporary periods, while their problems are being sorted out and suitable accommodation is being found for them. The essential feature of such a hostel would be that it would be at the disposal of the local probation service.

Such a scheme in which the needs of the homeless are graded along one dimension and society's response programmed accordingly has found favour in influential circles. NACRO has negotiated large grants in two conurbations to establish a range of hostel provision along these lines, and a working group in the Home Office arrived at very similar conclusions in 1972.[28]

> What is needed is 'variety of provision for offenders and the maximum possible flexibility within the system'. Urging more deliberate coordination, the Group advocates the development in all areas of what is referred to as 'a constellation system' which will provide 'a coordinated grouping of every type of accommodation within which the residents can progress and be helped through the various stages of development and rehabilitation' though it is recognised that some may need to stay for a very long time in protected surroundings and some perhaps to the end of their days.

Such ambitious schemes are so obviously well-intentioned, and the need for accommodation so self-evident that any expression of doubt about their viability or legitimacy is often regarded as tantamount to treachery among penal reformers. There are, nevertheless, dangers arising out of twin errors: first that of expecting the hostel system to achieve containment and rehabilitation when the evidence that it can do so is slight; and second that of underestimating the independence of residents by requiring them to conform to previously determined and externally imposed residential systems. Necessary shelter may be offered and even appreciated, but to expect after-care hostels to provide more is not only unwise; it may be a dangerous precedent for society in its evolutionary relationship with deviant minorities. 'It is easy to over-estimate the role of aid on discharge', says Hood in a rarely quoted but rigorous study of homeless borstal boys;[29] 'Borstal After-Care was incorrect in assuming that poor results for homeless cases were due to poorly organized after-care. Better organized help did not produce better results.' Hood suggests[30] that both homelessness and recidivism are reflections of the same circumstance, and that artificially to offer a solution to the former will not necessarily overcome the latter. Indeed if the main factor in achieving success is a personal commitment to settle down, the recognition that life in a sheltered hostel can, contrariwise, subject the resident to additional stresses and render him more liable to breakdown and further prosecution because of the proximity of support/control agents, suggests that the social planners' desire to provide 'rationally' designed total systems of accommodation on a continuum may be less successful in correctional terms than if they worked for the more normal absorption of the ex-prisoner into the society whence he came. He further suggests that it is the lack, not of sheltered accommodation that is the problem, but the absence of sufficient bed-sitters, flats and lodgings within society as a whole that is at its root. In other words, the solution is not for penal reformers to press for a proliferation of labelled hostels and homes of a clearly stigmatized kind, but for social policy makers to recognize a changing pattern of need in our society, and to make provision for the single man or woman in exactly the same way as provision is made for the homeless family – by means of council accommodation – which may certainly be stigmatized, but in a very much more broadly-based fashion. 'All I want is a room somewhere . . .' may well be an appropriate comment for the ex-prisoner, with the emphasis on *all*: no social worker, no warden, no artificial family atmosphere, no rules and regulations, no therapeutic group techniques, no segregation from ordinary people, and no subjection to further institutionalization at the very time when the ex-prisoner is expected to rediscover his independent role in society.

Homelessness is perhaps the most complex issue in the whole field of after-care, and yet in spite of the relatively extensive consideration that it has received in recent years, it has to be confessed that most of those people involved in it are working in the dark. Hood states the dilemma that is posed by his negative findings. 'To imagine that a new emphasis on after-care [for the homeless] will provide a panacea will only lead to the same type of disappointment that has been experienced after other penal experiments have failed to produce better results. Such a conclusion might delight the cynic, but it offers little to those whose job it is to improve the response of these most difficult boys.'[31] Hence, even if the various accommodation schemes that are being developed are fully utilized (and many existing hostels find difficulty in filling their beds every night), there is no guarantee that their availability will reduce reconviction rates, will provide for the felt needs of the majority of ex-offenders (especially those with the greatest problems), will be used by those for whom they are intended, will reduce the proportions of men coming out of prison with nowhere to go, or will remove the responsibility of local authorities to provide for the needs of the single homeless.

With the problem of the homeless ex-prisoner, there meet the administrative concerns of the Home Office (both regarding its departments of prisons and of probation and after-care), the local authorities, the DHSS (because of the psychiatric condition of many of the eligible residents), the Supplementary Benefits Commission, and innumerable voluntary organizations. The recipient of the services offered by all these powerful organizations cannot feel that his opinion about the appropriateness of the facilities available is of much consequence. In a discussion group at Pentonville, a visitor introduced the subject of after-care:[32]

> It was definitely the wrong term to use! After-care hostels, as we know them, have about as much attraction to the offender as prison itself. What was wanted was accommodation where independence is the keynote. 'When I've served my sentence I don't want people still telling me what to do', was the argument.

6 Employment

As well as disrupting a man's home life and taking him out of his own social community, imprisonment also destroys temporarily and sometimes damages permanently his capacity for economic survival. Some men sentenced to prison are already unemployed; some are virtually unemployable; but the majority have a capacity for work restricted only by the state of the labour market, the availability of appropriate jobs, their health and social stability, and the attitudes of employers towards them.

The breach in work routine is something that the Home Office has become increasingly self-conscious about in recent years, and in two respects it has sought to contribute to minimizing the effects of imprisonment: by developing prison industries and by experimenting with pre-release employment schemes.

Prison industries

> The aims of prison industries may be summarized as the provision of work for all persons in custody who are assigned for industrial employment, such work to be purposeful and efficiently organised and suited as nearly as possible to the needs of the prisoners and trainees so employed. The purpose is thus to contribute, through an appropriate industrial experience, to training and treatment needs whilst at the same time making the best economic use of labour and the other resources, and thereby to contribute to the cost of maintaining the penal system.[1]

It is recognized that these aims can often conflict, and although the facilities in some prisons and borstals are well developed (for example, at Albany, there is a punch-card operated machine capable of producing components for up to 1,200 dining chairs in a 40-hour week), it is admitted by the Home Office that the state of affairs in the local and some other prisons is far from ideal: 'in the meantime they will continue as areas where the pattern of employment is both penologically and commercially unsatisfactory'.

The unsatisfactoriness was reflected in the fact that in 1972,

2,160 men were employed in sewing mailbags – still the biggest single industry – and another 1,482 involved in metal recovery, the value of which 'lies chiefly in its capacity to employ a large number of unskilled men'.[2]

> They say they're building new shops and starting new industries. I've been doing bird for a long time now. I ought to know. The only new shop I've seen in my time in this type of nick is the dismantling shop – you know, pulling old GPO equipment to pieces. I suppose somebody at the Home Office tumbled to it one day that we were pretty useful at destroying things. Okay, fair enough; but don't talk about training and reform.[3]

In 1972, about 1,800 out of the manpower of 33,000 were engaged in vocational or industrial training.

The reality of a prisoner's working life can best be gauged by summarizing the average daily routine of an inmate who, serving a short- or medium-term sentence, has not been allocated to a special training establishment or open prison:

7.00 a.m. Cells are unlocked, and prisoners slop out; they collect warm water for washing and shaving. Later they collect their breakfast and take it back to their cells, before being locked up again while the staff have their meal.

9.00 a.m. The cells are unlocked again. More slopping out. The inmates go out to exercise yards where they walk in concentric circles for about 30 minutes.

9.40 a.m. Inmates go to the workshops or to their other jobs as cleaners, etc.

11.20 a.m. Inmates return to their wings, collect their dinner and take it to their cells. They are locked up again.

1.00 p.m. Some men are let out of their cells to start work.

2.00 p.m. The rest of the cells are unlocked, and the men slop out again. The inmates go to the exercise yards for more circular walks.

2.40 p.m. Inmates go to the workshops.

4.15 p.m. Inmates start to return to their wings. They collect their tea, take it to their cells and are locked up again for the night. All are locked away by 5.00 p.m.

This routine provides for a 16-hour working week. The Prison Department claims that just over half the prison population are employed for an average of 28 hours per week, but it admits that even this is far short of what is 'desirable penologically'. The 1969 White Paper describes the difficulties of developing an efficient employment policy in prisons where snags have to be faced quite different from those met by outside employers 'who can choose whom they will employ. Some prisoners are not inclined to work and others lack the adaptability to take on even fairly routine jobs. A small proportion would probably be regarded by any outside employer as unemployable. Some, like Mark Twain, "dislike work even when another person does it".' Similarly there is a 100 per cent turn-over in the labour force of an average workshop every three months, and most workshops are over-manned and over-crowded; security and discipline remain prime factors in determining organization and duties.

There is then small wonder that most men's experience of prison work confuses rather than facilitates the process of rehabilitation. Even where full-scale work and training are provided, it is now known that only a minute proportion of inmates will proceed on discharge into a similar form of activity with a view to utilizing their inside experience; the most depressing aspect of this is that it applies equally to ex-borstal residents whose sentence was intended primarily to provide them with some new skill through vocational training that might be of practical value on discharge.[4] Moreover, there is a suggestion from a preliminary attempt to evaluate post-release behaviour among inmates of Coldingley Industrial Prison – described by its Governor as an act of faith, and certainly the nearest Britain has yet got to building a model prison – that there is little improvement in terms of reduced reconviction rates, despite the high costs involved in running the prison as a factory.

Pre-release employment schemes

Implicit recognition of the damage that is done to a man's capacity to survive in the outside world by his experience of imprisonment is made by the Home Office's development since 1953 of pre-release facilities to ease an inmate back into the economic life of the community. Geared to the needs of men serving sentences of four years or more (including life-sentence prisoners), its purpose is avowedly to help inmates through the crisis period of transition from a closed institution to the open society. In essence, a man who is selected for the scheme is allowed to take work outside the prison for about the last six months of his sentence. He may live in normal accommodation within the prison, or in hostels attached to the prison; one hostel is a short distance away from the institution itself. The hosteller works for a private employer as if he were a free man and receives normal wages; but the system maintains control over his budget, allocating funds for the maintenance of his family, a contribution towards board and lodging, necessary fares, and savings; a specified sum is allowed for pocket money. Gradually the men are allowed some freedom in the evenings and the opportunity to visit their homes at weekends.

The pre-release hostel scheme demonstrates vividly the continuing conflict between the rehabilitative aim and the punitive aim. Rehabilitation is required with long-sentence men because of the known effects of institutionalization: after years (or even months) of a protected, controlled, restricted environment, the simple everyday tasks of handling money, travelling by bus, crossing the road, talking to a foreman, establishing and maintaining a human relationship with a friend, a wife, a son or daughter, are difficult for even the most socially competent person, while for one with low intelligence, personality disorders and a lifetime of experience as an inadequate social isolate, they represent monstrous hurdles to surmount. Hence, the prison hostel can ensure their gradual imposition. But men serving four-year sentences are more than likely to have committed acts of violence or serious property offences of a kind to outrage the leader-writers and the saloon bar conversationalist (not to mention the judiciary). Hence the fact that such men are 'let loose' in the community at a time when they are still serving a prison sentence contradicts the punitive aim of making a man pay the due penalty for his misdemeanour. In 1971, the dilemma was highlighted when the Prison Department reacted to public criticism following the commission of serious offences by prisoners in the hostel scheme; although less than two-thirds of those eligible were considered suitable for placement in hostels, a further special scrutiny was made, and two men already on the scheme were removed from it and twenty-four names on the waiting list were withdrawn. There is no better indication of the subtle administrative balance that is maintained by the Prison Department between responding to the known psychological and sociological needs of the prisoner and the equally well-known political and punitive demands of the public.

For some years the Home Office has been carrying out research into the hostel scheme, but publication of results has been subject to long delay. In 1971 the Annual Report showed that one-third of all those who left the hostels did so to return to prison for disciplinary reasons; almost all the remainder successfully completed their period, and left on discharge or on parole. In 1972 two hostels were closed because of the difficulty in finding employment in the vicinity, and this fact, together with the introduction of parole and 'the application of more stringent criteria for selection' led the Home Office to undertake a full review of the scheme in 1973.[5]

Experience in the USA

Taggart (1972) has carried out a review of the many attempts made in United States' corrections during the 1960s to improve the employment prospects for offenders (usually with the implicit or explicit aim of also reducing recidivism rates). Although he admits that his conclusions are contrary to what 'we want to believe', Taggart argues that his work[6]

> leaves little room for more than the most restrained optimism. There have been a wide range of projects to test the effectiveness of various strategies; and though the evidence which has been gathered is limited, very little of it is positive. There is no proof that any single manpower service or strategy has had more than a marginal impact on its recipients, and no proof that any combination of services can make a substantial contribution. On the basis of the existing evidence, it does not seem likely that the employment problems of offenders can be significantly alleviated by manpower programs, or that these programs will have a noticeable impact on the rate of crime.

In the course of his review, Taggart finds no evidence to suggest that prisoners are rehabilitated by their experience of normal prison industries or training programmes,[7] but, more important, he examines two ambitious experimental projects which set out to improve on the *status quo*.

Project Crossroads provided a counselling, job-development and placement service to disadvantaged offenders in the community, as an alternative to imprisonment.[8] There was slight improvement in employability and marginal gains were shown in a cost–benefit analysis; but an initial reduction in recidivism rates during the three months of the project disappeared during the next eleven months. Crossroads is said to provide some hope that such a strategy can be made to pay off, but the impact was undeniably modest, and a further note of caution is sounded by Taggart's description of another experiment and the larger programme which followed in its wake.

In New York, the Rikers Island Project combined a programme of vocational education and training in jail with a specialized support service after discharge. This intensive experiment involved training 137 borstal-age inmates to use IBM data-processing machinery; in addition they received remedial reading help, counselling, job-placement help, and some cash on release. Compared with a random control group, those who had received intensive training got more attractive jobs and had a lower reconviction rate afterwards. However, quite apart from the possibility that the control group's poorer response was influenced by the fact that it contained more and worse drug addicts in its number, there was one result which represented a serious disappointment: less than a fifth of those given specialized IBM training actually went into the job for which they had been prepared. In other words, it seems probable that such improvement that occurred was a result less of vocational training than of the counselling and support services that were an integral part of the project.

Rikers Island was an innovatory experimental project which showed some positive results, and it led directly to the Federal Department of Labor setting up more than fifty similar schemes under the Manpower Development and Training Act (MDTA); vocational training was extended on a wide front, but was now seen as a relatively routine operation within the existing prison setting, and a careful evaluation of twenty-five of the MDTA projects 'revealed that they had a very negligible impact on the post-release experience of participants'.[9] It seems as though the intensity of effort associated with Rikers Island could not be replicated within a more mundane operation. This finding has immense importance for correctional development, and not only in regard to the employment of offenders, for it demonstrates the hazards of placing too ready a reliance on the positive conclusions – especially where these are marginal – drawn from a unique penal experiment, carried out as a pioneering enterprise.[10]

Taggart's review indicates little cause for optimism, especially with regard to hard-core offenders, and where manpower programmes are to be utilized, they 'must be implemented aggressively and innovatively'.[11] There is little chance of success while corrections agencies are understaffed and underfunded, and while society retains its antipathy towards offenders even after they have served their sentence of imprisonment. Nevertheless, even in the most congenial conditions, previous experiments are sufficient to counteract any 'inflated hope of success in increasing employability or reducing recidivism'.[12]

Employment on release

Prisoners in Britain are well aware of the difficulties that await them so far as getting a job is concerned, and many of them express particular concern about the gaps in their insurance cards which they believe draw attention to their custodial experience. 'The blank insurance card was raised time and time again as an almost insurmountable obstacle to finding a reasonable job. . . . Gaps in a man's contribution record are a self-defeating additional punishment.'[13] Of prisoners who know about the availability of after-care facilities, 30 per cent expect the service to be able to offer help with employment, and it is true that the probation officer will often do what he can in this respect.[14] But in a study of two after-care units, less than 15 per cent of those coming to the office were directly helped in this way, although a much larger group might have been referred (possibly with a supporting letter or telephone call) to the Employment Office.[15] Moreover, evidence from a study of probationers suggests that even when probation officers spend considerable quantities of time and effort in securing work for their clients, the jobs are often not to the liking of the offenders and they rarely last for very long.[16] The fact is that the problems of marrying a man to a job are complex and that they are aggravated partly by economic conditions prevailing and partly by the circumstances peculiar to the ex-offender. One agency has emphasized three of these in particular:[17]

1. the fact that men serving a custodial sentence cannot attend for interview before release, and so cannot go through the normal processes of securing a job;
2. the fact that many employers (including a large number of government departments) are officially or unofficially unwilling to consider taking on a convicted offender, especially one straight from prison; and
3. the fact that the ex-prisoner has certain social and psychological characteristics associated either with his offence or with his

experience of imprisonment (or with both) which affects his ability to obtain and to hold suitable employment.

One of the major developments of after-care policy within the voluntary sector in recent years has been the recognition that the task of re-establishing an ex-prisoner in a regular work situation is one requiring intensive effort and heavy resources because of the complex and interacting psychological, social and economic determinants at play. Two organizations which have become involved are Apex and NACRO.

Apex

The prison cell is probably the most productive dream factory in the world. Into its embrace come all manner of men and women – the professional man struck off by his professional body, the young first offender, the elderly recidivist, the sexual offender, the drug addict, the alcoholic and those who are socially isolate and/or homeless. With the exception of the lifer, all these men and women have one thing in common – there is a known date in the months or years ahead for their release from prison. The nature of our society and the social pressures on them demand that they should obtain employment. But what? And how?

In the long hours in their cell the world of employment is far away. They forget the difficulties of obtaining a job in competition with a number of other applicants; the journey to work no longer exists; the length of their working day is very short compared with the eight hour shift of the factory or office; the pressure of the prison job is negligible compared to one in the City whilst changes in working methods and ideas (company law, factory acts, wage rates, etc.) do not register on their consciousness. Thus fantasies are born and may replace reality. The man who feels that he has gained an insight into prisoners denied to those without a conviction may seek social work; the man who has had a poem or an article accepted by the prison magazine may demand a career in journalism; the painter, praised by his prison visitor, may look for an opening in commercial art. The widening of possible horizons may well be an important feature of rehabilitation, but we must recognize that the matter is far beyond simple job placing. Few if any of these men have any

> knowledge of the training required or the competition to be faced in seeking such a post; so often failure to turn the fantasy into reality is blamed on society or the employer – that no 'con' will be considered for a decent job. Others will study the *Situations Vacant* columns in the newspapers and assure themselves that they will not have the slightest difficulty in obtaining a post on discharge for they are able to undertake most of the jobs being advertised. Another group will seek unrealistic salaries, employment in the antique business, open-air jobs or jobs where the restraints of office are less such as courier or guide; and others will go for self-employment without the skills required or the capital backing necessary to succeed.[18]

Thus does Apex, after seven years' experience as a voluntary agency committed to placing ex-prisoners in work, pin-point the crucial need for an honest recognition of reality in the employment sector, no matter how harsh an approach that might seem. Indeed it is Apex's total commitment to honesty in its dealings with ex-prisoners, employers and society as a whole that is its most impressive characteristic. It offers to place ex-prisoners in suitable posts, but insists that they agree to the employer being presented with full details of their personal history:[19]

> We are aware that a percentage of our clients will offend again. If an employer has the full history of a man and his problems, together with the Apex recommendation, it is possible to place him in a job where he will not be at risk, thus reducing the chance of his offending again. It is when a man offends again and the employer discovers that he was *not* in possession of the facts that the continuance of Apex could be at risk.

With the ex-prisoners, Apex is down-to-earth but totally involved, and so long as a client remains willing to be helped, he will be helped. And perhaps most impressive of all, the involvement of a full-time research worker in the project since its inauguration has ensured that Apex's work has been subjected to a degree of rigorous evaluation that puts it in the forefront of action–research pioneers. The existence of social problems (such as the unemployment of ex-prisoners) and the need for a social response (such as the offer of a service) may be self-evident, but the effect of the response and whether or not it achieves all that was hoped of it is rarely assessed; even when efforts are made to do so, the impression often left is one of half-heartedness or window-dressing. The work of Apex does not come into this category; indeed the research element clearly compels a continuing reassessment of the philosophy and ideals of the project, which may be disconcerting to the idealist but is refreshingly creative in the field of social administration. The philosophy of the Apex Trust was spelt out by Neville Vincent in 1967:[20]

> It is based on the principle that the State accepts that it has an obligation to rehabilitate and train the handicapped – those who are physically and mentally sick. Legislation by means of the Disabled Persons (Employment) Act 1944 implemented the idea that it was in the interests of society and the disabled that they could and should work. As a result a number of training establishments have been set up and are working successfully. The concept behind Apex is that this principle should be extended to the socially sick: men and women who are socially and emotionally handicapped as a result of having served prison sentences.
>
> There is a strong case on both humanitarian and economic grounds for the establishment of a central agency designed solely to assist ex-prisoners to find employment. Apex sets out to do exactly that, and in implementing this principle it is, perhaps, unique in that it attempts to find work for prisoners whilst they are still in gaol, so that jobs will be awaiting them as soon as they are released.

Two phases in the work of Apex have contributed most to its experience: one involving undifferentiated samples of prisoners and one focusing on white-collar offenders and sex offenders.

Phase I Apex initially wanted to see whether an active policy of finding suitable employment for men immediately on their release from prison effectively reduced their chances of reconviction. A well-designed experimental study was carried out in Wormwood Scrubs and Pentonville, and 450 men were offered the Apex service. Almost exactly half indicated their willingness to accept the help available; a quarter of these were given jobs, but less than a fifth actually took up the post. Only 9 per cent of those who accepted Apex's help stayed in their job for three months or more; the pay-off with hardened recidivists was particularly disappointing with only one man out of 65 settling for three months or more.[21]

In the report for 1970–1, Apex's research worker, Keith Soothill, confesses to three shocks: that only half of the men interviewed seemed to be really interested in the service on offer; that those who rejected the service appeared to perform marginally better after release in terms of reconviction than did the ex-prisoners who accepted help; and, most important of all, comparing the re-conviction rates of the prisoners offered help with those of similar prisoners randomly selected for control purposes, 'there is really very little evidence that in terms of reconviction the Apex service had any effect at all'.[22]

By the time Phase I had been completed, Apex was arguing that for an undifferentiated group of prisoners, 'it is fairly evident that the Apex service is by no means the complete answer to after-care',[23] and because of the complexity of the problems inherited by many an ex-prisoner on discharge, merely placing him in a job might often be insufficient to ensure his future stability:[24]

> It would probably be fair to say that none of us ever believed that simply finding employment would be a solution for every ex-prisoner, but we perhaps thought that the measurable effect would indicate that it was still economically worthwhile offering all ex-prisoners the services of a specialist employment service. From a humanitarian viewpoint one could still argue that it is a service which should be available to ex-prisoners.

The disappointment of these findings led Apex in two directions: its research emphasis switched to the attempt to develop a prediction formula which would serve to indicate those offenders most likely to make best use of the employment service, while its action team embarked on Phase II.

Phase II A decision was made to concentrate the Trust's limited resources on the relatively small numbers of white-collar and sex offenders on discharge from prison; it was believed that they presented particular difficulties in re-employment:[25]

> I would suggest that the position of the white collar offender is totally different to that of the tradesman, semi-skilled or unskilled man. With the latter groups employers are more concerned with what a man can do than with his past history. Such a man is only readily identifiable as an ex-prisoner when he has a blank or nearly blank National Insurance card. The white collar offender has many more obstacles to overcome.

> There are the problems of Fidelity Bonding, security checking, references and the complications of a four-page application form which frequently requires the names of referees.

As well as the problems particular to ex-offenders (for example, the difficulty of attending for interview before release; the restrictions that are imposed by society on the range of jobs open to him; the psychological problems related to his self-confidence and self-respect), the situation is aggravated both by any tendency for the overall rate of unemployment to rise and – for the white-collar offender – by the relatively recent trend towards large-scale redundancy among executive grades. In this situation, Apex has found that the greater the delay in securing a position, the more the problems tend to build up: 'Our evidence strongly indicates that problems accumulate rather than evaporate during the period after release';[26] 'not only is he an ex-prisoner but an ex-prisoner who cannot find work . . .'.[27]

The policy of Apex in Phase II certainly appears to have paid dividends in that by dint of long-term patient building of links with the working community, and by strictly keeping the referral rate down to a level at which the most intensive service necessary could be provided (there are approximately thirty ex-prisoners on the books at any one time, and an annual referral rate, mainly from prisons and probation officers, of about 225), the number of successful placings has risen steadily from 19 per cent in 1970 to 30 per cent in 1972. Nevertheless, the determination not to become carried away with self-congratulation remains strong: 'A steady increase in the numbers of successful placings has not, however, produced complacency for we continue to be disturbed at the number who break contact with Apex before a job is arranged by the Trust'.[28]

Lessons learned from Apex

1 The scale of the operation can be enormous. 'For a number of men over 100 employers were contacted by letter or by telephone before they were placed, the record being 207 letters – a figure we hope will never be exceeded';[29] the hope was not to be fulfilled, however, for in 1970, one man involved almost 400 such approaches.[30] Some men present virtually insuperable problems, and it is hoped that they can eventually be identified before excessive effort is spent on them; but for the moment, Apex's principle is to go to the end of the road with all referrals.

2 A growing awareness of the amount of effort required in order to place successfully 30 per cent of 200-plus ex-prisoners every year, coupled with the grim reality of 50,000 discharges per annum has led Apex increasingly to see itself as more than just a guide and counsellor to the ex-offender: its role also includes that of a pressure group, a publicity/public relations organization, and a body committed to educating society about its responsibilities towards the socially handicapped. Apex looks to the Department of Employment to provide a more effective service both within prisons and at Employment Exchanges. The Department is committed to the provision of a specialist service for the socially disadvantaged (including ex-prisoners), and will probably begin on an experimental basis. But Pentney of Apex is particularly concerned to see specialist employment officers with social work training appointed to all prison welfare departments; their task would be to make plans for employment provisions on discharge, and to fully utilize resources such as vocational guidance, training and educational facilities within the prison and the local community: 'We very much hope that this can be incorporated into the service envisaged by the Department of Employment.'[31]

3 Linked with the proposal that the responsible government department should adopt a more positive responsibility for ex-prisoners, is the notion that the prisons themselves should do more to prepare their residents for discharge. Of particular concern to Apex is the fact that, even with parole (despite its positive connotations), there are still many instances where inadequate time is allowed for arrangements to be made before release on licence; if parole decisions could be advanced (i.e. if the bureaucratic machine could be better oiled), then there might be fewer cases of parolees being out of work for considerable periods after their release.

4 'The staff of Apex have a difficult enough job without being asked to carry the additional burden of humility. However, the truth is that the enormous effort involved in placing ex-offenders into work does not have any easily measurable effect. One cannot say even of the apparent "successes" of the men who stay an appreciable time at a job arranged by Apex that they would have necessarily floundered without the help and support of Apex. It is one further difficult step to suggest that one has actually prevented a reconviction. Nevertheless, one creditable aspect of the work of Apex is the willingness to continue to try to evaluate the service it is offering. . . .'[32] Certainly a most important lesson from the project is that action–

research can be successful in its creativity even when the research element is discovering that some of the original hopes and expectations were not being fulfilled. Running right through the associated written material is the simple commitment to humanitarian ideals, irrespective of their impact on reconviction rates; and this in the sphere of after-care is quite something.

NACRO and New Careers

In the mid-1970s, the number of penal innovations is multiplying rapidly, although the question of which ones will make the most significant long-term impact on the system or in the lives of individual offenders is almost impossible to answer objectively.

Still in the field of employment, there could hardly be a more starkly contrasting innovation (when set alongside prison training schemes and the experimental Apex project) than that contained within the New Careers movement. Where traditional patterns of penal provision work largely within a strict institutional structure, and employ correctional or welfare agents to work with or on behalf of the so-called deviant, underprivileged or inadequate inmates or clients, New Careers takes the self-determination, self-help philosophy espoused by casework a step further and seeks to provide opportunities for ordinary young criminals to transform themselves into hard-working, highly respected social workers employed in the service system. The radical element in New Careers is reflected in a number of ways: it has employed group-work methods in which prison inmates play a major management role so far as their own affairs are concerned. Because of this, emphasis is laid on the need for isolation within the prison community in order to be protected against bureaucratic interference ('issuing manuals and procedures for the operation of projects is the kiss of death for innovation . . .');[33] the commitment of personnel and material resources must be considerable (as in Apex); and there is implied in much of the New Careers literature a recognition that the efforts of professional social workers in working with offenders have 'so far had little or no effect in changing criminal behaviour',[34] and indeed may be counter-productive. 'One of the greatest burdens faced by a parolee in California is represented by his parole agent.'[35]

Background to New Careers

The movement has slowly evolved over a period of two or more decades, and indeed, its background development is an intriguing case-history in the sociology of welfare innovation, involving as it does, the pendulum swing of party politics, the impact of economic affluence on contemporary social problems, an element of charismatic influence, and the cross-national fertilization of ideas. Some of the ideas in New Careers have been traced back as far as the 1940s when programmes were devised to re-socialize ex-prisoners-of-war, but the major elements explicitly recognized by those responsible for the original American penal programmes were twofold. First, the experience of Maxwell Jones (1968) in the Henderson Hospital in Surrey where the concept of the therapeutic community was fully employed from the early 1950s; and second, the attempts of American criminologists during the same period[36] to explore the sociological foundations of criminality and to speculate on the appropriateness or inappropriateness of different kinds of penal response.

The movement has had its largest expression, not specifically in the penal system at all, but as a part of the US poverty programme[37] in which the urban underprivileged were encouraged to become involved in community action on their own behalf; at this level, the concept of New Careers is very closely linked with the community action programmes of the 1960s. So far as offenders are concerned, however, the two best-known schemes are those at Chino and at Vacaville,[38] for both of which it is claimed that significant improvements were achieved both in respect of the ex-prisoners' offence-behaviour and in more general terms. The basic ideas in New Careers are:

1 the underprivileged have something positive to contribute to a treatment programme from the outset; their own life experience gives them a unique knowledge of people and problems from the 'inside', and not from above;

2 work and training should be simultaneous;

3 participants should be able to rise year by year, with increasing responsibility and salary, until they reach a stage equivalent to that of junior-trained professional welfare workers. When that point is reached they can continue normally up the promotion ladder.[39]

In the prison at Chino, a four-year project began with two years in which fairly conventional methods derived from social psychiatry were adapted to the prison setting; fifty-two medium-risk young adult prisoners participated in daily community and small group meetings, and worked with special counsellors to discuss and analyse the social interactions occurring within the situation. The innovation changed 'a small portion of the prison structure considerably, and the inmates developed impressive skills in working with one another'.[40] But the project did not succeed in separating itself sufficiently from the standard prison culture; correctional officers wanted disciplinary offences reported and punished, for example, whereas the project would choose to discuss them in the community group; and the prisoners retained their contact with the inmate culture which inevitably tended to undermine the experimental régime.

In its second phase, however, the project gained greater independence and established a functional role for correctional officers within the community; new work activities were developed, in place of the conventional laundry posting. Most significant of all, there was a general blurring of staff–inmate roles: the prisoners were fully involved in operating the unit and selecting candidates for vacant places; twelve of the men became social therapists in their own right, and some volunteered to remain in the project 'after they had finished their own rehabilitation to "put something back into it" – to help other residents to change.'[41]

At Vacaville, between February 1965 and June 1966, eighteen hardened criminals lived and worked together, in three phases, mainly concentrating their efforts on developing and using their skills in sociological research and focusing their attention largely on community welfare issues. On release from prison, the majority took jobs in the social services, in community action, and in further developing the New Careers movement. Those who, before prison, had had no chance because of their deprived surroundings were the ones who were best able to forge ahead once the opportunity was given them.

No-one who reads of the American experience can fail to be impressed with the freshness of the ideas and the dynamism of the activities, and it is not surprising that NACRO have initiated a New Careers scheme in Bristol, where twenty-eight young offenders over a 20-month period can be trained as social workers in a residential setting and as an alternative to a borstal sentence. Early progress reports[42] give a clear indication of both the opportunities and the problems that characterize the Bristol project. The overwhelming problem initially seemed to be in recruiting enough suitable young offenders as students. During the first quarter, out of nineteen in a remand centre eligible in terms of age and catchment area, eight opted out, four were moved to another prison, three were judged unsuitable because of maladjustment and a poor self-image, and another was later excluded because of his superficial involvement in the orientation phase. Three appropriate orders were eventually made by the courts, but one lad absconded after four days; the two 'successful' selections were still surviving after four months. Similar problems arose during the second quarter, and no further students joined, although it was hoped that five others would arrive later; a great deal of energy was spent on trying to determine how the original target could be reached.

Despite the inevitable difficulty of only working with two students, they were quickly involved in tasks with the mentally subnormal, on a community observation project and a playscheme, in a psychiatric hospital, and in work with senior schoolchildren. The acceptability of the students in different settings was not in question; and, apart from the numbers problem, the main concern of the project in its early months was to improve the quality and structure of the training syllabus; many of the placements seemed to suffer from a lack of clearly defined purpose, and the need was recognized for 'a more organised approach to programme planning and evaluation'.

Hinton[43] has said that New Careers 'is an educational rather than a treatment programme', and the early Bristol experience reflects the idea that its participants must be very carefully selected. Thus, the relevance of New Careers to our present discussion is not that it is a form of after-care, but that it is presented as a positive alternative to destructive incarceration or ineffective community supervision; however, its value must depend on the numbers of convicted offenders for whom it is considered suitable, and on satisfactorily clarifying its underlying objectives. If the Bristol project successfully explores these two issues it will have made an important contribution to penal thinking.

After-care was provided in the US New Careers experience, and indeed its extent and intensity far exceeds that generally available in either the British or American penal systems. For example, one New Careerist got into severe financial trouble and 'Doug Grant – the project director – made considerable personal loans to tide him over his various crises'; the general consensus seemed to be that without Grant's support – sometimes subtle, sometimes very direct – some at least of them would not have 'made it'.[44] Similarly it is anticipated that the Bristol scheme will back up the residents after they move into the community phase and beyond. But even more crucial will be the willingness of social services organizations to employ ex-offenders as full-time members of staff. Briggs has already criticized the Prison Service and the Probation and After-care Service for not doing what it expects other employers to do – give offenders the chance of a job – and has confessed that, as a social work teacher, he would 'be called more than daft' if he tried to persuade his academic colleagues to give a teaching place to a homeless borstal boy with no 'O' or 'A' levels and no good references. 'Clearly we must keep him in the client role', even though 'we could well use him now as a tutor on any residential course, or in social work methods courses – he knows them inside out. . . .'[45]

New Careers, like many radical presentations, has its inconsistencies and elements of confusion. In the American experiments described, just what was it that produced the results: the work of the social therapists, the powerful influence of exceptional innovators, the changed sociological base within which the community was allowed to develop? How successfully can apparently valuable innovatory projects be translated into situations where they would be the conventional norm? Does their value derive from the starkness of the contrast with the traditional prison culture? And what would be the implication for sentencing procedures if a sentence of imprisonment were generally interpreted as being a sentence to social psychiatry? How essential is an intensive after-care programme to the scheme? What is it that the New Careers movement is seeking to produce? Hinton refers to 500,000 New Careers aides now in post in the USA: how do these compare with the eighteen highly-privileged men from Vacaville whose experience, according to Hodgkin[46] is not likely to be repeated in the regressive atmosphere in California under the right-wing Governor Reagan? Is New Careers to be restricted to the creation of a new generation of welfare aides and social servants, and if so, are they likely to be more successful than contemporary borstal residents in being able to use their training for a relevant post in the world outside? Above all, although reference is made to the way in which the experiments have been evaluated in terms of reconviction rates and parole violation, there is an undeniable feeling that the full implications of the work have not yet been adequately subjected to rigorous research exploration.

New Careers is a segment of contemporary social and political revolution; it derives from a recognition of the gross inequalities of educational opportunity and cultural deprivation in the Western world, and belatedly seeks to make up for these; on a small scale it is suggested that it can succeed. What would be the effects if it went much further? Certainly the argument that there is, among the deviant, the distressed and the underprivileged, a vast potential army of social servants is an attractive one, but the concept of New Careers has such vast implications that, as Briggs puts it, 'there is no knowing where it would end'. It is easy, as the scheme's exponents readily do, to criticize society for its inequalities, to criticize social work and the professions for their closed shop attitudes; no doubt these will continue to change and evolve, but to draft in large numbers of ex-criminals would almost certainly have a number of unplanned and unintended consequences. If New Careers is concerned with improving the lot of the underprivileged, it really has to do with education, the occupational structure of society, and the relationship between different groups within society; as such it highlights clearly the way in which any consideration of the underlying issues in the penal system (and in particular, the way we deal with prisoners and ex-prisoners, and our consideration of alternatives to imprisonment) forces us to return to basic issues of social and political philosophy.

Conclusion

The offender and his job raise issues both general and specific, as we have seen; and it is incredibly difficult to separate them. If we discuss prison industries or the problem of fidelity bonding for the white-collar ex-prisoner, are we rashly accepting the reality of prison, and by working within contemporary penal confines, conniving at its worst iniquities? Or if we turn to the task of training offenders to hold responsible jobs (for example, as community development workers in a local authority), are we, for once, paying more than lip-service to the task of rehabilitation, or are we dangerously tampering with the finely balanced structure of our complex urban society? The problem for the penologist is a severe one, because the component parts in the puzzle reflect some of the most emotive and ever-present aspects of man's relationship with his social situation; and the prisoner – with his past record, his present plight and his future prospects – is a central figure in the continuing drama.

7 The prisoner's view

Traditionally, it has been one of the essential ingredients of imprisonment that inmates are denied the opportunity of influencing their surroundings to any significant extent: their cell accommodation, their food, their leisure-time activities, their work opportunities, their companions, their contact with the outside world, their mode of dress, hair-style, their movement within the prison system – all of these involve decisions that are very largely out of their hands. 'Prisonization' involves the inmate's acceptance of an inferior role: 'he becomes at once an anonymous figure in a subordinate group'.[1] Nevertheless, of course, within the confines of the social situation in which they find themselves, individual prisoners cling to as many opportunities as possible for small-scale decision-making: for example, in regard to the informal relationships existing within the inmate community, the tobacco economy of the institution, and manipulation of the system in order to get as comfortable a job as possible. Their essential powerlessness, however, persists. The prisoner quickly learns to accept his inferior role, and to behave in ways appropriate to the institutional culture. Only rarely does an inmate react violently in a desperate and necessarily futile striving for independence and freedom of choice; when this happens, the régime simply re-asserts its authority by imposing an even greater restriction of individual liberty – the withdrawal of privileges, minimum diet, close confinement, loss of remission.[2]

The good prisoner is one who quietly accepts the authority of the system, reconciles himself to the dreary routine and the unequal power structure within the institution, and never openly questions the conventional behaviour of the staff or the administration; such self-effacement may in turn be rewarded by a marginal increase in the area of personal freedom – by the achievement of red-band status or by referral to an open prison. (It should not be overlooked that such paradoxical demands are not made of prisoners alone; to a lesser extent, the same is true of a child at school, of a factory-hand, of a Civil Service clerk, or indeed of any junior employee in a large organization – in all these areas the notion of conformity to imposed demands can be seen in operation. However, although the difference may indeed be one of degree, the completeness of the prisoner's anonymity, his isolation from public view, and the fact of his residence in a total institution with no respite from the influence of the system renders the depersonalization process more complete.)

It is, then, perhaps not surprising that little weight is attached to the views of men and women in prison, despite the self-evident fact that their experience is more direct than that of many others whose views carry greater weight in policy-making circles. (Again, the analogy with low-status personnel in schools, factories and offices, indicates that ignoring the opinions of prisoners is only part of a much wider phenomenon in an unequal society. But there is an added factor: in so far as prisoners are where they are because of society's demand that they be punished, then it is argued by some that a proper part of that punishment consists of the denial of any natural right to self-determination to which the prisoner might lay claim).

Hence, prisoners are not expected to have valid opinions about their own circumstances; or at least they are not expected to express them openly. (In their correspondence, prisoners have usually been prevented from talking about conditions inside.) If they do have opinions, it is assumed that these are either irrelevant or unreliable. Not only, then, is there a dearth of research-based information about the nature of men and women in prison (see Chapter 2); there is very little material which enables the student to draw on the prisoner's own perception of his prison experience or his assessment of its effect on him when he returns to the community outside. This is partly a reflection of the greater ease with which the official line can be studied (by interviewing probation officers, for example, or by describing the *status quo* from the outside), and it is partly a reflection of the dominant position of administration-based research methods over the years. It is also an indication of society's attitude to the prisoner, and of the dangerous way in which the rights of human beings can be overlooked when one's concern is primarily with the maintenance of social stability by means of a penal response.

In this chapter, an effort is made to draw on autobiographical literature, research evidence and other material to reflect the prisoner's view of welfare and of the concept of after-care.

The validity of prison autobiographies

By 1967, the Home Office's own research unit had undertaken so little work in prisons that the House of Commons Estimates Committee felt obliged to express its concern that research was, accordingly, making virtually no contribution towards policy development in the Prison Department. Nevertheless, of course, there is in prison autobiographies a great wealth of first-hand evidence about institutional life. 'What's prison like? There's no excuse for people not knowing nowadays. So many books on the subject [have been written] by the people who've been there. . . .'[3] The weakness of these accounts for research purposes is not that they are necessarily untruthful or slanted, but that each presents only one person's view of a restricted range of prison establishments, and that, in sum, they represent the views of ex-prisoners who are themselves especially literate or who have access to a ghost-writer of some kind. But the net effect of reading a number of such volumes is to minimize the first of these problems, and to suggest that the second is not as important as it might seem at first sight, for although some of the authors went to prison as famous or notorious men,[4] others were quite unknown at the time of their sentence, and their experience of the reality of imprisonment is likely to have been relatively normal. In any case, one of the elements that emerges strongly in the literature is the way in which, for the most part, prisons depersonalize all those who go there and take little account of status in the outside world – which is not, of course, to imply that all prisoners are equal. One of the writers, in commenting on the general availability of prison biographies in the libraries of the institutions themselves, indicates his judgment that most books about prison experiences 'are, by and large, undeniably honest'.[5] Moreover, although the writer–prisoner is undeniably atypical (by virtue of the fact that he does set his experiences down on paper), there is sufficient variety among the authors to overcome any feeling that the evidence presented will be biased in exactly the same way in every book; there may be sections of the prison population markedly under-represented among the autobiographies, but a reading of, say, twenty such books, gives a wider range of experience than might at first be anticipated.

Finally, it is possible to supplement the personal descriptions with findings from the limited number of research studies that have been carried out in this area, and to show that, all in all, the consumer's view tends to be remarkably consistent – not only with regard to welfare and after-care, but also concerning the overall perception of prison life. Indeed, the consistency is so great that when it comes to factual details about food, work, classes, and social living, it is embarrassingly obvious that it is the official Home Office pronouncements that are sometimes at best only half true.[6]

The overall effect of reading prisoners' autobiographies is a very depressing one, and this applies at least as much to the area of welfare and after-care where one can perhaps recognize that there are good intentions on the part of those in authority. Hence, it is as well to bear in mind Wildeblood's comment that 'the prison is not always a gloomy place. . . . Nor are the people in it entirely bad; no one in the world is entirely good or bad.'[7]

Prisoners' attitudes towards, and experience of, the welfare service

The most relevant – and, one suspects, by no means accidental – fact is that the figure of the prison welfare officer is never central to the reality of prison life as described by those who have experienced it. The prison officers and the governor grades dominate the scene, with medical staff, chaplains and visiting committees allocated relatively clear roles at given points in time. But the welfare officer – even in the most recent accounts – rarely appears, and even when he does it is as a rather shadowy bureaucrat. Only Merfyn Turner, with perhaps a semi-professional interest in the subject, draws a detailed description of the old Discharged Prisoners' Aid official, Speedy Sam, who was always in a hurry, always had too much to do, too many people to see, too little in the way of resources to give.[8] And even then, following the introduction of 'professional' welfare officers to the prison, the change was for the worse, because, although Speedy Sam clearly couldn't cope with all the demands on his time, he had had a degree of personal contact with a proportion of the men, whereas the new welfare officers were seen to be much more formal in their approach to the job. At about the same time, Pauline Morris confirmed the impression with her research interviews focused on the needs of prisoners' families – one of the areas for which the welfare service was intended to be responsible: 'The men had very little faith in the prison welfare officers.'[9] She produced a lot of evidence about the plight of the men's wives and children to enable her to conclude that welfare provisions were totally inadequate.

Robert Allerton described the concept of welfare as 'the latest gimmick in a long dreary series of attempts at reforming prisoners' by the Home Office.[10] His view is typical. The 'welfare' is hardly noticed by the inmates; there is cynical resentment at the inflated claims made for its value in the correctional process; and, because of its identification with officialdom and with the 'screws', there is a general desire to have as little to do with welfare officers as possible. The most that any of them are thought able to give is advice, and generally this is unwanted and deemed to be inappropriate; occasionally there is a recognition that the welfare officers themselves – or some of them – are well-intentioned and non-punitive in their attitudes, but the harsh reality is that they have – or are thought to have – little to offer the serving inmate in the way of help. Only in cases of extreme crisis regarding the next-of-kin do prisoners think that welfare officers can come to their aid – and often then it is too late: you get to the point where 'you can never trust officials, even good-natured probation officers'.[11]

Of course, there is a slight but steady increase in the proportion of welfare officers to prisoners, but even in the most recent accounts, the basic facts remain the same: 'Welfare in prisons is practically non-existent.' The welfare officers are overworked and bound by red tape, and it is impossible for them to help you. Your problem goes on a list, no matter how urgent it is, and you may see the welfare a week later only to find that there is nothing they can do. . . . 'You never get any further with your problem.'[12]

A recent research study covering a representative sample of prisoners[13] showed that 20 per cent of all prisoners had not seen the prison welfare officer during their sentence, and that these tended to be the men with the greatest problems awaiting them on release.[14]

Attitudes towards, and experience of, the world outside

Absorption into prison is complete in all material respects; the outside world carries on as before, but the prisoner has no part of it, no influence over it, a greatly reduced awareness of it, and very little contact with it. Even with 1973 reforms, visits to prisoners by relatives are restricted to one a month – and even this is not always possible because of the geographical isolation of many men scattered through the prison system – and correspondence is still limited, even though censorship has been lifted.[15] Hence, most prisoners are largely cut off from society – a fact that is defended by the Government, because prison is 'a legitimate curtailment of civil rights, and, therefore, by definition and purpose a basically unpleasant experience'.[16]

However, it has been recognized on a wide front that such a deliberate policy can have a cumulatively damaging effect on the prospects for the prisoner when he returns to the outside world. For, while the prisoner is apart from it, the world moves on: his family struggles and perhaps breaks up, while he fluctuates between a depressed and an exaggerated concern for his wife and his children and a feeling of relief for the fact that he is no longer responsible for their welfare. Where prisoners discuss the world outside, it is mostly with regard to their wives or girlfriends, their fidelity and distress, and to the feeling of helplessness and shame that combine to reduce their own self-esteem even further than before. Pauline Morris, on the other hand, talks of men in prison having a 'roseate picture' of the situation in the world outside: 'Detention relieves him of many of his obligations.'[17]

The reality of prison life is that the internal system dominates the waking moments of virtually every prisoner's existence, and arguments that the prison welfare officer should be a vehicle for communication with the outside world would seem to be a rather artificial and unfruitful way of breaking down barriers; in any case, it places the welfare officer in something of an invidious position with the ability to award privileges on a rather haphazard basis – such a commodity would seem unlikely to improve the prospects for welfare officers in their developing casework role within the institution, although it would undoubtedly give them greater power.

Apart from those prisoners living in hostels and working outside, most seem to feel that all prisons involve equal isolation; indeed Willetts found that an open prison was, if anything, more oppressive than a closed institution.[18] The one element that means more than anything else to inmates is the visit – 'It takes your mind off other things'[19] – but of course the conditions under which visits are carried out only serve to emphasize the constricted nature of the relationship between the prisoner and his family. Television has brought the outside world in to the prisons in a totally new way, so that prisoners with access to it can at least remain reasonably up to date with social and political developments – including those impinging upon their own lives.

Perhaps the aspect of prison life which most emphasizes the isolation of prisoners from responsible society is the feeling that nobody cares about their circumstances – and this is heightened by the frequently described experiences when attempts are made by prisoners to draw attention to their plight. Restrictions have long been imposed on any kind of writing, and traditionally nothing may be written about prison life or any aspect of it; but more important, the prisoner is often denied any practical right to complain – although the theoretical right exists. Thus Baker, previously a Member of Parliament, was appalled to find that prison officers admitted that they entered any first letters that prisoners wrote to MPs in the correspondence book, and then tore them up: 'We enter them through the records as posted and then tear them up. You'd be surprised at the amount of trouble it saves.'[20] Prisoners, of course, generally assumed that their MP had simply ignored them, and few tried a second time.

Similarly, although prisoners have the technical right to petition the Home Office about the situation, Croft-Cooke[21] describes the practical difficulty of getting to see the Governor first, then obtaining the appropriate form, securing a pen and ink, filling it in, dealing with comments and criticisms made by the Deputy Governor, and finally sending it off. Frank Norman tells how, after his release and when he had become a respectable member of the establishment, he asked a Civil Servant 'what happened to petitions which were sent to the Home Office by geezers doing bird'. The only answer he got was that most of such men were 'nothing but trouble-makers' – a claim which Norman denied: 'Most of them have a real grievance or problem.'[22]

The prisoner is held in captivity: such a tautology is sufficient to summarize the degree of social isolation which he experiences. The world he lives in has its own emotions, its own language, its own social structure, its own norms of behaviour – but all of these are so different from those elsewhere that, come the day of release, the change of environment must present nothing less than a crisis for most men and women who have known only 'the nick' for anything from three months to ten years or more.

The day of release

There is a startling uniformity in prisoners' accounts of their experience of release. The appearance before the discharge board – the DPA or the welfare officer and other officials – and the feeling about its general worthlessness; the fact that 'until the very last minute, there was no change in the deadly machine-like routine of the place';[23] the meeting with the Governor in one's discharge suit, the proffered hand, and the headmasterly advice about not coming back; the solemn farewells with one's closest friends; the sleepless night immediately preceding discharge, fears and doubts crowding out the aspirations and the anticipated joys of the next day; the early awakening by the 'screw'; the drink and the porridge which you must, by prison lore, eat, because if you don't you're sure to return to finish it; and then the opening of the gate and the departure complete with the clothes provided and whatever sum of money was allocated to you under the Prison Rules. . . .

The first day out is undoubtedly, for the majority of ex-prisoners, a critical occasion. Partly because of their recent isolation from society, there are a whole range of problems and fears confronting them: the noise of the traffic, and the task of physical survival in busy streets; coping again with money, and with prices which may have changed out of all recognition; dealing with shops and shop assistants; coming to terms with the renewed presence of women in the environment; the semi-paranoid feeling that everybody is looking at them and recognizing their background. 'There were so many problems to be faced, so many fears to be brought out into the open that I almost wished I had never been given my freedom.'[24]

But in addition to this, there is the even more difficult task of surviving by one's own efforts. For so long, the prisoner has had no decisions to make, no responsibilities to carry, no problems to cope with. Now, if he is on licence, he is expected to report to a probation officer in the right place and at the right time; he has to go to the Supplementary Benefits office and the Employment Exchange – involving, the writers say, often hours of waiting, traipsing backwards and forwards from one set of officials to another; filling in forms in a dreary institutional room – spoken down to by women and bossy men who 'broadcast all over the place you've just come out of prison'.[25] It is clear from the biographies that the prisoners with families and friends to turn to quickly overcome their fears, their apprehensions, their doubts about survival in a hostile world, while those without suffer the most because of their isolation, and appear to be the least likely to avoid a return to crime and imprisonment. Those who are on their own continue to feel the stigma of imprisonment for longer than those with a social circle to which they can turn – an odd paradox, perhaps, but one which serves to aggravate the problems of those most in need of social support in any case. Lowson suggests that for his borstal boys, the day of release was a time of irritation (especially regarding the availability of cash and employment) rather than crisis; but there seems to be sufficient evidence in the literature to indicate a potential need for crisis support during the period immediately following release – providing the support is offered in such a way that it can be dissociated from the correctional stigma of the prison.

Attitudes towards after-care

A good deal of the detailed description of after-care by ex-prisoners in the literature is anachronistic because of the replacement of the work of the old Discharged Prisoners' Aid Societies during the 1960s by the probation service. Certainly, according to the men on the receiving end, the demise of the Discharged Prisoners' Aid Societies was no cause for weeping: 'The general opinion of all prisoners is that they are not worth a carrot',[26] and 'the whole thing is viewed in prison with the cynicism it deserves'.[27] If the Discharged Prisoners' Aid Societies did a good job, there is little or no appreciation of it in the contemporary accounts of their work by the men who were the intended beneficiaries.

What then of the probation officers who have taken their place? One undoubted problem is the ambiguous way they are perceived by prisoners who are never quite sure whether to regard them as friends or enemies;[28] the fact that probation officers are seen sometimes as having had a say in securing a custodial sentence does not help the situation, but the evidence about attitudes is somewhat variable.

Lowson's study of borstal boys in Liverpool is very clear in differentiating between the way they perceive probation officers as individuals and their opinion of after-care as a system.[29] In general, there was a positive response towards the professional agents of after-care: 'a man I can talk to, I like him'; 'I get on well with him, my parents think he's alright too'; 'a great help, he took an interest in my wife's problems when I was inside'. Only 3 out of 82 respondents were positively critical of their officer, while a further 13 spoke of the after-care relationship as being merely formal; in contrast, some lads showed 'a high enthusiasm for this official who had come into their lives'.

On the other hand, when asked about after-care as an institution, 'replies were markedly more critical'.[30] 47 out of the 82 were implicitly or explicitly critical, and there was particular resentment at the continuation of supervision long after they had served their sentence. In summary, Lowson concluded, 'the probation officer, as an individual, seemed to get through to the majority of lads though there was a generally unfavourable attitude to after-care as a system.'[31]

For the men in prison, however, especially for those with a lengthy experience of the penal system, attitudes appear to be harder. There is frequent criticism of those who give 'good advice': 'Sometimes I resent it, other times it bores me.'[32] There is reaction against a patronizing attitude or unsought familiarity. And, in particular, there is cynical realism about the inability of the after-care officer to deliver anything much in the way of material goods or practical assistance: 'Even when it was obvious I wasn't working, he didn't much want to know. . . .'[33] Silberman's interviews with prisoners from Pentonville reflect these attitudes in great detail. After-care had rarely helped the men to get a job, and was often confined to giving advice: 'The probation officer always thinks he knows your problems and the answers to them . . . the trouble is it is their answer, not yours.'[34] The men looked to the after-care for material aid, rather than verbal exhortations: 'At best, after-care and other forms of social work were regarded as a form of first-aid which helped them over a rough patch and failed to affect the basic position',[35] but instead of cash, they often got pep-talks: 'Those who told them how to manage their lives did not have the faintest idea of the conditions under which they had to live and did not greatly understand their problems.'[36]

As in Lowson's study – though not to the same extent – there was some recognition by the interviewees that individual probation officers were kind and helpful, but the system as a whole was subjected to scathing condemnation for its inherent inadequacies. The men's problems were so great and the resources available (time, money, personnel, social influence) so slight, that there was generally no hope of bridging the gap between the two.

In one of the most recent prison autobiographies, Fletcher (1972) very clearly and sympathetically defines the limitations of even the most intensive efforts on the part of a probation officer. The author had spent forty-four years in prison as a petty recidivist, and had long since lost all faith or interest in the ability of a social worker to serve a useful purpose in his life. But in 1970, the close working relationship between the probation service and the courts left him on probation with an exceptionally committed, patient and understanding woman officer: 'For the first time in my life I had found a PO who did what she promised to do.' Three times she helped him through the crises of further petty offences (usually involving a deliberate act of phone-box larceny, after which he sat down and waited for the police to pick him up) and loss of employment. But, says Fletcher, 'no matter how willing a probation officer is, they are so busy and so tied up with red tape that it is a wonder that they ever find time to talk to you'.[37] Moreover, the fact that probation officers are professionals means that they are only available for limited periods of time, and often not at the very moment of crisis when the need for support might be greatest. Fletcher says, with some justification, that for someone like him – thoroughly institutionalized, socially inadequate, and only too eager to return to the relative simplicity and the total security of prison, 'no one probation officer can possibly help on their own'.[38] He had, in addition, benefited from the active interest of a remarkable number of members of the community, and as a result was managing to survive.

To achieve this kind of breakthrough, there is no doubt that the community resources needed are enormous – and even then the achievements may be relatively slight. In Diana Norman's description (1970) of the work of John Dodd and his residential workers in the Langley House Trust, for instance, there is a heavy emphasis on the way in which totally committed hostel wardens and matrons simply run themselves into a state of exhaustion within a short space of time. For the Bill Fletchers of this world, survival outside a prison is not only a challenge to the individual, but can involve enormous cost to the wider community – or at least to selected groups within it. The gap between the 'normal' sort of after-care described by so many of the prisoners without enthusiasm, and the kind of resources pumped into Bill Fletcher's life in his late fifties, once a judge and a probation officer had determined between them to keep him in the community, is astronomical; and yet it is clear that such a step was the right social decision in an essentially ethical situation. It is also implicit in much that ex-prisoners say about after-care that they believe that only something on that scale can truly meet the needs of the most extreme isolates from the moment when the prison gate shuts behind them, and they emerge to face the confusing realities of the world outside.

For all the fact that there are now individuals like Bill Fletcher benefiting from intensive after-care in both the statutory and the voluntary sector, it is hard to avoid the conclusion that, seen with the eyes of the inmates themselves, the provision of after-care in Britain still falls far short of the minimum necessary to justify the term at all, let alone the kind of intensive long-term supportive style that is enabling one man at least to live a new life in society.

Other people's reactions to the prisoner following his release

There are major contrasts in priorities facing ex-prisoners on release. The sort of men that Silberman describes – 'the uncared-for children of deprived families belonging to an under-privileged class'[39] who had suffered from years of indifference and neglect, and whose lives were not sustained by stable social relationships of any kind – were concerned first and foremost with physical survival; social acceptance and the re-gaining of self-respect were luxuries beyond their imagination. This is not to say that such goals would be unattainable – Fletcher's account is of great value in showing just what is possible – but that the first concerns of many men on release are more basic, and that the common failure to meet their most elementary needs precludes an emphasis on social relationships and personal growth. On the other hand, a great many prisoners return to their parents on release, or to their wives and children, their old neighbourhoods, and sometimes to their former jobs. Such people are united in their feeling of shame and embarrassment at this time – especially in regard to employment, where the conflict between the desire to be honest about their prison sentence and the fear that it will lead to stigmatization by both workmates and bosses is almost always felt most deeply, and for which there appears to be no wholly satisfactory solution: 'I came to realise that the world is made up of two kinds of people – the helpers and those who will kick you in the teeth.'[40] But after the initial embarrassment (when handing in his railway warrant at the station near the prison, Norman felt that 'the geezer behind the burnt gave me a dodgy look, like I was made of dirt or something . . .'),[41] those men and women who had a family to turn to, even if they had not seen them for a decade or more, record how quickly and easily they were absorbed into it again. Both Morris (1965) and Martin and Webster (1971) have found that the actual experience of conviction and custody has an apparently less destructive effect on marriage than might be imagined: 'Generally speaking, relationships between husbands and wives appeared to improve while the husband was in custody',[42] but to a certain extent this appears to depend on an over-optimistic and fantasized view of the marital relationship. Morris found that after release the matrimonial pattern continued much as before,[43] but there was some evidence in Martin and Webster that, in the two years following discharge from jail, elements of conflict did break out in a number of cases; however, there is no evidence that this occurred *because* of the prison experience, and the main point remains unchallenged: that, at the time they return home, prisoners appear to have a helpful rather than a hostile family situation to contend with. Prison authors say they were surprised at the tolerance shown by most of those around them, although it is also true that they indicate that their experience of imprisonment is such as to make them feel 'different' from other people for a very long time. Willetts (1965) in particular, describes how she felt as though she had returned from the dead, and had in some way become a different person because of her imprisonment.

In summary then, for those not too taken up with the problems of material needs release from prison did not produce the anticipated sensation of social leprosy, but their experience was none the less a stigmatizing one, as much for their own self-perception as for the labelling processes of others.

Discussion

There is an odd feeling of familiarity about prison memoirs, in so far as they tend to go over much the same ground, and to express only slightly varying opinions; at the same time, they are strikingly at odds with most penological discussions, simply because the prisoner's view is rarely taken into account. Prisoners have been describing the depressing and inhuman sores and irritations of prison life for decades, and, more important, they have continually passed judgment on most of the reforms within the prison system, and have found them wanting. The most common emotion in the literature is not anger but resignation; the most common criticism is not about the punitive element in prison (which seems to be acceptable, so long as it is deemed to be fair and reasonably imposed), but – contrary to all the best hopes of the penal reformers – it is concerned with the hypocrisy of a system which claims to be reforming its inmates. The bitterest and most telling denunciations are against those members of the penal establishment who claim – in speech or in writing – that custodial sentences are achieving positive ends, by virtue of education and training, welfare and casework, therapy and good advice. On the contrary, the universal feeling among the men and the women is that they are 'doing time', and their prime aim is to get through it with a minimum of fuss. The prison which best facilitates this is seen as the best establishment – hence Norman speaks of one institution in glowing terms because it is so well organized that every prisoner is accorded his due rights without delay – while prisons which induce a deceptive sense of optimism while all the time maintaining the psychological reality of the prisoner's secondary status are the most disliked – as Willetts found in an open prison for women. Hence, role clarity would seem to be a crucial desire in the prisoner's mind, and any reform which removes this while still denying him his rights as a responsible citizen with control over his own destiny might well be a retrograde step – even though it might irrationally soothe the consciences of well-meaning but misguided liberal reformers.

Similarly, there would seem to be a need to differentiate between the traditional concept of after-care and the developing notion of through-care. The prison literature only serves to confirm the reality of the crisis at the time of discharge, and to reinforce the felt need for a gentler process of release, as distinct from the cold water plunge imposed on all but the 1 per cent of prisoners who go through the prison hostel scheme. To be a prisoner one day and a responsible citizen the next inflicts too great a strain on men and women whose capacity to cope with stress may already be suspect. For those with social support and material means, after-care would seem to be a private affair; for those without, the problem is compounded because, in addition to the cold plunge, there is added the fact that they have never learned to swim, and society provides them with virtually no aids to survival. It is manifestly clear that, despite all the talk of the 1960s, and despite the increased involvement of the probation service in after-care, the inmates themselves see hardly any improvement. With up to 50,000 men released every year, and a probation service less than a tenth that size, this is perhaps not surprising. But, more important, it indicates that society has by no means clarified the kind of service that it wants to provide for its most extreme social casualties, especially for those gradually deteriorating as they work their way through the penal (and perhaps the psychiatric systems). In Jeremy Sandford's vivid description (1973) of the plight of David Oluwale in the years before his death at the hands of two policemen, the helplessness of the prison welfare service and of the Leeds probation officers is made clear:

September 1967 David Oluwale was discharged from prison following a conviction for wandering abroad. The prison welfare officer said that 'he will be remaining in Leeds where he will seek his own accommodation. Does not have a job to go to.' Within a fortnight he was back inside, and spent most of the winter in prison.
April 1968 Given a conditional discharge for disorderly conduct, and sent to the Church Army hostel. But in August another prison sentence was imposed.
10 January 1969 Discharged from prison. The welfare officer said that 'he had been unemployed some time. Is of very low intelligence and could be very aggressive. He is going to have great difficulty in staying out of trouble on release.' In fact, David returned to prison almost immediately.
23 January 1969 Discharged again. The prison welfare officer said that he had not worked for six months and had no job to go to on release.
February 1969 Discharged again. The prison welfare officer: 'He has no settled way of life – no place to lodge when he is released. Deteriorating all the time.'
March 1969 Again discharged. Because of his need for accommodation, Oluwale called at the probation office. The probation officer tried to get him a place in a hostel, but none would have him.
April 1969 Discharged again. The prison welfare officer: 'David is rapidly becoming a social problem, unable to function on the outside.' The probation officer found it almost impossible to understand him, but sent him round to the Social Security, who agreed to help.
Eight days later, David Oluwale was dead.

The great danger with the idea of 'through-care' is that it will divert scarce resources away from the point of discharge, where it is perfectly clear they are needed as much as ever, and that it will be counter-productive if it involves the increased imposition of welfare staff within the prisons battling against the discipline role of the prison officer, as occurred in Phase I of the Chino project.[44] Through-care can only work if the concept of imprisonment is totally changed. Meanwhile, after-care remains an essential task in the penal system.

8 The dilemma of penal decision-making

Two underlying themes have emerged more than once in the foregoing text:

1 that any consideration of prison after-care must lead the student inexorably back towards a consideration of why men and women are given custodial sentences in the first place; and
2 that the nature and circumstances of such men and women are diverse in the extreme.

It is one of the myths of society, perpetuated – perhaps, it has to be admitted, inevitably – by public opinion and by the decision-making processes of the courts and the penal system, that there is an identifiable class of persons for whom the only appropriate place is a prison. This view is commonly expressed in the media: 'At present there are, on the one extreme, prisons containing the violent and truly criminal; while on the other hand there are residential homes with no security.'[1] This comment was made in respect of a criminal case which highlighted a great many of the dilemmas involved in correctional decision-making, and demonstrated the way in which a brief incident can precipitate a snowballing sequence of events with repercussions in numerous segments of the social system. In particular the case of Jacqueline Paddon illustrates the confusion that has arisen in discussions about criminals because of the failure to distinguish between what they have done, what sort of persons they are, what their contemporary social situation is, and what has happened to them in the past. Most disagreements in respect of penal decision-making stem from the fact that different people lay varying degrees of emphasis on each of these factors.

Jaqueline Paddon, the press and the public

One June day in 1972, a young mother was out shopping in Southend. Doreen Walsh was walking along, pushing her baby daughter Susannah's pram when she met a friend whom she had known since her schooldays. Jackie Paddon was a very simple sort of person and she had suffered the kind of institutional experiences which often make one's friends fearful and rejecting; but Doreen did not react to her in this way. She knew about Jackie's illegitimate son, born nearly two years earlier and in the care of the local authority for most of his life. She, too, had once been 'forced to hand over Susannah to foster-parents' and the intense pain of this experience, giving rise to a feeling that she *had* to have her baby back, gave her immense sympathy for Jackie's loss.

The father of Jackie's baby was in prison, and there was no question of any marriage pending. People had tried to persuade her to have her son Dean adopted, but Jackie would have none of it, and continued to hope that one day he might be returned to her. That very morning her parents had shown her some photographs of Dean with his foster parents and this had left her feeling very distressed. She told her friend about it, but Doreen could only suggest that they walk round to see the social worker in the civic centre; perhaps there might be more encouraging news about the prospect of Dean being given back to Jackie. . . .

Doreen allowed Jackie to take the pram handle and to push Susannah along. 'My baby, my baby . . .', she kept muttering to herself as they walked; she was in a rather dazed state and seemed to be trying to reconcile her crude notion of the rights of parental ownership of a child with the apparently competing powers of society to take one's baby away: 'If "my baby" was no longer *mine*, why should anybody's baby not be similarly open to another's possession?'

Doreen began to worry. Jackie, she knew, was a peculiar woman and her behaviour was not always predictable; she felt sorry for her and wanted to help if she could, but Jackie was acting very strangely and she didn't really know what she was letting herself in for. 'Would you take the baby – kidnap her, I mean?' she asked, as she began to realize what was happening. 'Why not?' replied Jackie, 'they've taken mine.' And with this, she strode quickly away past the shops; Doreen cried out after her, and ran, but she couldn't keep up with Jackie who was soon out of sight.

An incident had occurred; a crime had been committed against Section 56 of the Offences against the Person Act 1861. Doreen immediately telephoned the police; she carefully explained what had happened and where she and Jackie had been going. It was by no means the first time that the police had been asked to find Jackie, and either by luck or judgment, they soon located her. There she was, only 15 minutes after walking away from Doreen, by the civic centre, still with Susannah safe and sound in the pram, and still possibly thinking of going to see the social worker as Doreen had suggested. What had she in mind? To offer Susannah in exchange for Dean? Actually to keep Susannah for herself? To give her back as soon as Doreen caught up with her? No-one can now be certain. She insisted that the baby was her own when the police officer approached her, but she was still acting very strangely and there was no alternative but to take her along to the police station while everything was sorted out.

The policemen who interviewed Jackie were in no doubt about her mental condition; they decided there and then that 'she was mentally disturbed at the time of the offence'. Her behaviour was, to say the least, bizarre, and in any case, they knew that she had a recent history of psychiatric treatment. She had had a number of spells in South Ockenden Mental Hospital, and if this latest incident wasn't a demonstration of how much she still needed institutional care, they didn't know a symbolic 'cry for help' when they saw one. Moreover, it was known that a great many social workers were concerned with the Paddon family in one way or another; surely between them something might be done to help this unprepossessing nineteen-year-old girl. After all, no permanent damage had been done; Doreen Walsh had inevitably been rather shaken, and she would be unlikely to let Jackie Paddon push her pram again, but she was by no means anxious to see her friend brought to court. The officer in charge of the case therefore contacted the local probation office, where Jackie was already on probation, and subject to borstal after-care supervision.

The probation service knew her well; she had been the subject of a number of social enquiry reports for the court, had been on probation twice, but had had to be brought back to the court because of her refusal to accept the psychiatric treatment insisted upon by the court and prescribed for her by doctors. She had been sent to an approved school, served a borstal sentence, and had spent the previous Christmas in Holloway because of persistently absconding from the hospital which had been asked to achieve what the penal system itself had so far manifestly failed to achieve. The probation officer was sorry for Jackie, but what more could they do? As one of a caseload of 40, she could only be given a small amount of time each week, and for someone like her this was palpably not enough; and yet, when the question of hostel accommodation was considered, there was the over-riding problem of Jackie's unwillingness and apparent inability to co-operate in a voluntary situation. Even if she were to express her readiness to go into some hostel or house where she might be given help and understanding, the probation officer had only to look at the girl's previous behaviour patterns to know that the day after her arrival, or the next day, she would very probably change her mind and come home again. After all, she herself was not looking for support or understanding . . .; it is not even self-evident, as some were later to suggest, that she was looking for love. If she was asked her opinion, then and later, she would say that all she wanted was to be allowed to have Dean back and to look after him again; of course, the police and the probation officer alike had to balance this demand, made with her mother's backing, with their awareness that she had previously had two convictions for soliciting, and was known to have abandoned Dean on a number of occasions thus precipitating the court's order that he be placed in the care of the local authority. Jackie, for whatever reason, had not made the most of her earlier opportunities to prove herself capable of being a reasonable mother in her own right, and this latest incident could not lead those who knew her to feel that there had been much improvement.

What about going back to the hospital at South Ockenden? The policemen tried to enlist the help of the local authority mental health service, but with no greater success. The hospital would clearly be reluctant to accept Jackie as a voluntary patient unless she indicated her willingness to co-operate better than she had done previously. Jackie refused point blank. Moreover, her father indicated later that he too could see no benefit from a return to hospital; while she had previously been resident there, as a condition of a probation order, he had signed her out (as her responsible parent) because he was worried about her worsening mental state: 'She was becoming more depressed and suicidal. She was in the hospital wing with severely subnormal people. When we visited her she would be surrounded by patients who couldn't even talk. Any sane person would go round the bend in that sort of company. She was frequently heavily drugged. When we brought her home she was much happier.' Mr Paddon admitted that Jackie had absconded herself on one occasion, and in the end the probation officer had brought a summons for breach of probation because of her absence from the hospital. But nevertheless, said her father, 'she spent last Christmas in Holloway prison, and she was a lot better off there than in hospital. Her experiences in South Ockenden have turned her against any sort of hospital treatment.'

Sympathetic support for the mental health services in their failure to come to the rescue while Jackie was in the police station was later implicit in a comment made by Richard Fox, a psychiatrist in Severalls Hospital, not far from the Paddons' home town: 'In many cases, given existing facilities, it is impossible for a doctor to suggest a constructive way forward. It is also easier to be sorry for an offender than to know what one may usefully do to help.'

And so the police who had originally decided, according to one report, that Jacqueline Paddon was 'too ill to stand trial but too dangerous to be freed' found that they none the less had to bring a charge against her: that she unlawfully took away Susannah Walsh from her mother. It was later suggested that one possible outcome that the police had in mind was that the court might find suitable psychiatric provision of a kind that had proved impossible to secure for Jackie Paddon on an informal basis; but of course the police are realistic enough to know that once a case comes to court, the ultimate disposal is far from predictable, and the possibility of a prison sentence became a reality from the moment that the charge was made. The *Guardian* wondered eight months later whether the prosecution should ever have been brought, and indicated its disappointment at the failure of the social services to respond more positively to the police officers' appeal for help: 'What use is a welfare net that avoids the most difficult cases?'

The hearing began without much fuss in the Southend Magistrates' Court; limited national coverage was given to the preliminary hearing in June, but Jackie's remand to Chelmsford Crown Court was hardly big news. On 31 October there was a finding of guilt by the jury, and sentence was deferred to the next day by Mr Justice Boreham. When the court met, it was apparent that the judge had had to take a number of factors into account. First and perhaps foremost, there was Jackie's own background and personality, which reflected a growing crescendo of conflict with society in which both she and the community appeared to be getting more and more out of step with each other. Her own family history had presented a number of difficulties: her parents had lived first in a caravan and then in a one-roomed flat; there had been matrimonial trouble, and Jackie had twice been taken into care – at age six and again at ten. Because of her low intelligence, she had attended a special school where it was said that other children picked on her, and in her late teens she had five criminal convictions marked against her; each one was relatively minor, but their effect was cumulative, as much because of the penal system's response – however well-intentioned it might have been – as because of her own developing self-image. She had spells in an approved school and a borstal – both experiences which society intends to be helpful rather than damaging; she was remanded in custody on one occasion for medical and social enquiry reports, but the experience of prison is said to have precipitated a mental breakdown with the result that she was transferred on remand to South Ockenden Mental Hospital. It was this that had led to a probation order being made on condition that she remained in the hospital, and this in turn that produced breaches of probation and a consequent three-month prison sentence in Holloway.

But although penal policy is normally to sentence women on an individualized basis,[2] the judge had also to consider the nature of the offence. A few months previously there had been a quite different case in which a woman had been brought to trial for kidnapping a child and bringing it up as her own in a different part of the country. It seems probable that the judge took this previous case into account, and indeed the 21 months' imprisonment that he imposed on Jacqueline Paddon was identical to the sentence which had been passed in the previous case on appeal. The actual grounds for the decision were not spelt out, however, and the fact that the judge chose to concentrate on 'the fear and terror' that the loss of her baby put in the mind of Doreen Walsh seemed to most immediate commentators an inadequate reason to explain his action. It was unlikely that Jackie had intended to keep the child, and the cost of the police operation was minimal – both factors in sharp contrast to the earlier case of Pauline Jones.

The public reaction was almost wholly critical, with the *Guardian*, in its assumed role as the nation's main agent of penal reform, leading the way. MPs were quoted as describing the sentence as horrifying and reprehensible. The National Council for Civil Liberties called it savage and barbaric, and asked the Home Secretary to intervene. The Chairman of the National Association for Mental Health argued that no possible good could come from the sentence, and that Jackie was 'clearly in need of further help', and Doreen Walsh was quoted as saying that she could have cried when 'they sent her to prison. I am sure she would never have harmed my baby. I only called the police in because it was obvious she needed help.'

The Home Secretary did indeed concern himself with the matter – 'possibly a shade too promptly' according to one of his own back-bench supporters. He asked to see relevant background information; the Southend police and the Prison Department obliged. In the light of this, he decided that no further action on his part was appropriate. In the course of the next few days, with Jackie Paddon back in jail, much more information was being pieced together, and the dilemma that the judge had faced was beginning to be recognized by some of his critics: in passing sentence, he had to cope with the fact that nobody appeared to want her.

A fortnight after the court hearing, and after an appeal had been lodged against sentence, it was possible to have second thoughts, as one *Guardian* writer confessed. Like others, Catherine Storr had 'burned with indignation' at the sentence, but then observed that notes of caution began to appear in the Press stories. The news about the police efforts to avoid a court hearing emerged, and details of Jackie's difficult home situation were published; on the day after the sentence, Mrs Paddon said she wanted Jackie home, but what was she doing when the police were trying to find somewhere for Jackie in June? Jackie's relationship with her baby Dean and her abscondings from South Ockenden were described. In the light of all this, the judge's rejection of a non-custodial sentence (probably with the backing of probation and psychiatric reports) becomes comprehensible. Storr continues: 'To read, after all the hubbub, some "facts" now brought forward in [the judge's] defence might make some of us hesitate next time we feel like championing the sufferer in an obviously hard case at the expense of everyone else, and particularly of officialdom.'

In the meantime, the court hearing and its attendant publicity were having their inevitable side-effects. Jackie's invalid mother was very distressed, but went to visit her daughter shortly after she had started to serve her sentence: 'She was really dejected when I saw her. We met in a cold, bare visiting room and chatted across a green table while two stern-faced warders looked on. She hates the place. The food was bad and she didn't feel she could trust anyone. She is very worried about the lesbians in the jail.'

The Paddons had been so confident that Jackie would be placed on probation that they had even planned a party for her on the day of the court hearing; instead of a party, however, Mr Paddon found himself interviewed and photographed as the leader of a campaign to protest against the sentence. Backed by penal reformers and a local Women's Lib group, the campaign found that it could do little more than organize a march in Southend and await the outcome of the solicitor's efforts to lodge an appeal.

A more sinister development came with poison pen letters and photographs that were sent to the mother of the kidnapped baby. Doreen Walsh was plagued with letters which appeared to hold her responsible for the severity of Jackie's punishment; strangers tried to force their way into her house, and photographs of Susannah with her face slashed were pushed through the letter-box. She too, like the Paddon family, was unable to sleep and found her health deteriorating.

On 25 January 1973 – seven months after the offence and nearly three months after sentence – Jackie was given leave to appeal. On 9 February, Mr Lord Justice Roskill, with two of his colleagues, set aside the sentence of imprisonment and placed Jackie on probation for three years with a condition of residence in a probation hostel in Reading for twelve months. In doing this, the Appeal Court went out of its way to defend the Crown Court judge ('public criticism of him had been grossly unfair'), and to say that the original sentence was entirely justified. Because her period of time in Holloway had improved her (presumably on the evidence of a probation officer), the Court decided that it could do something 'which would have been utterly impossible for the trial judge to do'. (In fact, this implied that a three-month spell in prison had proved effective; nevertheless, had Jackie Paddon not appealed – as may well have been the case if there had been no publicity – she would have served her full sentence undisturbed.) Lord Roskill said to Jackie at the end of the hearing: 'Through no fault of your own, life has not been easy for you. But we are now giving you a fresh chance and letting you out into the world again. Off you go.'

Off Jackie went to Reading, with a general sigh of satisfaction from the *Guardian* and a few sympathetic comments elsewhere. Warning notes were sounded, however; specifically a penal reform campaigner, Kenneth Norman, who had set up the Portia Trust because of his concern about the lack of appropriate facilities for offenders like Jackie, was sceptical of the ability of a probation hostel to help or even to contain such a restless, disturbed character as she; while her mother put her finger on a sore spot by telling a reporter that 'the main thing Jackie wants now is to get her own baby back'. The one thing a girls' probation hostel cannot accommodate is babies, and in any case, it was known that the local authority who were caring for Dean 'would strongly oppose any attempt to have the child returned to her'.

Jackie's ten days in the Elizabeth Fry Hostel at Reading were eventful. The warden claimed that she had disrupted the life of the place from the time of her arrival; on three occasions she had tried to leave without permission. She had asked her probation officer if she could go and see her boyfriend, and he had said that he would consider the request; Jackie took the law into her own hands, 'presumed it was alright', went off for a weekend in London, returned to the hostel, and then in midweek absconded a second time. She was picked up in London and was remanded in custody to await a re-appearance at the Crown Court. The warden of the hostel told the magistrates that Jackie was 'most unsuitable for hostel treatment. Freedom is just too much for her to cope with.' When Jackie asked if she could be given bail and return to the hostel, the warden refused to consider the matter; they were having trouble with other girls at the hostel as a result of Miss Paddon's presence.

When Jackie returned to the Crown Court on 27 March 1973, Mr Justice Melford Stevenson summarized the position succinctly: 'You present almost every problem that a delinquent can.' But now few voices were raised against the sentence which, five months earlier, had induced an outraged response from all directions. The Portia Trust again protested, and claimed that arrangements could have been made for Jackie to be housed in conditions of stricter security while at the same time allowing her to be re-united with her baby: 'She is a very nice girl, but a bag of nerves now.' Her father too spoke out: 'Jacqueline needs help from people who understand. Putting her back in jail will only make matters worse. There will be a repeat performance if she gets parole. The judge has not given her a chance. They have written her off as a hopeless case.' And her defending counsel said of Jackie in court: 'The tragedy of the case is that the only place she behaved satisfactorily was in prison.'

It is one of the ironies of the legal system that Miss Paddon was eventually released following a further Appeal hearing – not because of any penal consideration, but because the complexity of the law relating to young offenders had led Mr Justice Melford Stevenson to commit a technical error in his re-imposition of the prison sentence following Jackie's absconsion from the Reading probation hostel. 'Lord Justice Lawton said that the court felt considerable reluctance in freeing her, but justice demanded it.'

There is little doubt that society's ambivalence and confusion is perfectly represented in the undulating reactions to Jacqueline Paddon. Perhaps many people do not care at all, but the initial emphasis of the media certainly depended on a crude notion of 'fair play' – or of the applicability of the tariff system. What Jackie had done did not deserve 21 months in prison, and she should be given another chance; but once that chance had been offered and thrown up, then the unfortunate girl had used up her legitimate supply of public goodwill, and could expect general sympathy no longer. After her absconsion from the Elizabeth Fry Hostel, and before the Crown Court sent her back to prison, a Portia Trust advertisement asking for funds to help her cost £180 and grossed £6·55.

And yet it is in this very area that the heaviest responsibilities of the penal system lie, and it is perhaps with clients like Jackie Paddon that the probation and after-care service will need to concern itself far more intensively and patiently than is at present possible.

The offence and its consequences

Jacqueline Paddon's offence was an uncommon one, but it has been suggested recently, both in the Press and elsewhere,[3] that though still rare, the offence is becoming increasingly common – possibly because of the publicity attendant upon either the crime itself or its consequent punishment. Criminal statistics, however, do not support the idea that baby-snatching is increasing out of proportion to the pattern of criminal behaviour as a whole. For although it is true, as Hunter has indicated, that the incidence of child-stealing has risen since the 1950s, the figures cannot be divorced from trends in other

Table 8.1 Child-stealing and all violent offences, 1966–72

	Child-stealing		Violent offences against the person	
	No.	Index	No.	Index
1966	28	100	26,716	100
1967	27	96	29,048	109
1968	37	132	31,850	119
1969	37	132	37,818	142
1970	43	154	41,088	154
1971	33	118	47,036	176
1972	45	161	52,432	196

Source: Annual Criminal Statistics, HMSO, London.

offence-categories. Thus, for the most recent years, table 8.1 shows the number of offences known to the police in regard to child-stealing and all violent offences against the person; the use of an index figure enables one to see relative movement in each line of statistics (1966 = 100).

The number of child-stealing offences has certainly undulated from year to year, but there is no evidence whatever to indicate that the growth in incidence is greater than that of other offences; indeed, since 1970 the trend has been to the contrary.

D'Orban (1972) has published the results of an exploratory analysis into thirteen cases of women child-stealers. Rather rashly, perhaps, but not without interest, he attempts to classify them into four groups:

1 Subnormal girls who seemed to want to play with the baby rather as if it were a doll;
2 Schizophrenic women with delusions, whose offences become intelligible 'in the light of their feelings of frustrated motherhood';
3 A psychopathic group, who stole children to compensate for their own emotional deprivation;
4 Manipulators, who sought to use the stolen baby to influence a man with whom they were emotionally entangled.

Not surprisingly, some psychiatrists have expressed doubts about the validity of D'Orban's classification-scheme, but there does seem to be agreement that the offence of baby-stealing (so far as it is committed by a woman, for the male offender is quite different) involves deep sociological, psychological and physiological factors of a kind which must defeat any attempt at a simple explanation of the deed, or, by corollary, any attempt at a simple response:[4]

> . . . a subject like baby-snatching is so emotive, so difficult to discuss rationally. Anything to do with a woman's biological function is liable to lead one into very diffuse and emotional arguments, so tied up is this with both sexual ignorance and prejudice, and the desperate possessiveness of the family structure.

The concern of the public, however, and to some extent that of the courts is as much with the victim as with the wrong-doer. In the cases of both Pauline Jones and Jacqueline Paddon, the respective mothers from whom the baby was stolen expressed initial sympathy and understanding for the offender, and then, under the stress of the situation into which they had been forced, became punitive – Mrs Weller in respect of Pauline Jones: 'I don't care . . . if she comes out worse after three years. I wouldn't have cared if the sentence had been 10 years.' Miss Walsh on Jacqueline Paddon: 'She got what she deserved.'

This, whether it is an attractive truth or not in the enlightened days of the 1970s, is what imprisonment is about. Attempts to define 'true criminality' must always fail, for the penal system only reflects the complexity of a society in which compassion and vindictiveness, possession and want, innocence and guilt are continually at war with each other; and the sentence of imprisonment is used primarily as a weapon legitimized by the reality of the conflict.

9 No alternative to imprisonment

If there were no prisons or correctional institutions, there would be no after-care or parole; and although there would still be a need for community work with offenders by the social work services, that element of after-care whose job it is to counteract the cumulative effects of the institutional experience could be redirected to more positive ends. To have been in a closed institution of itself may influence but not damage an individual: many men go through the army, the public school system or hospitalization and emerge socially and psychologically unharmed; but each of these has some redeeming feature to it. The unique quality of twentieth-century prisons compared with other total institutions is the almost wholly negative profile that they present to their inmates – no matter what the prison administration may intend, no matter what the hopes and aspirations of those intimately involved may be. There can be no denying the fact that there are many highly reputable and responsible men and women in the prison service at all levels; anyone who has met and talked with them – discipline staff, governors and assistant governors, chaplains, medical officers, teachers, trades instructors, welfare officers, clerical and executive staff, Home Office administrators – could not possibly regard them in the wildly pejorative terms that characterize some of the more extravagant criticisms of prisons. But the fact remains that they each participate in, and contribute to, the perpetuation of one of Britain's more corrupting social institutions of the late twentieth century. It is corrupting because of the innate purposelessness and dehumanization that appear to be the essential characteristics of the prison experience. Many men survive it, but those who are the least resilient in the outside world are often also the most damaged both by the mental and at times physical brutality of the prison culture and by the upheaval that is effected in their social situation.

There are few who would deny that the reality of imprisonment is harsh, potentially soul-destroying and at times brutal; the majority, however, would probably argue that it is as it should be, or that, if anything, the trend is towards too much comfort.[1] But among those who feel concern about the perpetuation of an essentially inhumane segment of society, there is disagreement and confusion when it comes to discussing alternatives; even among Cohen and Taylor's sample of long-sentence *category A* prisoners, 'the men are continually contradicting themselves and each other about what sort of regime they would like: a small wing or a large wing, concentration or dispersal, more work or less work, a soft governor or an old-fashioned governor'.[2] And when it comes to non-custodial or semi-custodial alternatives to imprisonment, the discussion is too often inadequately informed and unclear in its implications; in particular, it almost always neglects to take into account the social and political realities of the sentencing system. It also fails to draw a distinction between those who would make a frontal attack upon imprisonment as a penal response and those who argue simply that there are selective groups of men or women who need not be in prison.

In order to understand and come to terms with future after-care needs and policies, it is essential to identify some of the logical and empirical snags that must be confronted in the search for alternatives to imprisonment.

The penal reform lobby

The campaign against prison conditions has a long and respectable history (although that in itself is rather an indication of the campaign lobby's tenacity of purpose than of its effectiveness). Liberal–humanitarian organizations like the Howard League and NACRO (National Association for the Care and Resettlement of Offenders) have developed close working relationships with the Home Office and with parts of the penal system, and NACRO in particular has recently played an active part in the establishment and development of new enterprises intended to benefit prisoners before and after their release. By contrast, PROP (Preservation of the Rights of Prisoners) – the prisoner's union – offers full membership only to prisoners and ex-prisoners; recognizing the only limited achievements of previous pressure-groups in the field, PROP decided that it saw no benefit in becoming 'another group of social workers and academics'.[3] Inevitably it has had a shaky start to its existence, but Taylor argues that its[4]

> greatest initial achievement has been to transform the terms in

which a social problem is discussed. . . . No one uses words like 'inmates' or 'institutions' at PROP meetings now. The word prisoner is less and less a term of abuse. Another 'pathetic' section of the population is being slowly transformed into a group with self-respect.

However, it seems probable that the efforts of liberal–humanitarian groups are likely to continue unabated, because the perpetuation of the iniquities of prison are very much a part of the life of society as a whole, although their effects naturally hit the prisoner hardest. Whatever the motives of penal reformers, they remain to represent the conscience of society for the ills inflicted on the men in prisons, and they have, as yet, little to cheer: 'The fears and prejudices of society against the offender have changed very little and it is not surprising that individuals and charities who seek change should be dispirited by the time scale of change' in prisons or in after-care.[5] The arguments used against prison as an integral part of a modern penal system can be identified threefold: first there is the humanitarian case that no society should require any man or woman to live in the kind of conditions prevailing in places like Brixton, Holloway, Pentonville, Winson Green or Strangeways. Second there is the effectiveness argument that, partly because of the inhuman conditions but also because of the shortcomings of the training programme (especially for the short-term prisoner), prison is of no positive value in reducing crime: that it cannot reform and that it might conceivably even aggravate the situation by embittering a man, by destroying his spirit after a long sentence, by impoverishing his family and by making it more difficult for him to settle down again after his release. The economic argument is often thrown in (that it would be cheaper to keep a man in the community than in prison), but one suspects only because it is thought that it might successfully influence some politicians where more high-principled considerations have failed.

The humanitarian argument

The only truly valid argument against imprisonment is the humanitarian one, and the extent to which this is persuasive must depend on a personal and social assessment of the community's need for a truly unpleasant punishment in order to counteract criminal tendencies in society. Sykes has listed five pains of imprisonment:[6]

the deprivation of liberty; the deprivation of goods and services; the deprivation of heterosexual relationships; the deprivation of autonomy; and the deprivation of security. To these, Cohen and Taylor (1972) have added the loss of privacy; the obsession with time, not as a resource to be used, but as an 'undifferentiated landscape . . . to be traversed'; and the fear and reality of physical and mental deterioration.

Taking such aspects of prison life as given, do we in society believe that they are a regrettable but inevitable by-product of the need to guard against rape, political corruption, embezzlement, theft, baby-snatching, gang warfare, burglary, arson, hi-jacking, violent robbery, assault on the police, or manslaughter on the roads? The awful truth is that we simply do not know. The factors in the equation – deterrence, reform, retribution – are so complex, and the balance between them so different in the eyes of separate sectors of society, that the answer to the problem cannot be divorced from the political spectrum, and is in any case highly volatile (or dynamic) in the sense that it is likely to vary in response to a great range of social and economic factors in the situation.

In lieu of a radical humanitarian campaign to close down all prisons – the results of which might be disastrous or totally harmless – the same breed of argument is used to make minor inroads on the present system; and in recent years, pressure-groups have tended to concentrate on the belief that overcrowding in the prisons has been a major contributory factor to their inhumanity. Such an argument is of course something of an exaggeration: the Gladstone Report (1894), for example, expressed grave concern about the isolation of men alone in single cells; Cohen and Taylor's prisoners were not overcrowded and had some modern facilities, but suffered as much as or more than others because of the length of their sentences and the artificiality and insecurity of their private and social lives; and Willetts found that open prisons were more humiliating and had more of a deteriorating effect than she had found in Holloway.[7] Nevertheless, the problem of overcrowding and its effect on penal policy serves to illustrate the difficulty of planning in the correctional system.

For thirty years, up to 1971, the population of prisons rose fairly steadily; it had virtually quadrupled since the inter-war years, and increased by something like 45 per cent during the 1960s. Throughout most of this period there was reluctance in the Home Office to embark upon a major prison building programme, but from the middle-

Table 9.1 Sentenced prisoners: a comparison of receptions and population (1961 = 100)

Year	Receptions under sentence No.	Index	Average population No.	Index
1913	138,295	342	not available	
1938	30,646	76	7,674	37
1948	34,687	86	14,665	70
1958	34,009	84	17,817	85
1963	45,939	114	21,890	105
1968	36,020	89	21,401	103
1969	40,088	99	22,757	109
1970	45,014	111	25,634	123
1971	44,094	109	26,775	128
1972	41,655	103	25,887	124

Sources: *People in prison*, Cmnd 4214, HMSO, London, 1969, p. 14; Report on the work of the Prison Department, 1972, Cmnd 5375, HMSO, London 1973, p. 4.

1960s there was a recognition that the trend could no longer be denied, and capital expenditure rose from under £4m in 1966 to over £10m in 1971. During 1972, the Home Office indicated that it could see no alternative to making provision for a continuing increase both in population and in capital expenditure during the coming decade. (And yet at this very point in time, there emerged the possibility of a slackening in pressure. Both receptions and population fell in 1972, and, possibly of greater significance, in the first quarter of 1973 there were signs of a clear downward trend in the number of offences known to the police – the first indication for many years of a decrease in the general incidence of crime.)

There are two possible strategies to follow in seeking to combat overcrowded prison conditions: either some effort must be made to reduce the population, or a great deal of money has to be spent in developing new accommodation. The British Government has used both approaches.

The introduction of parole and suspended sentences in 1968 and the placing of further restrictions on the courts' power to commit fine-defaulters to prison were all part of an attempt to counteract the rising prison population; they succeeded in marginally reducing the pressure on the system during 1968 and 1969, but then the curve on the population graph started to rise again. The parole scheme effectively reduces the prison population by about 1,600 men and women at any one time (or about 4 per cent), and every place saved is said to cost the prison service something like 52 man-hours, plus the cost to the probation service and the expenses of the central administration, the Parole Board and the Local Review Committees.[8]

After the introduction of suspended sentences, some criminologists suggested that it may have led ultimately to an increase in the prison population rather than to the desired reduction. This is because of the probability that courts were making some suspended sentences in cases where previously a fine or a probation order would have been considered suitable, and that, because of the almost mandatory sentence of imprisonment that, under the 1967 Criminal Justice Act, followed the breach of a suspended sentence, many offenders were going to prison who would formerly have been dealt with in other ways. The Home Office recognized this unforeseen turn of events, and in 1971 acknowledged that if suspended sentences were intended to reduce the prison population, the attempt had failed, and 'the total number of men in custody in 1970 was about what might have been expected . . . if the suspended sentence had not been introduced'. The 1972 Criminal Justice Act attempted to rectify this error by giving courts greater freedom to choose not to activate a suspended sentence following a breach unless they thought the case was one in which 'a sentence of imprisonment would have been appropriate in the absence of any power to suspend such a sentence';[9] at the same time, however, the Act gave the courts greater freedom to make immediate sentences of imprisonment where the 1967 Act had required that the sentence be suspended and the Guide to the Act recognized that this clause would probably lead to some increase in the number of prison sentences. It has been further suggested that deferred sentences, introduced by the 1972 Act, could similarly have the opposite effect to that intended, if they were employed where previously a probation order or a fine would have been imposed without delay.[10]

The 1972 Act nevertheless contains, on an experimental basis, more ambitious alternative provisions in community service orders and day training centres, and further reiterates the argument that prison should only be used as a last resort; it seems probable that these provisions will have a marginal effect on numbers.

The difficulty of planning prison accommodation has been further highlighted, however, by the totally unexpected drop in the average population during 1972 – before the impact of the Criminal Justice Act could be fully felt. The drop occurred at the same time as an apparent levelling-off in crime figures, and must reflect a slight change in sentencing policy; in the absence of authenticated research exploration, one can only suppose that the decision-makers in the courts have been influenced both by the extensive public discussion about the need for alternatives to imprisonment and by their awareness of developing government policy in marginal areas. The outcome is a fall in the average total population – the first for many years – by 1,380 to 38,328. Whether this fall is an indication of the future pattern must depend partly on future crime statistics and partly on decisions in the courts; for all the work in criminology during the present century, it is yet impossible to make firm predictions about the former, while the latter have proved only marginally responsive to legislative and executive direction. The reduced pressure clearly provides a welcome respite for prison administrators, but whether it is an indication of more than that has yet to be seen.

Moreover, recent prison policy, as a result of which the least serious offenders and those with the most helpful social circumstances have either been kept out of prison or have been released early, has inevitably led to a reduction in the number of relatively good-risk offenders and to an increase in the proportion of hardened recidivists and socially alienated prisoners in the jail population – quite a rational thing to do, of course, in the light of the attempt to segregate risk-groups which has guided correctional policy in recent years, but an action which must have implications for the internal management of the prisons. As Cohen and Taylor note, there is general recognition of the 'fact' that there will continue to be an increase in the number of men needing to be coerced and controlled in conditions of maximum security.[11]

The pragmatic approach of the politicians and administrators appears then to be having limited success, even if its effects have not always occurred at the time and in the way expected, and although other external determinants have played an even more unpredictable part. Nevertheless, when the achievements are set against the efforts of the administration, the arguments of the pressure-groups and all the parliamentary ballyhoo that accompanies them, and when recognition is made of the difficulty of predicting probable developments in the years ahead, the story that emerges provides a salutary reminder of some of our weaknesses and our ignorance in the sphere of social administration, and represents a cautionary tale to anyone seeking to produce specified changes within the social system by means of legislation. Prisoners can perhaps hardly be blamed for seeing the Home Office as 'capricious and arbitrary, exerting their power, not with malice, but in a random, almost whimsical way';[12] but it seems probable that, in this respect, the Civil Service officials are only reflecting the arbitrariness, the indecision and the uncertainty of purpose that underpins the relationship between prisons and society as a whole.

The Government's second strategy employed to improve prison conditions by reducing the degree of overcrowding is concerned with capital development. The stated aim is 'to provide decent though austere, living conditions for inmates and tolerable working conditions for inmates and staff alike'.[13] The annual report for 1971 lists fifty-five schemes for new or extended premises, providing an additional 18,000 places. This represents easily the biggest capital expansion in the penal system since the nineteenth century, but whether or not it proves to be sufficient to overcome current problems of overcrowding probably depends on whether the Home Office is right or wrong in its expectations of a continuing increase in prison population. Unless the average figure really does level off at about 40,000 (as happened in 1973), it is acknowledged that the present building programme will be almost totally swallowed up by the demands of the next generation of prisoners; and even if the breathing-space is used to ameliorate conditions, there is always the danger that a radical improvement in the penal facilities available in the prisons might be self-defeating. If, for example, a great deal of money is spent on the provision of a sophisticated range of 'treatments' in custody the prison population might only rise again as a direct consequence because of the greater willingness of courts to sentence men to what they perceive as a more positive facility than had earlier been available; nothing is known about the reluctance of courts to make prison sentences because of the magistrates' and judges' concern about the inhumanity or purposelessness of the institutions available. In other words, there is a danger that, just as the provision for additional car-parks in cities may tend to increase traffic congestion because they attract extra vehicles, so the expenditure of large sums on an ambitious prison-building programme may be negated by the tendency of the supply of prisoners to rise in proportion to the availability of places.

It is important, too, not to lose sight of the fact that expenditure on prisons cannot be viewed in isolation from the growth of expenditure in the social services as a whole. Because three separate departments of State are involved (the Home Office, the Departments of Education and of Health and Social Security), the competition is not perhaps as tense as it might be if they were all vying for priority within a single departmental budget. Nevertheless, at a time when the needs of the mentally and physically handicapped, the hospital service, primary education and the growing numbers of old people are perpetually being pressed upon the country, it is surely unrealistic to expect that the penal system can succeed in getting a proportionately greater increase in capital development provisions than other equally deserving sectors of social need.

In December 1971 a Home Office minister announced that it was expected that prison capacity would have been raised to 44,000 by 1975–6. The state of overcrowding in the system depends entirely on whether, by then, the number of prisoners is greater or less than that amount. The projection at the time of the announcement was that there would be 59,000 prisoners at that time, but since then the figure has been scaled down considerably. It could be that overcrowding as a problem will not always be with us, and that we shall then again be forced to recognize that the inhumanity of prisons is much more basic. Robert Carr, then Home Secretary, put it:[14] 'being in prison is, by definition and purpose a basically unpleasant experience'. It is this assertion that makes the search for alternatives to prison so problematical and contradictory. If the purpose is to be unpleasant, then to seek more humane alternatives would seem to be unnecessary; the search for humanitarian alternatives must rather start from the argument that it is no part of society's aim to be unpleasant to any of its constituent members – but this then brings the debate back to the question of what the effect of such a policy would be on criminal behaviour.

There is no wonder that, faced with such a troublesome conundrum, the liberal campaigner turns rather to the effectiveness argument: that prison does not reform, and the courts ought rather to be imposing alternative sentences that do.

The effectiveness argument

Unfortunately the case for developing alternatives to imprisonment on other than humanitarian grounds is not straightforward. There are two problems in particular. For one thing, liberal critics of the present system are wrong is assuming that the sentence of imprisonment is used primarily to reform the individual offender. Thomas (1970) in his analysis of the sentencing policy of the Court of Appeal Criminal Division (which tends to influence decision-making in all courts throughout the country) has made the point that although the principle of individualization (in which 'the offender as an individual, whose needs, rather than whose guilt, would form the basis of the sentence passed') has made great impact in the last forty years, what we now have is a dual sentencing system in which the principle of individualization exists side by side with the older tariff system ('based primarily on the concepts of retribution and general deterrence'). 'The primary decision of the sentencer', says Thomas, '. . . is to determine on which side of the system the case is to be decided; is one of the individualized measures (if one is applicable) to be used, or is the case to be dealt with on a tariff basis? Once the primary decision has been made, the secondary decision follows – where on the tariff is the sentence to be located, or precisely what individualized measure is to be used?' Of course Thomas recognizes that there are border-line cases which make a clear-cut decision difficult to arrive at, but the distinction is none the less an important one because it clarifies just what is at issue when reformers call for a reduction in the prison population. Imprisonment is made possible by legislation, but only a small proportion of those offenders who could legally be sent to prison for what they have done actually receive a custodial sentence.

Within the statutory framework determined by Parliament, imprisonment is actually imposed because of court policies which decide (at least so far as the Court of Appeal goes) that certain types of case must be sentenced on the tariff system: for example, indecent assaults on small children, incest, or violent attacks on tradesmen or on people carrying sums of money in the street. In such cases the nature and circumstances of the offence make a prison sentence virtually certain; an expression of remorse might affect its length, but the social and personal circumstances of the offender are of relatively little consequence because the primary purpose of the court is to deter others from behaving in a similar fashion and to exact retribution from the perpetrator of the crime. Although the court might make reference to the hope that a term of imprisonment will have a salutary effect on the offender, this is very much a secondary consideration; hence the argument that the reform of the defendant can be secured by better means than imprisonment is in such a case largely irrelevant so far as the effective decision-makers (the court) are concerned. (The prisoner is much more sophisticated in his awareness of what prison is about: 'Prison is just what its creators meant it to be – mental torture and a hell of a punishment.' The criminal sanction as retribution 'involves the inflicting of hurts on the criminal to "make him pay" for his wrong acts; it seeks revenge rather than deterrence or reform. This ancient, barbaric ethic is still operative today. . . .'[15])

There is another hazard in the argument of those who want to replace imprisonment by other sentences in order the better to reform the offender. Evaluative research on the effectiveness of penal treatment is extremely difficult to undertake, and in Britain there has not yet been any opportunity to design a controlled comparison between custodial and non-custodial care; indeed, even in America, where much more has been attempted in the way of penal evaluation, direct comparison between traditional imprisonment and alternative allocations is still subject to a great many methodological problems. Nevertheless there is sufficient similarity between the British and American systems to enable one to look at the results obtained and draw tentative conclusions. In their review of evaluative studies, Hood and Sparks lament that a very large number of them have produced negative results,[16] although, as they indicate, any interpretation of their significance depends on what it is that is being sought. For example, the same 'negative' results are earlier presented by the authors like this: 'For many offenders, probation is likely to be at least as effective in preventing recidivism as an institutional sentence.'[17] In other words, if the campaigner is arguing that there are *better* alternatives to imprisonment, then the evidence is not strong; if on the other hand, he is arguing that release into the community appears to work *just as well* – i.e. that imprisonment does not itself act as a deterrent or reformative influence – then he can quote a good deal of empirical support for his argument, as well as asserting that the alternatives are probably cheaper. Hood and Sparks make two further comments, however: because of research design, it may be that some of the men sent to prison would not do so well as those who did not go to prison in the comparative studies, for few of the comparisons have used random allocation methods, but have rather had to rely on matching methods or prediction formulae:[18]

Moreover, even if *recidivism* rates did not rise, a shift to non-

> institutional sentences would lead to an increased *crime* rate, since it would mean that some offenders now sent to institutions (and so not 'at risk') for a time would instead be at liberty in the community during that time. The social cost of these extra offences would have to be balanced, in any policy calculation, against the excess cost of keeping offenders in institutions rather than leaving them in the community.

Nevertheless, although in 1966 Bailey could conclude that 'the evidence supporting the efficacy of correctional treatment is slight, inconsistent, and of questionable reliability',[19] some empirical material has begun to emerge to suggest that environmental engineering need not be quite so fruitless, in correctional terms, as might have been concluded a few years ago. (However, a corollary is that success is very much harder to come by than is sometimes suggested.)

Within institutions, Briggs has argued for the proven effectiveness of a therapeutic community approach (a one-year failure rate of 16 per cent, compared with the controls' 24 per cent),[20] and Shaw and Jarvis have indicated that the use of relatively intensive casework with prisoners also has a statistically significant effect on future reconviction rates.[21] These are both important findings, even if a possible interpretation of them is that they show how to overcome the pains of imprisonment rather than demonstrate ways in which the penal institution can actually reform offenders. Nevertheless, they have to be set against Sinclair's impressive study of adolescents in probation hostels (1971). The author there shows (1) the positive effect on individual patterns of criminal behaviour of a specified form of treatment, i.e. a change in the offender's residential setting, and the exercise of some control over him; (2) a differential effect: it works better with those who come from bad homes than with those who are known to have presented behaviour problems within their families, whether or not their homes were bad; and (3) most important of all, the effect of the hostel placement is entirely transitory. Once the twelve-month period of residence is completed the probationers who have been 'reformed' revert to the kind of law-breaking behaviour that would have been expected of them had they never been sent to the hostel in the first place but had simply been placed under the supervision of a probation officer. Thus, even a sentence (of a kind very like those intended when people refer to prison alternatives) which can be shown to affect the behaviour of some offenders while it remains in force loses its effect afterwards;

in other words, it has containment value, but apparently no long-term reformist element (and in addition there are a group of offenders – the behaviour problem group – for whom it appears to have no short-term effect either).

Given the validity of Sinclair's study, it is not surprising that most analyses of ordinary probation have indicated that it can hardly claim an interventionist effect. In one of the biggest experiments yet reported, in San Francisco, probationers were randomly allocated to caseloads receiving intensive, ideal, normal or minimum supervision.[22] Even so, it was found that in terms of reconviction, those given minimum supervision (in which they were required only to maintain contact with their probation officer by posting a report-card in every month) were no more likely to fail on probation than those receiving intensive care in a caseload of twenty-five which involved approximately one contact a week between client and supervisor. 'In the intensive caseloads, despite fourteen times as much attention as was provided for the minimum supervision cases, the violation rate not only failed to decline significantly, but increased with respect to technical violations.' Such a study must raise serious doubts about the reformist element in community supervision as it is currently practised; this is not to argue, of course, that probation has no value, but merely that it cannot be expected to play a reductivist role in the penal system, and that therefore those who seek reformative alternatives to imprisonment must look elsewhere than probation.

Because of figures contained in the Home Office's booklet *Sentence of the court* (1971), it is commonly asserted that there is evidence to show that fines are more effective than any other kind of sentence, and that they could usefully be used in place of imprisonment to better effect. Certainly a fine might do less damage to the offender than prison, and it must be more economical; but the comparisons in *Sentence of the court* are insufficiently trustworthy to enable one to argue firmly that fines are better at reducing the incidence of reconviction. In making the comparisons attempts were made to match offenders with others like them, but available data were limited and one cannot avoid the fact that those placed on probation or sent to prison were quite probably less capable persons, less adequate in the management of their affairs, and more likely to fail than those given fines – even though account was taken of their age and the number of their previous convictions. Another recent Home Office study attempted to look more closely at this question by concentrating on probationers alone: there it was found that offenders who were given financial penalties at the time they were placed on probation were certainly no more likely to succeed than those not given such a punitive sentence; indeed if there was any trend at all it was in the other direction.[23] This would tend to refute the general argument that fining a man has a more reformative effect than not fining him.[24]

In summary, then, it can be argued that conventional community disposals do no worse than prison, that hostels have been shown to contain some offenders, if not to reform them, and that some changes within penal institutions appear capable of influencing behaviour following release. So far as intensive community care programmes are concerned – which is the main form of alternative to imprisonment generally considered – positive evidence has been slow to emerge. A large number of negative findings can be listed,[25] but there are some positives among them, although these mostly refer to a younger age-group than would be concerned in relation to the British prison system. Stuart Adams (1967) has noted that glimmerings of light began to emerge in such experiments when treatment concepts and theoretical frameworks were clarified, and Palmer (1973) in particular has shown how a sophisticated system of matching client to supervisor can raise the success rate in the community from 51 per cent to 77 per cent over a fifteen-month period; the improvement carried over into a post-supervisory follow-up period. The Californian Community Treatment Project referred to by Palmer has had vast resources, and its clientele benefit not only from intensive supervision but also have access to group homes and other accommodation, specialized treatment facilities – individually, in groups, or in the family – and schooling or recreational facilities. In principle the work of the CTP is important because it claims to have demonstrated that failure rates can be lowered by the use of community resources and a theoretical design; but, even in respect of its published results, critical comments have been made.

Taggart, for example, has argued that the apparently positive impact of CTP[26]

> was to a large extent the result of the favorable treatment given to participants relative to other offenders violating the terms of probation or parole. For instance, in 1966, 68 per cent of control failures but only 29 per cent of experimental failures were accounted for by agents' recommendations that parole be

> revoked. When the offence is of low or moderate severity, experimentals are less likely to have their parole revoked, and they thus have a lower recidivism-rate.

Hence failure rates are as likely to be a function of the interaction between administrators and those with the power of decision-making as of the actual behaviour of the offender. The failure of a number of American research studies to deal adequately with this factor is a major cause of the ambiguity that characterizes much of the debate about the effectiveness of prison alternatives.[27] Indeed the problem of the legitimacy of success-measures has much wider repercussions. For example, Takagi[28] found that the failure rate of parolees depended largely on the willingness of agents to take bureaucratic action in referring them to the recall authorities, and that furthermore office *mores* tended to influence the behaviour of individual officers: to the extent that this was so, it is clear 'that recidivism rates cannot be utilised as the dependent variable in assessing correctional effectiveness; as the study demonstrates, apparent recidivism can be "controlled' by officials'. Conclusions such as these make it even more difficult than it appears at first sight to arrive at valid conclusions about the efficacy of penal treatments – whether innovatory or traditional: if the apparent 'success' achieved by programmes of community supervision were partially or wholly the result of parole revocation variations, then these expensive experiments would merely be able to claim that they were influencing the decision-making behaviour of correctional officials, and not the offence-behaviour of delinquents.

If, however, such methodological criticisms were to be satisfactorily countered, the next danger to be faced would be that the practical implications would be in danger of being lost if those who sought to replicate the experiments elsewhere tried to do so without ensuring the availability of equivalent resources. CTP provided a systems approach to the treatment of the young offender; there is no reason why the same should not be attempted for older men, but it must be done on both an intensive and a long-term basis, with inevitably higher costs than are often thought to be involved when there is talk of alternatives to imprisonment.

The economic argument

The truth is that, even given that treatment outside the prison system is feasible, its cost is likely to be rather more than is usually imagined. Obviously it is cheaper not to send a man to prison if the alternative is to fine him, place him on probation or offer him 'intensive community contact' at the rate of one interview a week, but even this assertion needs to be qualified. Its validity depends on the numbers of men involved. Nuttall (1973) has shown that the marginal cost per week of a single prisoner might be very much less than the £35 that is often quoted; indeed it could be less than £4. Thus the economic argument cannot be used to support small-scale schemes in which the numbers of inmates transferred to the community number a hundred or less. To achieve any economy, 'radical transfers have to be made'.

The Californian Probation Subsidy scheme is often quoted for its economic attractions, and there is no doubt that it has reduced the need for capital expenditure in the state prison system, and enabled many offenders to be released on probation who would otherwise have gone to prison. It is not argued that any offenders have been reformed by the scheme; indeed its main architect is quoted as saying that its rationale is essentially organizational: it is 'a form of behaviour modification applied to social institutions', and as such it belongs more to the area of parliamentary and administrative manipulation than to therapeutic casework or corrections. In this respect, it is significant that there was no evaluation built into it. It was sufficient that it relieved pressure on the prison system without leading to greatly increased violation rates. The scheme is an excellent demonstration of a social administrative approach to a penal treatment problem; the results are impressive in financial and organizational terms, if rather nonsensical in relation to the notion of individualized sentencing and diagnostic treatment.

The Dutch prison system, which has been widely respected for its humane therapeutic approach to the needs of inmates, places an emphasis on intensive personal contact. The results are impressive but the cost per head is double that of the British system, although there are proportionately many fewer kept in jail than is the case in the UK.

The options are quite clear. If the prison system is to be maintained at its present level or thereabouts, because of demands by society – as represented by the judiciary and the legislature – that wrongdoers shall continue to be punished by custodial sentences, then there would seem to be a need for vastly increased expenditure on prisons, and for it to be used for purposes other than security measures (which is where much of the extra cash has gone since the publication of the Mountbatten Report). On the other hand, if society accepts the need to bring down the level of the prison population – irrespective of its association with crime statistics – then either the sentencers must be induced (presumably by legislation, for there is no similar link between them and the local administration as exists in California, and which has made it possible for the state authorities to exchange promises of correctional grant–aid for changes in sentencing policy) to diminish the proportion of custodial decisions, or the responsibility for decision-making must pass from the judiciary to the penal arm of the political authority, with a view to sentencing being replaced by a treatment-based individualized process of diagnosis and allocation.

But even here it would be dangerous to assume a cost advantage. Writing in 1967, Warren argued that the Community Treatment Project (of which she was then Director) was enabling capital development costs to be cut. However, she recognized that CTP running costs were not only much higher than normal parole or probation costs, but more surprisingly, they were higher per head than normal institutional disposals because 'CTP cases tend to remain in intensive treatment longer than Control cases spend in institutions'. The economic value of CTP is dependent upon its success in achieving a correctional improvement: 'Since CTP shows fewer failures and thus fewer returns to institutions, career costs for the Experimental program are apt to be less than for the regular program.'[29] Hence, the validity of the economic argument appeared to be dependent on the success of the project in achieving its reductivist objectives.

It may be politically essential to argue the case for prison alternatives on economic grounds, but administratively it is important to recognize that the cost equation is every bit as complex as the effectiveness argument. To respond to the needs of offenders, whether they are underprivileged, deviant, disturbed or dangerous, may prove to be an expensive business however it is tackled; the need is all the greater for both law-makers and administrators to clarify just what it is they are seeking to achieve.

Clarification or confusion?

What then is the difference between community release and imprisonment? The former can be cheaper than the latter, although it need not be so, especially if intermediate forms of treatment are involved on any extensive scale. Community care is probably less destructive of family life and less likely to disturb a man's social position, although some research[30] has suggested that the social consequences of imprisonment – especially short-term sentences – might not be so universally devastating as is sometimes claimed. It is more humane in most cases not to shut a man away in an artificially imposed community, but the inhumanity could perhaps be reduced by a willingness to spend more money on improving prison conditions and by allowing more scope for inmate decision-making within the institution; moreover, there are a minority of cases where it would be more sadistic to potential victims to give a man his freedom than it would be to lock him up. The evidence that community care reforms offenders is slight, and even where it is positive, it applies only to a small proportion of potential recidivists; on the other hand, there is every reason to believe that imprisonment works no better, although while an offender is cooped up, his crimes against society are confined within the walls of the institution.

None of the arguments against imprisonment, persuasive though they may be in the minds of reformers, can be seen in isolation from the context in which sentencing takes place. In their primary decision, the courts are influenced not by the need to reform a man nor to save money, but rather by their self-perceived role of exercising control in a complex modern society – by exacting retribution, deterring others and ensuring the protection of citizens. Those who are campaigning against the numbers of men in prison are campaigning against a central element in society's control system, and are thus engaged on a major task of social reorganization.

Within the court's response there can be identified – very crudely – two quite different emotional elements, but both reflecting the felt need to control behaviour: the first is one of exasperation, the second one of anger.

In any prison population, there is a group of men and women who are there because of the exasperation of the court at seeing them appear before them time and time again. Thomas (1970) carefully documents the change in policy regarding 'inadequate recidivists' – old lags who may have spent more time in prison than out of it, but who rarely commit a serious offence.[31] In the late 1950s the Court of Appeal started in a number of cases varying sentences of preventive detention to probation with the aim of avoiding institutionalization, and from about 1963 the emphasis shifted even further towards probation until today 'it is the policy of the Court in the case of the inadequate recidivist to investigate every possibility of a rehabilitative approach and to use probation even though the chance of success does not appear to be high'.[32] Here then are a group of men, traditionally sentenced to prison out of exasperation, for whom the higher courts are now advised to adopt a non-punitive approach if at all possible.

However, the realities that surround such old lags are well documented, and serve to illustrate the dilemmas still facing the well-intentioned reformer. They are incredibly difficult to supervise in the community: the probation officer frequently has neither the time nor the resources that may be needed to nursemaid a truly inadequate man through his daily trials in lodging houses, hostels, temporary jobs, upsets at the Employment Exchange and occasional drinking sprees. The hostels contain some men, but for every one who stays six months in a stable environment, there are a dozen or more who keep on the move. The Appeal Court has nevertheless decided that they are rarely a danger to society: they may be a nuisance, but provided they don't appear too often before the bench, and provided they express a willingness to be helped by the probation officer, they are a nuisance that society must learn to live with and need not lock away. However, the provisos are such that some at least still return to prison – because of the exasperation not only of the sentencers, but also perhaps of their would-be helpers in the probation service and in voluntary organizations.[33]

The case of Jacqueline Paddon was also primarily one of exasperation – at her failure to use opportunities given to her, and at her failure to respond to society's so-called helping agencies.

The second response – of anger – is the more difficult to counteract. For whereas in exasperation cases, those who seek alternatives may tend to over-simplify the situations confronting them and to have an exaggerated view of the potential helpfulness and effectiveness of a planned social work response (preferring not to acknowledge, for example, that some men might prefer to do time than to suffer at the hands of over-fussy, semi-authoritarian do-gooders), when it comes to the group in prison because of society's anger at their actions, there is the much greater danger that reformers will completely underestimate the functional nature of the penal response. The fact of the matter is that we simply do not know what effect (if any) the liberalization or destruction of the prison system would have on standards of public morality or on the stability of society as a whole. The evidence – such as it is – is contradictory: Holland's experience tends to suggest that fears about the outcome of such reforms can be over-stated, and that a good deal could be achieved without undermining the social structure; on the other hand, there is some indication that the concept of general deterrence has meaning in society, and that a hard-line sentencing policy can be used to control some crimes like vandalism and petty theft – although other factors may be just as important, or even more so. It might be an expensive experiment to remove the punitive sanction from the courts entirely, and we have no means of knowing whether, for example, it would lead to an increase of scapegoating hostility against minority groups, or to the growth of a hard-to-control private enterprise system of justice by an aggrieved populace.

Where individuals challenge the security of life and property, what does the community do? Neither the explanations of psychology nor sociology have served to provide a key to social reaction as it ought to be legitimized within the penal system; political theory and ideology have made their contribution but empirical evidence in support of one alternative or another is slight. The concerned critic cannot turn away from this discussion with any feeling of satisfaction. Prison never corrects, but that is not what it is there for. . . . It could be made more humane, though there are dangers even in this. If one again looks at the Californian experience, and especially at the attempts made there to produce a more enlightened approach to custodial sentences – or even to do away with the punitive element altogether – one finds yet another example of the unintended consequences of social reform. Godfrey Hodgson (1971) has commented wryly on conditions in Soledad – the erstwhile show prison but now synonymous with some of the worst iniquities of the total institution: the prison was meant to be 'progressive'; the penal system is 'enlightened' and prisoners tend to get indeterminate sentences so that they can be released as soon as they are 'ready'. 'In practice, this system puts the prisoners at the mercy of the guards. Any guard can, for almost any reason, give a prisoner a bad conduct mark which will prevent him getting a date to appear before the parole board.' Moreover, frequent bad conduct marks may land a prisoner in the adjustment centre. 'The Californian prison system', comments Hodgson 'is fond of euphemism. Guards are "correctional officers". The prison itself is a "training facility". And the adjustment centre at Soledad was in fact a particularly barbaric deterrent', which was criticized by a Federal court in 1966 because it thought it likely to result 'in a slowburning fire of resentment until it finally explodes in open revolt'.

This is not to argue that all improvements are bound to be disappointing or counter-productive – but that the liberal reformer and the progressive administrator cannot assume that all benevolent innovations will have the intended effect, especially if they are imposed upon existing structures and administered within a punitive context.

It seems probable that we shall see a continuing gentle swing towards individualized treatment in selected cases (with parole, day training centres, and deferred sentences recent manifestations of the trend), but, by a process of social homeostasis, the prison population will continue to reflect the apparent desire of society that it should punish its wrong-doers in the only way open to the courts other than by fining them. Perhaps the efforts of liberal reformers would prove more fruitful if they were to recognize the legitimacy of the concepts of punishment and the tariff as elements of social control. Such recognition – normally associated only with the right wing – is implicit in relation to motoring offenders and to the development of learned skills in childhood; it is employed without question in sport, in matters of professional conduct and academic development, and in the application of behaviourist techniques to a wide range of social practices. If its validity in the penal system were to be acknowledged by those seeking alternatives to it, there could be serious consideration given to devising forms of punishment – like financial penalties and the expression of public disapproval or the withdrawal of privileges – that were free from the depersonalized and corrupting elements of imprisonment, and that did not create, by their very imposition, a built-in requirement to provide extensive after-care facilities in order to overcome the damage imposed by the state. This would enable society's response to the identified offender to be separated from its response to his needs for social support, education or therapy, which have too often become confused with the penal treatment, to the detriment of both.

In the meantime, so long as the tariff remains the primary basis of penal law (as it is in well over 90 per cent of sentences), imprisonment will remain the ultimate sanction, the prison population will not fall significantly, and the job of the prison welfare officer and the after-care officer will remain as necessary and as futile as ever.

10 After-care – an apology for vengeance

The sentence of imprisonment is very largely an act of vengeance and of retribution. As a statement of social fact, this seems to me probably true; and although one may deplore it because of its negative implications, or because of an awareness of the elements of injustice sometimes contained within it, I have argued that to ignore it, and in particular to exaggerate the importance accorded to reform and rehabilitation in the minds of those who send men to prison, can only lead to confusion in any attempt to understand the sentencing process and to seek alternatives to imprisonment.

However, once the sentence has been passed, the reality of imprisonment can be analysed rather differently. The experience of retribution may still be an influential factor in the prisoner's mind, in the cohesiveness of the inmate community, in the administration of the institution and in the range of decisions that continue to be made about each man's movement through and eventually out of the correctional system. But there is much more to the experience of imprisonment than this, and the numerous attempts that have been made to study it have each tended to reflect differing foci. For example, the prison community exists and can be observed as a social organization with both formal and informal elements; the individual prisoners seek ways of adjusting to the depersonalizing process of incarceration, and constantly struggle for their sanity and self-respect especially in the face of long sentences – 'to survive is to succeed' – and, despite the scepticism of many critics and whatever the absurdity of some of the claims made officially, it even seems likely that some inmates may indeed be helped, trained, treated or brought face-to-face with their other selves as a result of the prison experience.

But above all, for those concerned with the prisoner's relationship with the outside world and with his eventual discharge into it, the most important fact is his regression, his enforced dependence, his almost total freedom from responsibility and decision-making. The prisoner is propelled into an infancy role, and has no choice but to come to terms with it. Cohen and Taylor[1] have identified four distinct modes of adaptation to the prison régime, but although these variations indicate the heterogeneity of the likely responses, the fact remains that adaptation of some kind is demanded by the situation, and that the adaptation is necessarily to a form of dependency totally divorced from the way of life awaiting them on release when once again they will be required to accept responsibility for their own welfare and possibly for that of other people. Malleson (1973) has argued that, following an accident or illness, the process of hospitalization – once it is accepted by the patient – can lead to a similar form of regression in his behaviour:

> There are advantages in being sick. If these advantages are large, then recovery is more difficult. . . . Sickness excuses failure and provides the right to be looked after. The monotony of work can be avoided and tiresome responsibilities shelved. . . . When patients are being [rewarded] for being sick rather than for getting well, both they and the rehabilitation staff who look after them become demoralised. The patients stay sick and the rehabilitation staff get fed up.

The analogy needs little clarification for us to see its applicability to the unintended consequences of imprisonment – despite the very different sequence of events that lead a man to prison instead of to hospital. Many of the autobiographical accounts by ex-prisoners describe how speedily the new inmate overcomes his first feelings of abhorrence at the institutional experience, and learns to play a dependent role *vis-à-vis* the staff. Even for the most competent of men, the task of re-adjusting to an independent role after discharge can prove awesome, but for those who are usually thought of as the target-group for after-care – the needy, the recidivist, the unsupported, the lonely – it is apparent to any but the most stubborn and blinkered defender of incarceration as a means of 'teaching the offender a lesson' that prison may bring about, not perhaps bitterness or alienation, but a dangerous inability to manage in the open society, an unwillingness to persevere, and an awareness that, for a price, society is willing to free the man or woman of his responsibility for himself and to provide a form of permanent shelter which, though unattractive to many, may in prospect nevertheless offer a legitimate means of escape from the reality of living.

If this is so, the challenge to the after-care service is seen to be not so much excessive as absurd; for if the effect of imprisonment is to produce regression and dependence, what hope has the ordinary probation officer in his semi-officially defined task of 'starting all over again' (see p. ix)? Presumably the prison service is still in need of its Florence Nightingale who, a century ago, amazed the military hospital medical officers by 'treating their men as if they were human beings'; certainly this is the view of Whiteley and his co-authors who refused in their work 'simply to suppress the deviant', but argued that the offender needed 'to establish an identity as somebody who is acknowledged by society as an integral part of society'.[2]

After-care now is little more than an apology for vengeance, and those who argue for reform in the prison system are well aware of its inadequacies. But few critics are willing to recognize that revenge is an element in society which many people (perhaps most) are happy to retain. Whiteley spells out the two options: 'Either deviants are suppressed and contained, which is seen as an authoritarian control, or they are allowed to work towards change, which is seen as liberal and progressive.'[3] Each of these, he argues, has its attendant theoretical base – either functionalist or social conflict theory and there is no doubt that the latter is the more appealing in liberal–humanitarian eyes. But what matters about sociological theory is not which is the more attractive ethically but which is the more valid in practice, and a little later, Whiteley recognizes that, among other more pleasant attributes, 'there are needs in all of us to punish wrong-doers, to elect scapegoats'.[4] If that is so, then like it or not, functionalist theory may lead inexorably to the conclusion that society is doomed perpetually to reap the harvest of its own punitive sanctions, and that this harvest must inevitably include men and women whose lives have been recurrently and cumulatively damaged partly by their own actions but concomitantly by the responses of the judicial and penal systems to what they have done. In that sense, the activities of the after-care officer, and of ever more extensive systems of therapy and support, may be seen primarily as responses by a minority element in society to counter-balance the large-scale dynamic process that begins with the arrest of an offender and that incorporates a range of interactions most of which are totally divorced from the liberal–humanitarian concern that characterizes much 'informed' discussion about the plight of the prisoner in society.

In this concern, there are currently two main planks of reform: one which seeks to improve the effectiveness of treatments given within the system, and one which argues for an improvement of conditions for the prisoner, and a defence of his human rights whilst in custody. In some ways, the two might overlap, but there is no necessary reason for them to do so; the development of the specialized psychiatric prison at Grendon Underwood illustrates the difficulties. Smedley[5] has described the humane therapeutic régime there:

> It was amazing to see all the doors open. Some of the rooms as they called them [i.e. not 'cells'] had about four blokes in playing cards, while others were listening to their own portable radios, or record players, which they were permitted to have sent in from outside. Blokes were walking around with jugs of tea, which they had just made for themselves. There they were with Ronson lighters, and wearing rings and wrist-watches, and I began to wonder whether I was really in prison or a holiday camp. . . . Nobody ever told me what they were trying to do at Grendon. You just joined in the meetings and were left to draw your own conclusions as to what it was all about.

Smedley himself argues that the 'think and talk' approach enabled him, a compulsive gambler, to change his basic nature and his outlook on life, 'to accept advice and criticism gratefully, and try to improve myself generally. It is very hard work.' But he attributes to one of the psychiatrists in the prison rather more modest aspirations: 'We feel that if a man is a burglar, at least we hope that when he leaves Grendon he will be a better thinking burglar.' This is about all they could guarantee, and the doctor's humility is supported by a study carried out by prison psychologists in the Home Office which found no improvement in success rates after men had served their sentence at Grendon. The author reported a very much more humane régime than that found in many prisons, but did not feel that this in itself was sufficient, 'for we do little service to the inmates if we treat them kindly for a while and then release them just as likely as before to commit further offences and serve further terms of imprisonment'.[6]

The pressure to move towards a treatment-orientated policy is strong; and it may be that the administration and the public have to believe in its potential effectiveness in order to justify radical improvements in basic conditions. But there are great dangers in such an approach. For one thing, it flies in the face of sociological research evidence concerning the nature of crime and the circumstances of the criminal, the greater part of which would suggest that institutional 'treatment' is almost certainly irrelevant to the offence act committed; and second, the search for treatment techniques can surreptitiously lead in directions totally divorced from considerations of humane and civilized behaviour; for example, the fact that methods of persuasion employed by the authorities in Northern Ireland, and enquired into by the Parker Committee,[7] were used for purposes of interrogation is no guarantee that, in different circumstances, they could not equally be used for alleged treatment purposes. It is significant that possibly the most stark contrast between official versions of imprisonment and consumer accounts of it relates to its supposed intention. As Frank Norman puts it, 'nobody wants to be corrected';[8] and yet the *correctional system* is increasingly the way that Home Office administrators and penal reformers view what has traditionally been the *penal system*. Turner[9] has commented on the way that lay clients of psychiatrists assess 'the efficacy, necessity and propriety of the treatment operations that practitioners bring to bear on the problem'; but usually in such situations, the patient or client can withdraw from the relationship, if it is not what their pre-conceptions had led them to expect or if they feel that it has no value. The prisoner has no such choice, and he might justifiably be suspicious of any undue extension of 'treatment' aspirations within the prison system. Winchester (1973) has referred to one Federal programme in the USA which has a title to delight the eyes of the most demanding penal reformer: Special Treatment and Rehabilitative Training. The START programme 'involves a complicated series of psychological and physical processes for altering the "antisocial behaviour" of certain selected inmates. All normal prison rights are taken away, such as visiting, bathing, reading, keeping personal belongings, and taking exercise, and in an atmosphere of almost total physical isolation, men are taught how to "behave".' There are reports that men are being given drugs to modify their behaviour, and 'reformers consider the START programme is a gross violation of what few rights a prisoner has'.

It is significant that two of the prison experiments that claim to have led to slight reductions in post-release reconviction rates shared the common characteristics that they attempted to improve the quality of communications with the outside world, and to treat the offender as a responsible individual within the institution.[10] It may be that the most positive policy for the administration to pursue would be to increase the involvement of the prisoner in his own affairs, with a view to minimizing the degree of his alienation from the world outside. The empirical evidence is, in truth, not strong enough to suggest that such an approach would universally reduce the impact of institutional damage, and it is almost certain that it would have at best only a marginal reformative effect, if indeed any at all. 'Prison destroys'; more humane régimes might reduce the level of destruction; but no-one has yet satisfactorily demonstrated that prison can build or repair previous damage.

At the end of the day, we are faced – as the probation officer is faced – with the reality of total separation, with the emptiness of 'doing time', and with the fact that, sooner or later, the prisoner must once again resume his place in society. For some the transition is easier than anticipated; but for many it is a time of crisis, when their inadequacies, their isolation and their low status all seem to have been magnified in the interim period since last they were struggling for survival outside. The development of after-care through the twentieth century represents a recognition of the need for crisis support at a time of stress, and the available evidence suggests that the need today is certainly no less, and is probably greater than ever before, because of the complexity of social support provisions and the worsening of the accommodation problem.

In recent years, however, the probation service has had its attention drawn to another new role in relation to prisoners – the idea of *through-care*. There is evidence that through-care is now being practised in isolated cases: for example, an offender in one northern city, described as 'a good family man' was given four years for deception; following sentence, the probation officer undertook intensive work in the home, helping the prisoner's wife come to terms with reality and re-adjust to her own enlarged responsibilities while her husband was away; two prison visits were made (including one abortive one, as the prisoner had been transferred to another institution without the probation officer being told), and a lot of practical assistance was given to the wife with regard to Social Security and material aid. Voluntary associates were allocated to both husband and wife. The record showed that the probation officer was involved in roughly one item of work every week during the time the man was inside.

Such an instance represents a radical change of approach for the probation service, but it also illustrates an intrinsic danger in the after-care officer's position in the developing penal system; for it is important to ensure that through-care does not deflect the service from its still emerging responsibility for after-care. The two concepts are quite different. Through-care is essentially a way of involving the probation officer even more actively in the prison; after-care is a way of employing an agent to reduce the pains of transition. The notion of through-care is clearly an important breakthrough in the humanization of imprisonment if it can be developed in such a way that it is universally available, is not struggling for survival in a hostile system, and – what may well be the same point – is acceptable to the main body of prison officers. If, however, through-care were to be under-resourced and merely imposed upon an unwilling system, it could hardly hope to fulfil the aspirations expressed by those who advocate it.

The half-hearted use of through-care would be even more damaging if it were to involve a re-direction of resources from the after-care service. The work of Apex, of the hostels, and of the probation service's own after-care units have all shown how much effort is needed in many of the most intransigent situations facing ex-prisoners. For the homeless, the inadequate, the elderly, the unemployed, there is as great a need for a service on discharge as there ever was, and the task of crisis intervention will remain of critical importance for the ex-prisoner for as long as imprisonment remains society's answer to its feelings of exasperation or anger. The idea of through-care is a well-intentioned attempt to reduce the impact of imprisonment, especially perhaps on the family of the offender, but it would be unfortunate if it deflected energies away from the still under-developed, under-resourced after-care service which, it can be argued, represents an important attempt by society to repair the damage inflicted without undermining the punitive nature of the original sentence – something which some might not wish to see brought about.

Even with after-care, though, there is a final note of caution – and this applies equally to the provision of all social services. Far too little has been done to determine the true area of need as felt by the intended recipients of care, and then to create a service around these needs. 'After-care has always been an after-thought – a beneficent extra after punishment has been inflicted',[11] but if it has been beneficent, rather than punitive or even reformative, there is everything to be said for ensuring that what is offered is what is needed. Story (1973) has expressed the position vividly, in relation to a parallel situation involving Lorel, his subnormal daughter living in a hospital for the mentally handicapped:

> Compassion of the most genuine sort can be polluted by conceit (who's normal?) or the need to shine in a dim light. 'I'm trying to teach them drama therapy but they keep telling me to piss off', said Therese [one of the hospital staff].

> If they finally take me away and anyone comes to visit me on Sunday afternoons let it be to bring me whisky or to have sexual intercourse. Let's not have any strolling round the grounds exchanging vacant smiles with blissfully vacant people. 'Haven't you brought Beauty? I wanted to see Beauty!' Lorel would say, after I'd driven 60 miles and forgotten the dog. Piss off, daddy.

The fact that the average after-care service cannot provide whisky, sex, or a dog to love, but is restricted not even to drama therapy and conceited compassion but often to a letter to the WRVS, a ticket to the Salvation Army hostel and a few telephone calls to possible employers is something which ought to keep our view of the social services for ex-prisoners in clear perspective. Offenders have no special right to facilities not ordinarily available to non-offenders; but in two ways after-care services are needed in much greater proportion than are currently available: first, as a readily accessible crisis resource at the time of discharge, and second, in the light of the recognition that many ex-prisoners belong to a severely underprivileged sector of society, as an ongoing provision, in association with the wider band of social services normally on offer.

The study of prison after-care, then, brings us face-to-face, not only with the harsh realities of society's punitive commitment, but with the apparent problems that are involved in offering a service to those in greatest need of help. Similar difficulties arise in other fields where, for example, there may be severe conditions of mental handicap, physical disability, addiction or terminal sickness. Slowly our society is moving to a position where it can choose to provide forms of social support and material aid irrespective of the probable response from the recipient, but the movement is as yet tentative and hesitant, its wider implications for the economics of social policy and the efficiency of its implementation are as yet barely recognized, and the viability or validity of an approach to professional social work based entirely on service is far from clear. Nevertheless, a clear commitment to an extension of after-care provisions would represent an important step forward in the establishment of a compassionate society.

Notes

Preface

1 Expenditure Committee, 1971, p. 22.
2 ACTO, 1963.

Chapter 1 The reality of after-care

1 ACTO, 1963.
2 Ibid., p. 71.
3 Ibid., p. 72.
4 Ibid., p. 72.
5 Ibid., pp. 61–2.
6 Ibid., p. 4.
7 Ibid., pp. 35–8.
8 Report on the work of the Probation and After-Care Department, 1969–71, p. 45.

Chapter 2 Before release

1 Report on the work of the Prison Department, 1972, p. 2.
2 Home Office, *People in prison, England and Wales*, 1969, para. 24.
3 Ibid., para. 38.
4 Ibid., para. 93.
5 Ibid., p. 119.
6 Unscripted paper delivered to a conference of the Howard League, York, 1973.
7 Home Office, *People in prison, England and Wales*, 1969, para. 15.
8 Ibid., para. 34.
9 Ibid., para. 35.
10 Willetts, 1965, p. 17.
11 Ward, 1973, p. 389.
12 Wilshaw, 1973.
13 *Daily Mail*, 1 November 1973.
14 PROP, *Report on Strangeways*, p. 2.
15 Norman, Frank, 1970, p. 25.
16 Ibid., p. 22.
17 PROP, *Report on Strangeways*, p. 2.
18 Buxton and Turner, 1962, pp. 6, 192 and 13.
19 RAP, *The Case for Radical Alternatives to Prison*, p. 7.
20 PROP, *Report on Strangeways*, p. 1.
21 Ellis, 1973, pp. 142–3.
22 Evans, 1972.

23 Buxton and Turner, 1962, p. 133.
24 Willetts, 1965, p. 5.
25 PROP, *Report on Strangeways*, p. 9.
26 Ibid., and RAP Newsletters.
27 In Speed, 1973.
28 Buxton and Turner, 1962, p. 111.
29 PROP, *Report on Strangeways*, p. 3.
30 RAP, *The Case for Radical Alternatives to Prison*, p. 8.
31 PROP, *Report on Strangeways*, p. 3.
32 O'Hara, 1967.
33 Turner, Anne, 1973.
34 PROP, *Report on Winchester*.
35 Turner, Merfyn, 1964, pp. 47, 114, 115.
36 RAP, *The Case for Radical Alternatives to Prison*, p. 8.
37 Phelan, 1967, p. 131.
38 Sykes, 1967, pp. 66 and 126.
39 PROP, *Report on Winchester*.
40 PROP, *Report on Strangeways*, p. 7.
41 Ibid., p. 8.
42 Willetts, 1965, p. 12.
43 Parker, 1963, p. 22.
44 Home Office Circular 130/1967.
45 Reports on the work of the Probation and After-Care Department, 1966–8 and 1969–71.
46 1971, pp. 9–10.
47 Ibid.
48 Expenditure Committee, 1971, p. 103.
49 Shaw and Jarvis, 1971.
50 Plant, 1970.
51 Shaw and Jarvis, 1971.
52 Ibid.
53 Ibid.
54 National Association of Probation Officers, 1971, p. 6.
55 Shaw and Jarvis, 1971.
56 Expenditure Committee, 1971, p. 146.
57 Ibid., p. 154.
58 Parsons, 1967, p. 366.
59 Report on the work of the Prison Department, 1972, p. 33.
60 National Association of Probation Officers, 1971, p. 26.
61 McWilliams and Davies, 1971, p. 394.
62 Ibid., pp. 389–90.
63 Ibid., p. 391.
64 Paterson.
65 National Association of Probation Officers, 1971, p. 25.

Chapter 3 Voluntary after-care

1 ACTO, 1963, p. 73.
2 McWilliams and Davies, 1971, p. 403.

3 Silberman and Chapman, 1971.
4 Ibid., p. 34.
5 Ibid., p. 31.
6 Ibid., p. 42.
7 Ibid., p. 20.
8 Taggart, 1972, p. 69.
9 Oliver, 1969, p. 60.
10 Taggart, 1972, pp. 71–2.
11 McWilliams and Davies, 1971, pp. 397–9.
12 Monger and Pendleton, 1970.
13 Cook, 1973; and Totten, 1973.
14 Morris, 1965, pp. 100–1.
15 Ibid., p. 259.
16 Ibid., p. 300.
17 Totten, 1973.
18 Croft-Cooke, 1955, p. 241.
19 Parker and Allerton, 1962, p. 138.
20 Seebohm Report, paras 495–500; Aves Report, *passim.*
21 Morris, Terence, 1964.

Chapter 4 Release on licence

1 ACTO, 1963, p. 74.
2 Report on the work of the Probation and After-Care Department, 1966–8, p. 42.
3 Bottoms and McClintock, 1973, p. 404.
4 Powell, 1969, p. 20.
5 Pentney, 1972 and 1973b.
6 Reconviction rates are discussed in detail in pp. 78–81 above.
7 Bottoms and McClintock, 1973; Davies, 1973a. The study by Davies was distributed within the probation and after-care service, but was never published. A separate small-scale study was carried out privately during 1972 and 1973, and produced results similar in all material respects to those obtained in the earlier Home Office project; the details given in this chapter relate to the later study. Morris, forthcoming, has also analysed in detail the work of probation officers with parolees.
8 Smith, *et al.*, 1972, p. 163.
9 Bottoms and McClintock, pp. 473–4.
10 Ibid., pp. 338–9.
11 Report of the Probation and After-Care Department, 1966–8, para. 209.
12 Powell, 1969, p. 56.
13 Report of the Prison Department, 1971, p. 33.
14 Bottoms and McClintock, pp. 376–7.
15 Davies and Knopf, 1973.
16 Bottoms and McClintock, pp. 180–8.
17 Report of the Prison Department, 1971, p. 24.
18 Annual Report for 1972 of the Principal Probation Officer for south-east Lancashire.

19 Alper, 1968, p. 13.
20 Ibid., p. 14.
21 For example, Smith, *et al.*, 1972.
22 See Hirschi and Selvin, 1967, in particular.
23 Report of the Parole Board, 1972, para. 29.
24 Hood, 1966, pp. 65 and 72.
25 Cockett, 1967, p. 19.
26 Ibid., p. 20.
27 Bottoms and McClintock, p. 410.
28 Ibid., p. 412.
29 Sinclair, 1971.
30 A governor, quoted in the Report of the Prison Department, 1964.
31 Report of the Parole Board, 1972, para. 61.
32 Ibid., para. 62.
33 Elkin, 1957, p. 267.

Chapter 5 The homeless offender

1 McWilliams and Davies, 1971.
2 Walmsley, 1972.
3 Carr-Saunders, *et al.*, 1958, p. 3.
4 Adams, Barbara, 1973, pp. 4–5.
5 See, for example, Walker and McCabe, 1973.
6 Fox and Fogg, 1973.
7 The Department of Health and Social Security has recently recognized the general problem of homelessness among single people, and in 1972 issued a Circular, 37/72, which asked local authorities to investigate whether there was adequate hostel accommodation in their areas. This narrow interpretation of need has come under growing criticism, however, and critics are calling for a greater emphasis on the provision of one-person housing units by local authority housing departments. See, for example, Diamond, 1973.
8 *The homeless offender*, a Report prepared for the South West Regional Group Consultative Committee for After-Care Hostels, Southampton, 1969.
9 Norman, Diana, 1970, p. 210.
10 In Whiteley, 1972, pp. 223–4.
11 Norman, Diana, 1970, p. 214.
12 *The homeless offender*, p. 34.
13 Ibid., p. 36.
14 Whiteley, 1972, pp. 214–15.
15 Ibid., pp. 220–1.
16 Griffiths, 1970, pp. 17–18.
17 Ibid.
18 Ibid., p. 18.
19 Sinclair and Snow, 1971, p. 74.
20 Ibid., p. 77.
21 Sinclair, 1971.
22 Sinclair and Snow, 1971, p. 78.

23 Ibid., p. 98.
24 Expenditure Committee, pp. xvi–xvii.
25 Walmsley, para. 14.1.
26 Ibid., para. 12.4.1.
27 Ibid., para. 12.4.2.
28 Home Office Bulletin, no. 22, 1972.
29 Hood, 1966, p. 72.
30 Ibid., p. 66.
31 Ibid., p. 73.
32 *Residential Care*, November 1972.

Chapter 6 Employment

1 Report on the work of the Prison Department, 1971, para. 188.
2 Ibid., para. 209; Report on the work of the Prison Department, 1972, p. 88.
3 Turner, Merfyn, 1964, p. 63.
4 Bottoms and McClintock, 1973, pp. 365–6.
5 Report on the work of the Prison Department, 1972, para. 96.
6 Taggart, 1972, pp. 96–7.
7 Ibid., p. 56.
8 Rovner-Pieczenik, 1970; Holahan, 1970.
9 Taggart, 1972, p. 41.
10 Sullivan and Mandell, 1967; Abt Associates, 1971.
11 Taggart, p. 104.
12 Ibid., p. 109.
13 NACRO, South Wales and Severn, 1970.
14 McWilliams and Davies, 1972, p. 390.
15 Silberman and Chapman, 1971, p. 25.
16 Davies, 1974.
17 Pentney, 1973a, p. 3.
18 Ibid., pp. 4–5.
19 Pentney, 1971, p. 5.
20 Apex, Annual Report, 1966–7, p. 2.
21 Apex, Annual Report, 1969–70, p. 7.
22 Apex, Annual Report, 1970–1, p. 14.
23 Apex, Annual Report, 1967–8, p. 13.
24 Apex, Annual Report, 1970–1, p. 15.
25 Ibid., p. 11.
26 Pentney, 1972, p. 10.
27 Ibid., p. 14.
28 Pentney, 1973a, p. 7.
29 Apex, Annual Report, 1969–70, p. 4.
30 Apex, Annual Report, 1970–1, p. 8.
31 Pentney, 1973a, p. 17.
32 Keith Soothill, the research worker, in Apex, Annual Report, 1971–2, p. 9.
33 Briggs, no date, p. 12.
34 Ibid., p. 1.

35 Hodgkin, no date, p. 29; a quotation from Irwin in *The felon.*
36 See, for example, Cloward and Ohlin, 1961; and Cressey, 1964.
37 Pearl and Reissman, 1965.
38 Described in summary form in the Howard League publication referred to in notes 33 and 35 above.
39 Hodgkin, no date, p. 18.
40 Briggs, no date, p. 7.
41 Ibid., p. 11.
42 New Careers Progress Reports, April–July 1973, and July–September 1973.
43 Hinton, 1973, p. 10.
44 Hodgkin, no date, p. 30.
45 Briggs, 1973, p. 5.
46 Page 35.

Chapter 7 The prisoner's view

1 Clemmer, 1958, p. 298.
2 This is not the place to discuss the numerous attempts that have been made to categorize the varieties of response that prisoners can and do make to their prison experience. Morris and Morris, 1963, pp. 169–83, discuss the question at length, and use an adapted version of Robert Merton's typology of reaction in their study of Pentonville: conformity/innovation/ritualism/retreatism/ rebellion/ manipulation. More recently, Cohen and Taylor, 1972, p. 178, have identified four styles of adaptation among long-term prisoners: rebellion/subverting/retreatism/giving in.
3 Parker and Allerton, 1962, p. 169.
4 For example, Baker, 1961; Vassall, 1973; Wildeblood, 1955.
5 Lonsdale, 1965, p. 151.
6 O'Hara, 1967, p. 164, provides a useful example of the sharp contrast between the Home Office's public description of a newly opened prison and the reality as it was experienced by the inmates when they moved in.
7 Wildeblood, 1956, p. 11.
8 1964, p. 93.
9 1965, p. 70.
10 Parker and Allerton, 1962, p. 138.
11 Fletcher, 1972, p. 13.
12 Ibid., p. 128.
13 McWilliams and Davies, 1972, p. 393.
14 A major investigation of prison welfare practice has been carried out by the Home Office Research Unit in three Midlands prisons, but the detailed results are not yet published; a preliminary report by Shaw and Jarvis, 1971, indicates that one of the aims of the experiment was to compare the normal pattern of prison welfare with one in which casework contacts were established on a more regular footing with selected prisoners.
15 *Guardian*, 13 June 1973.

16 Robert Carr, Home Secretary, reported in the *Guardian*, ibid.
17 Morris, Pauline, 1965, p. 71.
18 Willetts, 1965, p. 103.
19 Norman, Frank, 1972, p. 196.
20 Baker, Peter, 1961, p. 31.
21 1955, p. 240.
22 1972, p. 251.
23 Croft-Cooke, 1955, p. 248.
24 Allen, 1952, p. 185.
25 Parker and Allerton, 1962, p. 132.
26 Ibid., p. 130.
27 Croft-Cooke, 1955, p. 239.
28 Silberman, 1969, p. 86.
29 Lowson, 1970, p. 91.
30 Ibid., p. 92.
31 Ibid., p. 124.
32 Parker and Allerton, 1962, p. 117.
33 Ibid., p. 132.
34 Silberman, 1969, p. 87.
35 Ibid., p. 89.
36 Ibid., p. 87.
37 Fletcher, 1972, p. 123.
38 Ibid., p. 138.
39 Silberman, 1969, p. 90.
40 Allen, 1952, p. 191.
41 Norman, Frank, 1972, p. 237.
42 Martin and Webster, 1971, p. 111.
43 1965, p. 297.
44 Whiteley, 1972, pp. 118 ff.

Chapter 8 The dilemma of penal decision-making

1 *Southend Evening Echo*, Editorial, 27 March 1973.
2 Thomas, 1970.
3 Hunter, 1973, for example.
4 Mooney, 1973, p. 61.

Chapter 9 No alternative to imprisonment

1 An NOP survey of public opinion in 1970, published in the *Daily Mail*, and quoted by Cohen, 1973, indicated that 70 per cent thought that prison conditions should be made harsher than they now are.
2 Cohen and Taylor, 1972, p. 196.
3 Taylor, 1972, p. 618.
4 Ibid., p. 620.
5 Pentney, 1973a, p. 19.
6 Sykes, 1967, pp. 65–78.
7 Willetts, 1965, p. 103.
8 Report on the work of the Prison Department, 1971, para. 95.

9 Section 11(3).
10 Davies, 1973b.
11 Cohen and Taylor, 1972, pp. 187–8.
12 Ibid., p. 116.
13 Report on the work of the Prison Department, 1971, para. 24.
14 Quoted in the *Guardian*, 13 June 1973.
15 Hunt, 1973, p. 302.
16 Hood and Sparks, 1970, p. 191.
17 Ibid., p. 186.
18 Ibid., p. 189.
19 Bailey, 1966, p. 157.
20 In Whiteley, 1972, p. 169.
21 1971, p. 76.
22 Described in Lohman, *et al.*, 1967.
23 Davies, 1971.
24 A useful discussion of this issue has been published by Bottoms, 1973.
25 Reviews of the literature can be found in Adams, Stuart, 1967, and in Grey and Dermody, 1972.
26 Taggart, 1972, p. 37.
27 For further discussion of this complex but crucial issue, see Bottoms and McClintock, 1968, and Robison and Smith, 1971.
28 Takagi, 1969, pp. 198–9.
29 Warren, Marguerite, in Yefsky, 1967, p. 198.
30 For example, that reported by Martin and Webster, 1971.
31 Men like Fletcher, 1972.
32 Thomas, 1970, p. 23.
33 The case examples presented in Chapter 5 are both illustrative of this situation.

Chapter 10 After-care – an apology for vengeance

1 1972, p. 178.
2 Whiteley, 1972, pp. 228 and 238.
3 Ibid., p. 11.
4 Ibid., p. 12.
5 1973, p. 228.
6 Newton, 1971, p. 36.
7 Parker Report, 1972.
8 Norman, Frank, 1958, p. 199.
9 Turner, Roy, 1969.
10 Whiteley, 1972; Shaw and Jarvis, 1971.
11 Morris, Terence, 1971, p. 9.

Further reading

Chapter 1 The reality of after-care

For those seeking a detailed knowledge of the developing reality of after-care, there must be a willingness to come to terms with the stodgy lay-out and presentation of Government blue books. The official history is well documented, and it is quite easy to detect the problems and ambiguities that have characterized policy-making and planning during the last decade. Special reference should be made to *The organisation of after-care*, report of the Advisory Council on the Treatment of Offenders, HMSO, London, 1963, and Reports on the work of the Probation and After-Care Department: 1962–5, Cmnd 3107, HMSO, London, 1966; 1966–8, Cmnd 4233, HMSO, London, 1969; 1969–71, Cmnd 5158, HMSO, London, 1972.

The two principal books making direct reference to the probation service's involvement in after-care are King, Joan F. S., ed., *The probation and after-care service* (third edn), Butterworth, London, 1969, and Monger, Mark, *Casework in after-care*, Butterworth, London, 1969.

Chapter 2 Before release

Factual details should be sought in *People in prison, England and Wales*, the Home Office White Paper, Cmnd 4214, HMSO, London, 1969, and Annual Reports on the work of the Prison Department, HMSO, London.

The best collection of papers is in Johnston, Norman, *et al.*, eds, *The sociology of punishment and correction* (second edn), Wiley, London, 1970, especially Section 3, 'The Prison Community', and Section 4, 'Treatment in Institutions', pp. 383–571.

On the work of prison welfare officers, there are the Government references suggested for Chapter 1, together with *Probation Officers in Prison*, the report of a survey by the National Association of Probation Officers, London, 1971, and Priestley, Philip, 'The prison welfare officer – a case of role strain', *Br. J. Sociol.*, *23*, 2, 1972, pp. 221–35.

Chapter 3 Voluntary after-care

The best general introduction to what voluntary after-care means is to be found in a Home Office Research Unit publication, Sinclair, Ian, *et al.*, *Explorations in after-care*, HMSO, London, 1971. Two NACRO papers stimulate thinking: Vercoe, Kate, *Helping prisoners' families*, NACRO, London, 1968, and Morris, Terence, *After-care in the seventies*,

NACRO, London, 1971; and for those interested in the use of voluntary associates with ex-prisoners, there is a detailed account of one such project in Barr, Hugh, *Volunteers in prison after-care*, Allen & Unwin, London, 1971.

Chapter 4 Release on licence

The twin topics discussed in this chapter have a relatively extensive research literature, and, especially with regard to parole, this is likely to grow during the next few years. The following are most useful: The Annual Reports of the Parole Board, from 1968, HMSO, London; West, D. J., ed., *The future of parole*, Duckworth, London, 1972; *British Journal of Criminology*, special issue on parole, *13*, 1973; Carter, R. M., and Wilkins, Leslie T., *Probation and parole, selected readings*, Wiley, New York, 1970, especially Section II, pp. 177–276; Hood, Roger, *Homeless borstal boys*, Bell, London, 1966; Hood, Roger, *Borstal re-assessed*, Heinemann, London, 1965; Bottoms, A. E. and McClintock, F. H., *Criminals coming of age*, Heinemann, London, 1973.

A research study of a group of young offenders who are similarly subject to statutory after-care, but who have not been considered in detail in this chapter, was made by Dunlop, Anne and McCabe, Sarah, *Young men in detention centres*, Routledge & Kegan Paul, London, 1965.

Chapter 5 The homeless offender

The standard national review of the problem of homelessness as it affects ex-prisoners is that presented in the Reading Report, 1966. The papers by Sinclair and Snow and by Leissner in *Explorations in after-care*, Home Office Research Unit, HMSO, London, 1971, review some of the problems involved in providing hostel accommodation for single men, and references by Merfyn Turner, 1961, and Diana Norman, 1970, provide personal accounts of residential work. For the rest, the student will have to search out more specific studies, such as those by Walmsley, 1972 and Griffiths, 1970. The National Association of Voluntary Hostels has published a number of lectures and essays, including one by John Greve on 'The problems of the single homeless person'.

At the present time, there is some research being done into the realities of life as perceived by the homeless themselves, and this should ultimately make a considerable contribution to our understanding of the problem. Jeremy Sandford's *Down and out in Britain*, New English Library, London, 1972, is a useful beginning.

Chapter 6 Employment

Both Apex and the New Careers projects in the UK have yet to be reported in detail. Until they are, the following must serve as introductions: Pentney, F., *Employment for the ex-offender*, Apex, London, 1971; Pentney, F., *The employment future of the ex-offender*, Apex,

London, 1973; Annual Reports from Apex, 1966–72; *New careers for ex-offenders*, Howard League, London, n.d.; Pearl, A., and Reissman, F., *New careers for the poor: the non-professional in human service*, Free Press, New York, 1965.

For an excellent review of research in this area and a book which carries its implications over into the whole sphere of corrections, see Taggart, Robert, *The prison of unemployment: manpower programs for offenders*, Johns Hopkins University Press, Baltimore, 1972.

The Annual Reports of the Prison Department present an official version of developments in Britain.

Chapter 7 The prisoner's view

The nearest to a consumer survey of prisoners' attitudes towards the institution and post-release provisions are Silberman, Martin, *Care or crime*, Royal London Discharged Prisoners' Aid Society, London, 1969, and Lowson, D. M., *City lads in borstal*, Liverpool University Press, 1970.

For prisoners' own accounts of their experiences inside and afterwards, any of the references made in the text can be examined. A rather arbitrary selection of three with particular interest for their references to after-care would be Fletcher, J. W., *A menace to society*, Elek, London, 1972; Parker, T. and Allerton, R., *The courage of his convictions*, Hutchinson, London, 1962, and Turner, Merfyn, *A pretty sort of prison*, Pall Mall, London, 1964.

For a vivid description of the whole penal process from the prisoner's angle, there is Hunt, Morton, *The mugging*, Secker & Warburg, London, 1973.

Chapter 8 The dilemma of penal decision-making

On baby-snatching, there is nothing save D'Orban, P. T., 'Baby stealing', *Br. Med. J.*, 10 June 1972, pp. 635–9. Nor is there anything which begins to tackle the intricate nature of the relationship between an offender's behaviour and the society of which he or she is a part, although Hunt's *The mugging* (recommended for Chapter 7) touches on it. Little is known about the true impact of the news media on patterns of criminal behaviour or even upon arrest processes, and the failure of the helping services to help those at the very bottom of the pile is equally unexplored, although Sandford's play, *Oluwale*, highlights the problem.

The reader is recommended to learn more from the Press's handling of cases similar to that of Jacqueline Paddon, and those involved with the administration of such cases could do worse than consider more carefully the nature of what they are doing with a view to bringing their experiences into the arena of public discussion.

Chapter 9 No alternative to imprisonment

The Press coverage and concentration of conference agendas have been extensive so far as alternatives to prison are concerned. Rigorous examination of the issues has been much rarer. An excellent start could be made by looking at Sections 6, 7 and 8 of Hood, Roger and Sparks, Richard, *Key issues in criminology*, Weidenfeld & Nicolson, London, 1970.

The reference to Taggart for Chapter 6 is relevant here too, but from there the reader has to be prepared to give careful consideration to each particular alternative said to be on offer. Some claim success, but have been criticized on methodological grounds; others admit disappointment; some report selective success for some types of offender; others record overall improvement but only at a marginal level; some define success in terms of further offences, others in relation to re-imprisonment, and still others adopt broader criteria concerned with social behaviour or personal improvement. Section 5 of Norman Johnston, *et al.*, *The sociology of punishment and correction* (second edn), Wiley, London, 1970, brings together a selection of the best-known experiments.

A quite different volume that is crucial to the argument of this chapter is Thomas, D. A., *Principles of sentencing*, Heinemann, London, 1970.

Since completion of the manuscript two important texts have appeared. *Young adult offenders*, HMSO, London, 1974 is a review of the borstal system by the Advisory Council on the Penal System, and is relevant to Chapter 4. *The prisoner's release* by Keith Soothill, London, Allen & Unwin, 1974 is the full evaluation of Apex referred to in Chapter 6.

Bibliography

Abt Associates, Inc. (1971), *An evaluation of MDTA training in correctional institutions*, vols 1–3 and final summary, AAI, Washington.

ACTO (The Advisory Council on the Treatment of Offenders) (1963), *The organisation of after-care*, HMSO.

Adams, Barbara (1973), 'Housing the single person is a growing social need', *Social Worker*, *2*, 64, 16 August, pp. 4–5.

Adams, Stuart (1967), 'Some findings from correctional caseload research', *Federal Probation*, *31*, 4, December, pp. 48–57.

Allen, John E. (1952), *Inside Broadmoor*, W. H. Allen.

Alper, B. S. (1968), 'Borstal briefly re-visited', *Br. J. Crim.*, *8*, 1, pp. 6–19.

Apex Charitable Trust, Annual reports, 1966–1972, Apex.

Aves Report (1969), *The voluntary worker in the social services*, the report of a committee set up jointly by the National Council of Social Service and the National Institute for Social Work Training, Allen & Unwin.

Bailey, Walter C. (1966), 'Correctional outcome – an evaluation of a hundred reports', *J. of Crim. Law, Criminol. and Pol. Sci.*, *67*, pp. 153–60.

Baker, Peter (1961), *Time out of life*, Heinemann.

Barr, Hugh (1971), *Volunteers in prison after-care*, Allen & Unwin.

Beresford, Peter (1973), 'Without a home', *New Society*, *25*, pp. 212–13.

Bottoms, A. E. (1973), 'The efficacy of the fine – the case for agnosticism', *Crim. Law Rev.*, September, pp. 543–51.

Bottoms, A. E. and McClintock, F. H. (1968), 'Research into the institutional treatment of offenders'. Paper to the Third National Conference on research and teaching in criminology, Cambridge.

Bottoms, A. E. and McClintock, F. H. (1973), *Criminals coming of age*, Heinemann.

Briggs, D. L., n.d., 'A transitional therapeutic community for young violent offenders', in *New careers for ex-offenders*, Howard League, London.

Briggs, D. L. (1973), 'De-clienting social work', *Social Work Today*, *3*, 21, January, pp. 3–6.

Buxton, J. and Turner, Margaret (1962), *Gate fever*, Cresset.

Carr-Saunders, A. M., Jones, D. C. and Moser, C. A. (1958), *Social conditions in England and Wales*, Oxford University Press.

Clemmer, Donald (1958), *The prison community*, Holt, Rinehart & Winston, New York.

Cloward, R. A. and Ohlin, L. E. (1961), *Delinquency and opportunity*, Routledge & Kegan Paul.

Cockett, R. (1967), 'Borstal training – a follow-up study', *Br. J. Crim.*, *7*, pp. 150–83.
Cohen, S. (1973), 'Living with crime', *New Society*, 8 November, pp. 330–3.
Cohen, S. and Taylor, L. (1972), *Psychological survival*, Penguin.
Cook, Judith (1973), 'Prisoners by marriage', *Guardian*, 21 May.
Cressey, D. R. (1964), *Delinquency, crime and differential association*, Martinus, Nijhoff.
Croft-Cooke, R. (1955), *The verdict of you all*, Secker & Warburg.
Davies, Martin (1971), *Financial penalties and probation*, Home Office Research Unit, HMSO.
Davies, Martin (1973a), *Parole and the probation service*, Home Office Research Unit (for restricted circulation).
Davies, Martin (1973b), 'The Criminal Justice Act 1972 as an expression of social policy', *Social Work Today*, *4*, 7, pp. 195–8.
Davies, Martin (1974), *Social work in the environment*, To be published by HMSO.
Davies, Martin and Knopf, Andrea (1973), *Social enquiries and the probation service*, HMSO.
Department of Health and Social Security, Circular 37/72.
Diamond, Gillian (1973), 'Homelessness', *New Society*, 27 September.
D'Orban, P. T. (1972), 'Baby stealing', *Br. Med. J.*, 10 June, pp. 635–9.
Elkin, W. A. (1957), *The English penal system*, Penguin.
Ellis, Mary (1973), 'The experience of Borstal', *New Society*, 18 October, pp. 142–4.
Estimates Committee, Eleventh report, 1966–7 (1967), *Prisons, borstals and detention centres*, HMSO.
Evans, Peter (1972), 'Clockwork life of shunting and shuffling', *The Times*, 18 January.
Expenditure Committee (1971), *First report from the House of Commons, 1971–1972*, HMSO.
Fletcher, J. W. (1972), *A menace to society*, Elek.
Fox, James and Fogg, Nicholas (1973), 'Crisis on Skid Row', *Sunday Times Magazine*, 24 June.
Gladstone Report (1894), *Report of the Departmental Committee on Prisons*, C7702, HMSO.
Goldberg, E. M. (1971), *Helping the aged*, Allen & Unwin.
Grey, A. L. and Dermody, H. E. (1972), 'Reports of casework failure', *Social Casework*, *53*, 9, November, pp. 534–43.
Griffiths, W. A. (1970), *After-care hostels – a critique of the family model*, NACRO.
Hinton, N. (1973), 'Offenders as social workers', *Social Work Today*, *3*, 21, January, pp. 9–11.
Hirschi, T. and Selvin, H. C. (1967), *Delinquency research*, Free Press.
Hodgkin, Nancy, n.d., 'The New Careers project at Vacaville', in *New Careers for ex-offenders*, Howard League, London.
Hodgson, Godfrey (1971), Feature article on the American Penal System, *Sunday Times*, 8 August.

Holahan, J. F. (1970), *A benefit–cost analysis of Project Crossroads*, National Committee for Children and Youth.

Home Office (1965), *The adult offender*, Cmnd 2852, HMSO.

Home Office (1969), *People in prison, England and Wales*, Cmnd 4214, HMSO.

Home Office (1971), *Sentence of the court* (revised edn), HMSO.

Home Office (1972a), Bulletin Number 22, issued by the Probation and After-Care Department, 9 August.

Home Office (1972b), *Guide to the Criminal Justice Act 1972*, HMSO.

Hood, Roger (1965), *Borstal re-assessed*, Heinemann.

Hood, Roger (1966), *Homeless borstal boys*, Bell.

Hood, Roger and Sparks, Richard (1970), *Key issues in criminology*, Weidenfeld & Nicolson.

Hunt, Morton (1973), *The mugging*, Secker & Warburg.

Hunter, Joan (1973), 'The problem of baby stealing', *Social Work Today*, *4*, 9, pp. 266–8.

Jones, Maxwell (1968), *Social psychiatry in practice*, Pelican.

Kelmanson, Andrea (1973), *The experience of giving – borstal boys in full-time community service*, Community Service Volunteers.

Lacey, A. (1964), 'The Citizen and After-Care', *Howard Journal*, *XI*, 3, pp. 194–202.

Lohman, J. D., Wahl, A. and Carter, R. M. (1967), *The San Francisco Project – the intensive supervision caseload*, Research Report, no. 11, School of Criminology, University of California, March.

Lonsdale, Gordon (1965), *Spy*, Spearman.

Lowson, D. M. (1970), *City lads in borstal*, Liverpool University Press.

McKee, John, *et al.* (1970), *Barriers to the employment of released male offenders*, Rehabilitation Research Foundation, Elmore, Alabama.

McWilliams, W. and Davies, Martin (1971), 'Communication about after-care', *Br. J. Social Wk*, *1*, 4, pp. 381–407.

Malleson, Andrew (1973), *Need your doctor be so useless?* Allen & Unwin.

Martin, J. P. and Webster, D. (1971), *The social consequences of conviction*, Heinemann.

Maxwell Report (1953), *Report of the Committee on Discharged Prisoners' Aid Societies*, Cmnd 8874, HMSO.

Merton, Richard (1949), *Social Theory and Social Structure*, Free Press.

Monger, Mark and Pendleton, John (1970), 'The Nottingham Prisoners' Families Project', *Probation*, *16*, 3, November, pp. 84–6.

Mooney, Bel (1973), 'Baby snatchers', *Nova*, June, pp. 58–61.

Morris, Pauline (1965), *Prisoners and their families*, Allen & Unwin.

Morris, Pauline, *Report of research into parole supervision* (forthcoming).

Morris, Terence (1964), quoted by H. M. Holden in 'The implications of after-care', a paper to the Principal Probation Officers' Conference, Oxford.

Morris, Terence (1971), *After-care in the seventies*, NACRO.

Morris, Terence and Morris, Pauline (1963), *Pentonville*, Routledge & Kegan Paul.

Mountbatten Report (1966), *The report of an enquiry into prison escapes and security*, Cmnd 3175, HMSO.

NACRO (National Association for the Care and Resettlement of Offenders) (1970), *South Wales and Severn: a regional report. The prisoner's view of after-care.*

NACRO (1973), *New Careers progress report, April-July 1973*, NACRO.

NACRO (1973), *New Careers progress report, July-September 1973*, NACRO.

NAPO (National Association of Probation Officers) (1971), *Probation officers in prison*, NAPO.

Newton, M. (1971), *Reconviction after treatment at Grendon*, Home Office.

Nokes, Peter (1967), *The professional task in welfare practice*, Routledge & Kegan Paul.

Norman, Diana (1970), *Road from Singapore*, Hodder & Stoughton.

Norman, Frank (1958), *Bang to rights*, Secker & Warburg.

Norman, Frank (1970), *Lock 'em up and count 'em*, Knight.

Norman, Frank (1972), *The lives*, Penguin.

Nuttall, Christopher (1973), paper to the Howard League Conference, York.

O'Hara, P. (1967), *I got no brother*, Spearman.

Oliver, E. L., *et al.* (1969), *A future for correctional rehabilitation?* Division of vocational rehabilitation, Coordinating Service for Occupational Education, Olympia, Washington.

Palmer, Ted B. (1973), 'Matching worker and client in corrections', *Social Work*, *18*, 2, March, pp. 95–103.

Parker Report (1972), *Report of the committee of privy counsellors appointed to consider authorised procedures for the interrogation of persons suspected of terrorism*, Cmnd 4901, HMSO.

Parker, Tony (1963), *The unknown citizen*, Hutchinson.

Parker, Tony and Allerton, R. (1962), *The courage of his convictions*, Hutchinson.

Parole Board Reports, 1968–72, HMSO.

Parsons, Talcott (1967), *Sociological theory and modern society*, Free Press.

Paterson, Sir Alexander (1965), quoted in Home Office: *The adult offender*, Cmnd 2852, HMSO.

Pearl, A. and Reissman, F. (1965), *New careers for the poor: the non-professional in human service*, Free Press.

Pentney, F. (1971), *Employment for the ex-offender*, Apex, February.

Pentney, F. (1972), *A survey to determine the value of a service offered prior to discharge compared with a similar service offered subsequently*, Apex, September.

Pentney, F. (1973a), *The employment future of the ex-offender*, Apex, February.

Pentney, F. (1973b), personal communication to the author, 3 April.

Phelan, J. (1967), *Nine murderers and me*, Phoenix.

Plant, Raymond (1970), *Social and Moral Theory in Casework*, Routledge & Kegan Paul.

Powell, Eileen (1969), 'The parole system – initial reactions and early experience of some probation officers', thesis submitted for the diploma in social and administrative studies, University of Oxford, May.

PROP (Preservation of the Rights of Prisoners) (1973a), *Report on General Conditions in Her Majesty's Prison, Strangeways, Manchester*, PROP.

PROP (1973b), *Report on General Conditions in Winchester Prison*, PROP.

RAP (Radical Alternatives to Prison), n.d., *The Case for Radical Alternatives to Prison*, RAP, Christian Action.

RAP Newsletters, *Radical Alternatives to Prison*, monthly.

Reading Report (1966), *Report of the working party on the place of voluntary Service in After-care: residential provision for homeless discharged Offenders*, HMSO.

Report on the work of the Prison Department (1964), Cmnd 2708; (1971), Cmnd 5037; (1972), Cmnd 5375.

Report on the work of the Probation and After-Care Department (1962–5), Cmnd 3107; (1966–8), Cmnd 4233; (1969–71), Cmnd 5158.

Residential Care (1972), *1*, 1, November, p. 10, 'Opinion'.

Robison, J. and Smith, G. (1971), 'The effectiveness of correctional programs', *Crime and Delinquency*, *17*, 1, pp. 67–80.

Rovner-Pieczenik, R. (1970), *Project Crossroads as pre-trial intervention – a program evaluation*, National Committee for Children and Youth, Washington, D.C.

Rutherford, A. and Rogerson, M. (1971), 'The after-care workshop and its implications', *Probation*, *17*, 3, November, pp. 68–74.

Sandford, Jeremy (1973), 'Oluwale, deceased', Part 4, *Residential Care*, *2*, 5, May, pp. 4–8.

Seebohm Report (1968), *Report of the Committee on local authority and allied personal social services*, Cmnd 3703, HMSO.

Shaw, Margaret and Jarvis, Fred (1971), 'Casework with prisoners', *Probation*, *17*, 3, November, pp. 74–6.

Silberman, Martin (1969), *Care or crime*, Royal London Discharged Prisoners' Aid Society.

Silberman, Martin and Chapman, Brenda (1971), 'After-care units in London, Liverpool and Manchester', in *Explorations in after-care*, Home Office Research Unit, HMSO.

Sinclair, Ian (1971), *Hostels for probationers*, Home Office Research Unit, HMSO.

Sinclair, Ian and Snow, David (1971), 'After-care hostels receiving a Home Office grant', in *Explorations in after-care*, Home Office Research Unit, HMSO.

Smedley, Ted (1973), 'A year inside', *Social Work Today*, *4*, 8, 12 July.

Smith, C., Farrant, M. and Marchant, H. (1972), *The Wincroft Youth Project*, Tavistock.

South West Regional Group Consultative Committee for After-Care Hostels (1969), *The homeless offender: a report*, Southampton.

Speed, Dorothy, ed. (1973), *The Medical Care of Prisoners and Detainees, A CIBA Foundation Symposium*, Associated Scientific Publishers.

Story, Jack Trevor (1973), 'Looking to Lorel', *Guardian*, 31 March.
Sullivan, C. E. and Mandell, W. (1967), *Restoration of youth through training*, Wakoff Research Center, New York.
Sykes, R. (1967), *Who's been eating my porridge?*, Leslie Frewin.
Taggart, Robert (1972), *The prison of unemployment*, Johns Hopkins University Press, Baltimore.
Takagi, Paul T. (1969), 'The effect of parole agents' judgments on recidivism rates', *Psychiatry*, *32*, 2, pp. 192–9.
Taylor, Laurie (1972), 'Prison splash', *New Society*, 28 September, pp. 618–20.
Thomas, D. A. (1970), *Principles of sentencing*, Heinemann.
Totten, Eileen (1973), 'Wives in the wings', *Guardian*, 6 June.
Turner, Anne (1973), 'Library services in four West Riding prisons', *Howard Journal*, *XIII*, 4, pp. 288–96.
Turner, Merfyn (1961), *Safe lodging*, Hutchinson.
Turner, Merfyn (1964), *A pretty sort of prison*, Pall Mall.
Turner, Roy (1969), 'Some formal properties of therapy talk', in Sudnow, David, ed., *Papers in Interaction*, Free Press.
Vassall, William (1973), *Sunday Times Magazine*, 7 January.
Walker, Nigel and McCabe, Sarah (1973), *Crime and insanity in England, 2: new solutions and new problems*, University Press, Edinburgh.
Walmsley, Roy (1972), *Steps from prison*, Inner London Probation Service.
Ward, Joyce (1973), 'Women inside', *New Society*, 16 August, pp. 388–90.
Whiteley, Stuart, *et al.* (1972), *Dealing with deviants*, Hogarth.
Wildeblood, Peter (1955), *Against the law*, Weidenfeld & Nicolson.
Wildeblood, Peter (1956), *A way of life*, Weidenfeld & Nicolson.
Willetts, Phoebe (1965), *Invisible bars*, Epworth.
Wilshaw, Harold (1973), 'Nosh in the jug', *Guardian*, 3 October.
Winchester, Simon (1973), 'Crime out of mind', *Guardian*, 31 August.
Yefsky, S. A., ed. (1967), *Law enforcement, science and technology*, vol. 1, Thompson, Academic Press.

Index of names

Index of subjects

International Library of Sociology

Edited by
John Rex
University of Warwick

Founded by
Karl Mannheim

as The International Library of Sociology and Social Reconstruction

This Catalogue also contains other Social Science series published by Routledge

Routledge & Kegan Paul London and Boston

68-74 Carter Lane London EC4V 5EL
9 Park Street Boston Mass 02108

Contents

● *Books so marked are available in paperback*

All books are in Metric Demy 8vo format (216 × 138mm approx.)

GENERAL SOCIOLOGY

Belshaw, Cyril. The Conditions of Social Performance. *An Exploratory Theory. 144 pp.*

Brown, Robert. Explanation in Social Science. *208 pp.*

● Rules and Laws in Sociology.

Cain, Maureen E. Society and the Policeman's Role. *About 300 pp.*

Gibson, Quentin. The Logic of Social Enquiry. *240 pp.*

Gurvitch, Georges. Sociology of Law. *Preface by Roscoe Pound. 264 pp.*

Homans, George C. Sentiments and Activities: *Essays in Social Science. 336 pp.*

Johnson, Harry M. Sociology: *a Systematic Introduction. Foreword by Robert K. Merton. 710 pp.*

Mannheim, Karl. Essays on Sociology and Social Psychology. *Edited by Paul Keckskemeti. With Editorial Note by Adolph Lowe. 344 pp.*

Systematic Sociology: *An Introduction to the Study of Society. Edited by J. S. Erös and Professor W. A. C. Stewart. 220 pp.*

Martindale, Don. The Nature and Types of Sociological Theory. *292 pp.*

● **Maus, Heinz.** A Short History of Sociology. *234 pp.*

Mey, Harald. Field-Theory. *A Study of its Application in the Social Sciences. 352 pp.*

Myrdal, Gunnar. Value in Social Theory: *A Collection of Essays on Methodology. Edited by Paul Streeten. 332 pp.*

Ogburn, William F., and **Nimkoff, Meyer F.** A Handbook of Sociology. *Preface by Karl Mannheim. 656 pp. 46 figures. 35 tables.*

Parsons, Talcott, and **Smelser, Neil J.** Economy and Society: *A Study in the Integration of Economic and Social Theory. 362 pp.*

● **Rex, John.** Key Problems of Sociological Theory. *220 pp.*

Urry, John. Reference Groups and the Theory of Revolution.

FOREIGN CLASSICS OF SOCIOLOGY

● **Durkheim, Emile.** Suicide. *A Study in Sociology. Edited and with an Introduction by George Simpson. 404 pp.*

Professional Ethics and Civic Morals. *Translated by Cornelia Brookfield. 288 pp.*

● **Gerth, H. H.,** and **Mills, C. Wright.** From Max Weber: *Essays in Sociology. 502 pp.*

Tönnies, Ferdinand. Community and Association. *(Gemeinschaft und Gesellschaft.) Translated and Supplemented by Charles P. Loomis. Foreword by Pitirim A. Sorokin. 334 pp.*

SOCIAL STRUCTURE

Andreski, Stanislav. Military Organization and Society. *Foreword by Professor A. R. Radcliffe-Brown. 226 pp. 1 folder.*

Coontz, Sydney H. Population Theories and the Economic Interpretation. *202 pp.*

Coser, Lewis. The Functions of Social Conflict. *204 pp.*

Dickie-Clark, H. F. Marginal Situation: *A Sociological Study of a Coloured Group. 240 pp. 11 tables.*

Glass, D. V. (Ed.). Social Mobility in Britain. *Contributions by J. Berent, T. Bottomore, R. C. Chambers, J. Floud, D. V. Glass, J. R. Hall, H. T. Himmelweit, R. K. Kelsall, F. M. Martin, C. A. Moser, R. Mukherjee, and W. Ziegel. 420 pp.*

Glaser, Barney, and **Strauss, Anselm L.** Status Passage. *A Formal Theory. 208 pp.*

Jones, Garth N. Planned Organizational Change: *An Exploratory Study Using an Empirical Approach. 268 pp.*

Kelsall, R. K. Higher Civil Servants in Britain: *From 1870 to the Present Day. 268 pp. 31 tables.*

König, René. The Community. *232 pp. Illustrated.*

● **Lawton, Denis.** Social Class, Language and Education. *192 pp.*

McLeish, John. The Theory of Social Change: *Four Views Considered. 128 pp.*

Marsh, David C. The Changing Social Structure of England and Wales, 1871-1961. *288 pp.*

Mouzelis, Nicos. Organization and Bureaucracy. *An Analysis of Modern Theories. 240 pp.*

Mulkay, M. J. Functionalism, Exchange and Theoretical Strategy. *272 pp.*

Ossowski, Stanislaw. Class Structure in the Social Consciousness. *210 pp.*

SOCIOLOGY AND POLITICS

Hertz, Frederick. Nationality in History and Politics: *A Psychology and Sociology of National Sentiment and Nationalism. 432 pp.*

Kornhauser, William. The Politics of Mass Society. *272 pp. 20 tables.*

Laidler, Harry W. History of Socialism. *Social-Economic Movements: An Historical and Comparative Survey of Socialism, Communism, Co-operation, Utopianism; and other Systems of Reform and Reconstruction. 992 pp.*

Mannheim, Karl. Freedom, Power and Democratic Planning. *Edited by Hans Gerth and Ernest K. Bramstedt. 424 pp.*

Mansur, Fatma. Process of Independence. *Foreword by A. H. Hanson. 208 pp.*

Martin, David A. Pacificism: *an Historical and Sociological Study. 262 pp.*

Myrdal, Gunnar. The Political Element in the Development of Economic Theory. *Translated from the German by Paul Streeten. 282 pp.*

Wootton, Graham. Workers, Unions and the State. *188 pp.*

FOREIGN AFFAIRS: THEIR SOCIAL, POLITICAL AND ECONOMIC FOUNDATIONS

Mayer, J. P. Political Thought in France from the Revolution to the Fifth Republic. *164 pp.*

CRIMINOLOGY

Ancel, Marc. Social Defence: *A Modern Approach to Criminal Problems. Foreword by Leon Radzinowicz. 240 pp.*

Cloward, Richard A., and **Ohlin, Lloyd E.** Delinquency and Opportunity: *A Theory of Delinquent Gangs. 248 pp.*

Downes, David M. The Delinquent Solution. *A Study in Subcultural Theory. 296 pp.*

Dunlop, A. B., and **McCabe, S.** Young Men in Detention Centres. *192 pp.*

Friedlander, Kate. The Psycho-Analytical Approach to Juvenile Delinquency: *Theory, Case Studies, Treatment. 320 pp.*

Glueck, Sheldon, and **Eleanor.** Family Environment and Delinquency. *With the statistical assistance of Rose W. Kneznek. 340 pp.*

Lopez-Rey, Manuel. Crime. *An Analytical Appraisal. 288 pp.*

Mannheim, Hermann. Comparative Criminology: *a Text Book. Two volumes. 442 pp. and 380 pp.*

Morris, Terence. The Criminal Area: *A Study in Social Ecology. Foreword by Hermann Mannheim. 232 pp. 25 tables. 4 maps.*

● **Taylor, Ian, Walton, Paul,** and **Young, Jock.** The New Criminology. *For a Social Theory of Deviance.*

SOCIAL PSYCHOLOGY

Bagley, Christopher. The Social Psychology of the Epileptic Child. *320 pp.*

Barbu, Zevedei. Problems of Historical Psychology. *248 pp.*

Blackburn, Julian. Psychology and the Social Pattern. *184 pp.*

● **Brittan, Arthur.** Meanings and Situations. *224 pp.*

● **Fleming, C. M.** Adolescence: Its Social Psychology. *With an Introduction to recent findings from the fields of Anthropology, Physiology, Medicine, Psychometrics and Sociometry. 288 pp.*

● The Social Psychology of Education: *An Introduction and Guide to Its Study. 136 pp.*

Homans, George C. The Human Group. *Foreword by Bernard DeVoto. Introduction by Robert K. Merton. 526 pp.*

Social Behaviour: *its Elementary Forms. 416 pp.*

Klein, Josephine. The Study of Groups. *226 pp. 31 figures. 5 tables.*

Linton, Ralph. The Cultural Background of Personality. *132 pp.*

Mayo, Elton. The Social Problems of an Industrial Civilization. *With an appendix on the Political Problem. 180 pp.*

Ottaway, A. K. C. Learning Through Group Experience. *176 pp.*

Ridder, J. C. de. The Personality of the Urban African in South Africa. *A Thematic Apperception Test Study. 196 pp. 12 plates.*

● **Rose, Arnold M.** (Ed.). Human Behaviour and Social Processes: *an Interactionist Approach. Contributions by Arnold M. Rose, Ralph H. Turner, Anselm Strauss, Everett C. Hughes, E. Franklin Frazier, Howard S. Becker, et al. 696 pp.*

Smelser, Neil J. Theory of Collective Behaviour. *448 pp.*
Stephenson, Geoffrey M. The Development of Conscience. *128 pp.*
Young, Kimball. Handbook of Social Psychology. *658 pp. 16 figures. 10 tables.*

SOCIOLOGY OF THE FAMILY

Banks, J. A. Prosperity and Parenthood: *A Study of Family Planning among The Victorian Middle Classes. 262 pp.*
Bell, Colin R. Middle Class Families: *Social and Geographical Mobility. 224 pp.*
Burton, Lindy. Vulnerable Children. *272 pp.*
Gavron, Hannah. The Captive Wife: *Conflicts of Household Mothers. 190 pp.*
George, Victor, and **Wilding, Paul.** Motherless Families. *220 pp.*
Klein, Josephine. Samples from English Cultures.
1. Three Preliminary Studies and Aspects of Adult Life in England. *447 pp.*
2. Child-Rearing Practices and Index. *247 pp.*

Klein, Viola. Britain's Married Women Workers. *180 pp.*
The Feminine Character. *History of an Ideology. 244 pp.*
McWhinnie, Alexina M. Adopted Children. *How They Grow Up. 304 pp.*
Myrdal, Alva, and **Klein, Viola.** Women's Two Roles: *Home and Work. 238 pp. 27 tables.*
Parsons, Talcott, and **Bales, Robert F.** Family: Socialization and Interaction Process. *In collaboration with James Olds, Morris Zelditch and Philip E. Slater. 456 pp. 50 figures and tables.*

SOCIAL SERVICES

Bastide, Roger. The Sociology of Mental Disorder. *Translated from the French by Jean McNeil. 260 pp.*
Carlebach, Julius. Caring For Children in Trouble. *266 pp.*
Forder, R. A. (Ed.). Penelope Hall's Social Services of England and Wales. *352 pp.*
George, Victor. Foster Care. *Theory and Practice. 234 pp.*
Social Security: *Beveridge and After. 258 pp.*
● **Goetschius, George W.** Working with Community Groups. *256 pp.*
Goetschius, George W., and **Tash, Joan.** Working with Unattached Youth. *416 pp.*
Hall, M. P., and **Howes, I. V.** The Church in Social Work. *A Study of Moral Welfare Work undertaken by the Church of England. 320 pp.*
Heywood, Jean S. Children in Care: *the Development of the Service for the Deprived Child. 264 pp.*
Hoenig, J., and **Hamilton, Marian W.** The De-Segration of the Mentally Ill. *284 pp.*
Jones, Kathleen. Mental Health and Social Policy, 1845-1959. *264 pp.*

King, Roy D., Raynes, Norma V., and **Tizard, Jack.** Patterns of Residential Care. *356 pp.*

Leigh, John. Young People and Leisure. *256 pp.*

Morris, Mary. Voluntary Work and the Welfare State. *300 pp.*

Morris, Pauline. Put Away: *A Sociological Study of Institutions for the Mentally Retarded. 364 pp.*

Nokes, P. L. The Professional Task in Welfare Practice. *152 pp.*

Timms, Noel. Psychiatric Social Work in Great Britain (1939-1962). *280 pp.*

● Social Casework: *Principles and Practice. 256 pp.*

Young, A. F., and **Ashton, E. T.** British Social Work in the Nineteenth Century. *288 pp.*

Young, A. F. Social Services in British Industry. *272 pp.*

SOCIOLOGY OF EDUCATION

Banks, Olive. Parity and Prestige in English Secondary Education: a Study in Educational Sociology. *272 pp.*

Bentwich, Joseph. Education in Israel. *224 pp. 8 pp. plates.*

● **Blyth, W. A. L.** English Primary Education. *A Sociological Description.*

1. Schools. *232 pp.*
2. Background. *168 pp.*

Collier, K. G. The Social Purposes of Education: *Personal and Social Values in Education. 268 pp.*

Dale, R. R., and **Griffith, S.** Down Stream: *Failure in the Grammar School. 108 pp.*

Dore, R. P. Education in Tokugawa Japan. *356 pp. 9 pp. plates*

Evans, K. M. Sociometry and Education. *158 pp.*

Foster, P. J. Education and Social Change in Ghana. *336 pp. 3 maps.*

Fraser, W. R. Education and Society in Modern France. *150 pp.*

Grace, Gerald R. Role Conflict and the Teacher. *About 200 pp.*

Hans, Nicholas. New Trends in Education in the Eighteenth Century. *278 pp. 19 tables.*

● Comparative Education: *A Study of Educational Factors and Traditions. 360 pp.*

Hargreaves, David. Interpersonal Relations and Education. *432 pp.*

● Social Relations in a Secondary School. *240 pp.*

Holmes, Brian. Problems in Education. *A Comparative Approach. 336 pp.*

King, Ronald. Values and Involvement in a Grammar School. *164 pp.*

School Organization and Pupil Involvement. *A Study of Secondary Schools.*

● **Mannheim, Karl,** and **Stewart, W. A. C.** An Introduction to the Sociology of Education. *206 pp.*

Morris, Raymond N. The Sixth Form and College Entrance. *231 pp.*

● **Musgrove, F.** Youth and the Social Order. *176 pp.*

● **Ottaway, A. K. C.** Education and Society: An Introduction to the Sociology of Education. *With an Introduction by W. O. Lester Smith. 212 pp.*

Peers, Robert. Adult Education: *A Comparative Study. 398 pp.*

Pritchard, D. G. Education and the Handicapped: *1760 to 1960. 258 pp.*
Richardson, Helen. Adolescent Girls in Approved Schools. *308 pp.*
Stratta, Erica. The Education of Borstal Boys. *A Study of their Educational Experiences prior to, and during Borstal Training. 256 pp.*

SOCIOLOGY OF CULTURE

Eppel, E. M., and M. Adolescents and Morality: *A Study of some Moral Values and Dilemmas of Working Adolescents in the Context of a changing Climate of Opinion. Foreword by W. J. H. Sprott. 268 pp. 39 tables.*
● **Fromm, Erich.** The Fear of Freedom. *286 pp.*
The Sane Society. *400 pp.*
Mannheim, Karl. Essays on the Sociology of Culture. *Edited by Ernst Mannheim in co-operation with Paul Kecskemeti. Editorial Note by Adolph Lowe. 280 pp.*
Weber, Alfred. Farewell to European History: *or The Conquest of Nihilism Translated from the German by R. F. C. Hull. 224 pp.*

SOCIOLOGY OF RELIGION

Argyle, Michael. Religious Behaviour. *224 pp. 8 figures. 41 tables.*
Nelson, G. K. Spiritualism and Society. *313 pp.*
Stark, Werner. The Sociology of Religion. *A Study of Christendom.*
Volume I. *Established Religion. 248 pp.*
Volume II. *Sectarian Religion. 368 pp.*
Volume III. *The Universal Church. 464 pp.*
Volume IV. *Types of Religious Man. 352 pp.*
Volume V. *Types of Religious Culture. 464 pp.*
Watt, W. Montgomery. Islam and the Integration of Society. *320 pp.*

SOCIOLOGY OF ART AND LITERATURE

Jarvie, Ian C. Towards a Sociology of the Cinema. *A Comparative Essay on the Structure and Functioning of a Major Entertainment Industry. 405 pp.*
Rust, Frances S. Dance in Society. *An Analysis of the Relationships between the Social Dance and Society in England from the Middle Ages to the Present Day. 256 pp. 8 pp. of plates.*
Schücking, L. L. The Sociology of Literary Taste. *112 pp.*

SOCIOLOGY OF KNOWLEDGE

Mannheim, Karl. Essays on the Sociology of Knowledge. *Edited by Paul Kecskemeti. Editorial Note by Adolph Lowe. 353 pp.*

Remmling, Gunter W. (Ed.). Towards the Sociology of Knowledge. *Origins and Development of a Sociological Thought Style.*

Stark, Werner. The Sociology of Knowledge: *An Essay in Aid of a Deeper Understanding of the History of Ideas. 384 pp.*

URBAN SOCIOLOGY

Ashworth, William. The Genesis of Modern British Town Planning: *A Study in Economic and Social History of the Nineteenth and Twentieth Centuries. 288 pp.*

Cullingworth, J. B. Housing Needs and Planning Policy: *A Restatement of the Problems of Housing Need and 'Overspill' in England and Wales. 232 pp. 44 tables. 8 maps.*

Dickinson, Robert E. City and Region: *A Geographical Interpretation. 608 pp. 125 figures.*

The West European City: *A Geographical Interpretation. 600 pp. 129 maps. 29 plates.*

● The City Region in Western Europe. *320 pp. Maps.*

Humphreys, Alexander J. New Dubliners: *Urbanization and the Irish Family. Foreword by George C. Homans. 304 pp.*

Jackson, Brian. Working Class Community: *Some General Notions raised by a Series of Studies in Northern England. 192 pp.*

Jennings, Hilda. Societies in the Making: *a Study of Development and Re-development within a County Borough. Foreword by D. A. Clark. 286 pp.*

● **Mann, P. H.** An Approach to Urban Sociology. *240 pp.*

Morris, R. N., and **Mogey, J.** The Sociology of Housing. *Studies at Berinsfield. 232 pp. 4 pp. plates.*

Rosser, C., and **Harris, C.** The Family and Social Change. *A Study of Family and Kinship in a South Wales Town. 352 pp. 8 maps.*

RURAL SOCIOLOGY

Chambers, R. J. H. Settlement Schemes in Tropical Africa: *A Selective Study. 268 pp.*

Haswell, M. R. The Economics of Development in Village India. *120 pp.*

Littlejohn, James. Westrigg: *the Sociology of a Cheviot Parish. 172 pp. 5 figures.*

Mayer, Adrian C. Peasants in the Pacific. *A Study of Fiji Indian Rural Society. 248 pp. 20 plates.*

Williams, W. M. The Sociology of an English Village: *Gosforth. 272 pp. 12 figures. 13 tables.*

SOCIOLOGY OF INDUSTRY AND DISTRIBUTION

Anderson, Nels. Work and Leisure. *280 pp.*

● **Blau, Peter M.,** and **Scott, W. Richard.** Formal Organizations: *a Comparative approach. Introduction and Additional Bibliography by J. H. Smith. 326 pp.*

Eldridge, J. E. T. Industrial Disputes. *Essays in the Sociology of Industrial Relations. 288 pp.*

Hetzler, Stanley. Applied Measures for Promoting Technological Growth. *352 pp.*

Technological Growth and Social Change. *Achieving Modernization. 269 pp.*

Hollowell, Peter G. The Lorry Driver. *272 pp.*

Jefferys, Margot, *with the assistance of Winifred Moss.* Mobility in the Labour Market: *Employment Changes in Battersea and Dagenham. Preface by Barbara Wootton. 186 pp. 51 tables.*

Millerson, Geoffrey. The Qualifying Associations: *a Study in Professionalization. 320 pp.*

Smelser, Neil J. Social Change in the Industrial Revolution: *An Application of Theory to the Lancashire Cotton Industry, 1770-1840. 468 pp. 12 figures. 14 tables.*

Williams, Gertrude. Recruitment to Skilled Trades. *240 pp.*

Young, A. F. Industrial Injuries Insurance: *an Examination of British Policy. 192 pp.*

DOCUMENTARY

Schlesinger, Rudolf (Ed.). Changing Attitudes in Soviet Russia.

2. The Nationalities Problem and Soviet Administration. *Selected Readings on the Development of Soviet Nationalities Policies. Introduced by the editor. Translated by W. W. Gottlieb. 324 pp.*

ANTHROPOLOGY

Ammar, Hamed. Growing up in an Egyptian Village: *Silwa, Province of Aswan. 336 pp.*

Brandel-Syrier, Mia. Reeftown Elite. *A Study of Social Mobility in a Modern African Community on the Reef. 376 pp.*

Crook, David, and **Isabel.** Revolution in a Chinese Village: *Ten Mile Inn. 230 pp. 8 plates. 1 map.*

Dickie-Clark, H. F. The Marginal Situation. *A Sociological Study of a Coloured Group. 236 pp.*

Dube, S. C. Indian Village. *Foreword by Morris Edward Opler. 276 pp. 4 plates.*

India's Changing Villages: *Human Factors in Community Development. 260 pp. 8 plates. 1 map.*

Firth, Raymond. Malay Fishermen. *Their Peasant Economy. 420 pp. 17 pp. plates.*

Gulliver, P. H. Social Control in an African Society: a Study of the Arusha, Agricultural Masai of Northern Tanganyika. *320 pp. 8 plates. 10 figures.*

Ishwaran, K. Shivapur. *A South Indian Village. 216 pp.*

Tradition and Economy in Village India: *An Interactionist Approach. Foreword by Conrad Arensburg. 176 pp.*

Jarvie, Ian C. The Revolution in Anthropology. *268 pp.*

Jarvie, Ian C., and **Agassi, Joseph.** Hong Kong. *A Society in Transition. 396 pp. Illustrated with plates and maps.*

Little, Kenneth L. Mende of Sierra Leone. *308 pp. and folder.*

Negroes in Britain. *With a New Introduction and Contemporary Study by Leonard Bloom. 320 pp.*

Lowie, Robert H. Social Organization. *494 pp.*

Mayer, Adrian C. Caste and Kinship in Central India: *A Village and its Region. 328 pp. 16 plates. 15 figures. 16 tables.*

Smith, Raymond T. The Negro Family in British Guiana: *Family Structure and Social Status in the Villages. With a Foreword by Meyer Fortes. 314 pp. 8 plates. 1 figure. 4 maps.*

SOCIOLOGY AND PHILOSOPHY

Barnsley, John H. The Social Reality of Ethics. *A Comparative Analysis of Moral Codes. 448 pp.*

Diesing, Paul. Patterns of Discovery in the Social Sciences. *362 pp.*

Douglas, Jack D. (Ed.). Understanding Everyday Life. *Toward the Reconstruction of Sociological Knowledge. Contributions by Alan F. Blum. Aaron W. Cicourel, Norman K. Denzin, Jack D. Douglas, John Heeren, Peter McHugh, Peter K. Manning, Melvin Power, Matthew Speier, Roy Turner, D. Lawrence Wieder, Thomas P. Wilson and Don H. Zimmerman. 370 pp.*

Jarvie, Ian C. Concepts and Society. *216 pp.*

Roche, Maurice. Phenomenology, Language and the Social Sciences. *About 400 pp.*

Sahay, Arun. Sociological Analysis.

Sklair, Leslie. The Sociology of Progress. *320 pp.*

International Library of Anthropology

General Editor Adam Kuper

Brown, Paula. The Chimbu. *A Study of Change in the New Guinea Highlands.*

Van Den Berghe, Pierre L. Power and Privilege at an African University.

International Library of Social Policy

General Editor Kathleen Jones

Holman, Robert. Trading in Children. *A Study of Private Fostering.*
Jones, Kathleen. History of the Mental Health Services. *428 pp.*
Thomas, J. E. The English Prison Officer since 1850: *A Study in Conflict. 258 pp.*

Primary Socialization, Language and Education

General Editor Basil Bernstein

Bernstein, Basil. Class, Codes and Control. *2 volumes.*
1. *Theoretical Studies Towards a Sociology of Language. 254 pp.*
2. *Applied Studies Towards a Sociology of Language. About 400 pp.*

Brandis, Walter, and **Henderson, Dorothy.** Social Class, Language and Communication. *288 pp.*
Cook-Gumperz, Jenny. Social Control and Socialization. *A Study of Class Differences in the Language of Maternal Control.*
Gahagan, D. M., and **G. A.** Talk Reform. *Exploration in Language for Infant School Children. 160 pp.*
Robinson, W. P., and **Rackstraw, Susan, D. A.** A Question of Answers. *2 volumes. 192 pp. and 180 pp.*
Turner, Geoffrey, J., and **Mohan, Bernard, A.** A Linguistic Description and Computer Programme for Children's Speech. *208 pp.*

Reports of the Institute of Community Studies

Cartwright, Ann. Human Relations and Hospital Care. *272 pp.*
Parents and Family Planning Services. *306 pp.*
Patients and their Doctors. *A Study of General Practice. 304 pp.*
● **Jackson, Brian.** Streaming: *an Education System in Miniature. 168 pp.*
Jackson, Brian, and **Marsden, Dennis.** Education and the Working Class: *Some General Themes raised by a Study of 88 Working-class Children in a Northern Industrial City. 268 pp. 2 folders.*
Marris, Peter. The Experience of Higher Education. *232 pp. 27 tables.*
Marris, Peter, and **Rein, Martin.** Dilemmas of Social Reform. *Poverty and Community Action in the United States. 256 pp.*
Marris, Peter, and **Somerset, Anthony.** African Businessmen. *A Study of Entrepreneurship and Development in Kenya. 256 pp.*
Mills, Richard. Young Outsiders: *a Study in Alternative Communities.*

Runciman, W. G. Relative Deprivation and Social Justice. *A Study of Attitudes to Social Inequality in Twentieth Century England. 352 pp.*

Townsend, Peter. The Family Life of Old People: *An Inquiry in East London. Foreword by J. H. Sheldon. 300 pp. 3 figures. 63 tables.*

Willmott, Peter. Adolescent Boys in East London. *230 pp.*

The Evolution of a Community: *a study of Dagenham after forty years. 168 pp. 2 maps.*

Willmott, Peter, and **Young, Michael.** Family and Class in a London Suburb. *202 pp. 47 tables.*

Young, Michael. Innovation and Research in Education. *192 pp.*

● **Young, Michael,** and **McGeeney, Patrick.** Learning Begins at Home. *A Study of a Junior School and its Parents. 128 pp.*

Young, Michael, and **Willmott, Peter.** Family and Kinship in East London. *Foreword by Richard M. Titmuss. 252 pp. 39 tables.*

The Symmetrical Family.

Reports of the Institute for Social Studies in Medical Care

Cartwright, Ann, Hockey, Lisbeth, and **Anderson, John L.** Life Before Death.

Dunnell, Karen, and **Cartwright, Ann.** Medicine Takers, Prescribers and Hoarders. *190 pp.*

Medicine, Illness and Society

General Editor W. M. Williams

Robinson, David. The Process of Becoming Ill.

Stacey, Margaret. *et al.* Hospitals, Children and Their Families. *The Report of a Pilot Study. 202 pp.*

Monographs in Social Theory

General Editor Arthur Brittan

Bauman, Zygmunt. Culture as Praxis.

Dixon, Keith. Sociological Theory. *Pretence and Possibility.*

Smith, Anthony D. The Concept of Social Change. *A Critique of the Functionalist Theory of Social Change.*

Routledge Social Science Journals

The British Journal of Sociology. *Edited by Terence P. Morris. Vol. 1, No. 1, March 1950 and Quarterly. Roy. 8vo. Back numbers available. An international journal with articles on all aspects of sociology.*

Economy and Society. *Vol. 1, No. 1. February 1972 and Quarterly. Metric Roy. 8vo. A journal for all social scientists covering sociology, philosophy, anthropology, economics and history. Back numbers available.*

Year Book of Social Policy in Britain, The. *Edited by Kathleen Jones. 1971. Published Annually.*

1373